W9-AEY-336

# THE PANTHER PARADOX:
## A Liberal's Dilemma

Also by DON A. SCHANCHE:

*Mister Pop*

E185.615
S27

# THE PANTHER PARADOX:

## A Liberal's Dilemma

*by* DON A. SCHANCHE

169599

JUN 22

DAVID McKAY COMPANY, INC.  New York

THE PANTHER PARADOX: A LIBERAL'S DILEMMA

COPYRIGHT © 1970 BY DON A. SCHANCHE

All rights reserved, including the right to reproduce this book, or parts thereof, in any form, except for the inclusion of brief quotations in a review.

Quotations from *Soul on Ice* by Eldridge Cleaver (Copyright © 1968 by Eldridge Cleaver) used with permission of McGraw-Hill Book Company.

Quotations from the speech made at Stanford University from *Eldridge Cleaver: Post-Prison Writings and Speeches,* ed. by Robert Scheer. Copyright © 1967, 1968, 1969 by Eldridge Cleaver. Reprinted by permission of Random House, Inc.

(A portion of the Foreword of this book appeared originally in *The Atlantic Monthly,* May, 1970, Copyright © 1970 by The Atlantic Monthly Company.)

Library of Congress Catalog Card Number: 70-135585

MANUFACTURED IN THE UNITED STATES OF AMERICA

VAN REES PRESS • NEW YORK

"The awakened Negro will forget his moment of Christian hope and Christian inspiration . . . There will be no more hymns and no more prayer vigils. He will become a Samson whose African strength flows ominously back into his arms. He will suddenly pull the pillars of white society crashing down upon himself and his oppressor."

—Thomas Merton
*Ramparts*, 1963

# Contents

# *Foreword*

MOST of the Black Panthers I have met are naive,
malleable ghetto kids, angry and despairing, but not naturally
vicious or mean-spirited men and women. They have been
driven by white society to their insanity; they have not
marched to it by choice. Watching their haphazard close-
formation drill on a makeshift parade ground in Oakland,
listening to their banal, adolescent chatter as they bundle
copies of the obscene and Jew-baiting *Black Panther* weekly,
even shuddering as they go through precisely coordinated
public demonstrations of ferocity with clearly implied goals
of assassination and guerrilla warfare, one catches the bizarre
mirror image of Boy Scouts. Like Tenderfeet, new to the
troop (their party, after all, is very young and most of them
are teenagers, quite a few not yet halfway through adolescence), they seem both awed and securely warmed by the
first good feelings of fraternity and solidarity that inevitably
accompany mild military or quasi-military discipline. I'm sure
that Hitler's Brown Shirts felt it; so did Mao's Fourth Route
Army, the original American Minutemen, the present-day nuts
of the same name, the Kerensky revolutionaries, the Bolshe-
viks, the officers of the Bolivian General Staff, the Pathet Lao
and the Vietcong, among others. The analogy may seem ludi-
crous, but it is apt, because while the goals of good Scouts
and Black Panthers are appallingly disparate, the raw material

ix

in which they are implanted is not: little kids, for the most part, indoctrinated in the flush of fraternity and solidarity to suspend critical judgment in areas that are vital to the greater organization and the ideals of its leaders.

What will happen to the Boy Scouts when some bright Eagle reflects on the population explosion and decides that it is an antisocial act to guide old ladies safely across the street when overcrowded mankind might better urge them to stroll in heavy traffic? What will happen to the Black Panthers when some farsighted Captain decides that Huey Percy Newton, the party's founder, was better off remaining in jail where he could continue to work at overcoming his functional illiteracy, therefore the Free Huey campaign was counterrevolutionary?

All militants—whether they are black revolutionaries or white, middle-class Boy Scouts—are by nature enwrapped in the sweet feelings of righteousness, doing good deeds according to the revelations of their leader, no matter whether he is Lieutenant General Sir Robert S. S. Baden-Powell who used the unassailable rightness of being kind to elderly women as a means of implanting quasi-military Imperial British patriotism in ordinary kids who would never reach Sandhurst, or Eldridge Cleaver who is so fed up with that kind of patriotism that as an act of scorn for it he wants to remove the head of Senator John McClellan of Arkansas (although he would settle for simply "kicking the Senator in the ass if I could get to him," he says).

Both groups indoctrinate their young members in the classic military virtues of *unquestioning* duty, loyalty, and physical courage, and the chief difference may be only that from one, as any Army commander will tell you, you get excellent battlefield soldiers, while from the other you get unpredictable urban guerrilla fighters whose willingness to commit suicide scares hell out of their immediate opponents, the cops.

That's quite a difference. Most Scouts get over their boyish gullibility and adopt a pragmatic regard for self-preservation that doesn't always include doing their duty for God and their Country (Jerry Rubin was a Boy Scout). I doubt whether many Panthers will develop self-serving critical minds, because, to the everlasting regret of the white society that made them what they are, the kids who become Black Panthers have been motivated by life, as well as indoctrinated by their party, to emulate Samson, whose historical first act of suicidal blind rage they can understand better than Boy Scouts understand patriotism. Unhappily, it probably won't occur to many of them that Samson didn't accomplish much beyond the immortality of his own name when he brought the Philistines' building down on his unshorn head.

The Samsonian thirst for retributive suicide appears in everything the Panthers do, from their children's breakfast program, which really is only a front like the Cubs and the Brownies for implanting party dogma in ever-younger minds, to the deliberately self-defeating courtroom tactics of the Panther 21 or Bobby Seale, an impassioned man who has shown extremely limited vision. Their ineptly constructed party doctrine, which borrows selectively from Mao (the power of the gun), Che (death with honor, many Vietnams), Karl Marx (death to capitalism), Ho Chi Minh (feed on the brutality of the occupying army), Al Fatah (terrorize, disrupt, destroy), and Bakunin (all revolutionaries are doomed), is suicide, too, in a country that yearns at present for peace and quiet above all else. The doctrine grows like a thalidomide Topsy around malformed slogans, fatally nurtured on corrupted body chemistry so that each added day of gestation only accelerates its ultimate death: Free Huey, Off the Pigs, Free Eldridge, Power to the People, Free Bobby, Pussy Power, Avenge Bobby Hutton, Pick up the Gun, Off the Zionist Imperialists, Burn the Motherfucker Down, Destroy Babylon, Wring Dick Nixon's Neck, Right On!

Charles Garry, the radical San Francisco lawyer whom the Panthers call the only true White Panther, tried in 1968 to explain their almost hopeless state of mind to the Oakland jury that convicted Huey Newton of manslaughter in the death of an unacceptably disagreeable patrolman named John Frey. It may have been the last orderly courtroom trial of a Panther. After painstaking days of questioning, cross-examination, and argument that established the dismal life conditions of black people in a ghetto where the police feel perfectly free to harass, break into homes without warrants, brutalize, and even kill, he moved on to the unconscious racism of the society at large. "Take a look at our language, our vocabulary: White denotes charity, innocent truth. Black is sin, fiendish, devilish, infernal, monstrous, atrocious, horrible, nefarious, treacherous, venal. Blackballs. Blacklists. We can whitewash anything except a black mark; black is a badge of shame. Even the white flag takes a back seat to black death, black heart, black need, black outlook, black sheep." Certainly, white America prepares fertile ground for the incubation of a social death wish among desperate black youth, inspiring them to want to tear it all down.

Eldridge Cleaver, with less than his life at stake (he said he was writing to expunge from his soul his own rage and private guilt over the crime of raping white women), drew a far more eloquent picture of the systematic alienation and conscious oppression of black people by white society. From his own deep pain he expressed in *Soul on Ice* the outrage of the stifled black man. "We shall have our manhood," he wrote. "We shall have it or the earth will be leveled by our attempts to gain it." Death to Oppressors is but a short step away from that angry cry for attention, and Cleaver, living today in the Alice-in-Wonderland world of exiled international revolutionaries in Algeria, has taken that step. I had known him before his exile and had become accustomed to his sometimes violent rhetoric. But when I visited him in Algiers after his flight from the United States, the rhetoric had a harder and less coherent sound. He spoke of a list of marked victims (whether he was literally writing a list or mentally toting up the names, I'm not sure). It included all the obvious targets: President Nixon

("Break his little fuckin' neck"), Senator McClellan ("We'll take off his head"), Mayors Daley and Alioto, Police Chief Charles Gain of Oakland, and "a lot of targets that I actually want to aim at and pull the trigger." He is almost as contemptuous of many unsuspecting white liberals like Leonard Bernstein and Arthur Goldberg who have tried to help in the name of civil liberties, as well as some otherwise sympathetic journalists, including me, I suppose, who have been slow to understand just what the Panthers have against them.

"If you're not part of the solution, you're part of the problem," says Cleaver, who would rather see you dead than see you standing around watching innocently, even writing sympathetic articles or dropping contributions into the Panther legal defense fund, while the Panthers feel the power structure grind its foot ever deeper into their collective necks. He is not kindly disposed toward those who contribute money for legal defense while announcing their total opposition to everything that the Panthers stand for. "You must accept us as a liberation movement that is seriously trying to deal with the problems of the people," he says. He means *must* accept, too. Very few whites or blacks of any political stripe this side of the extreme radical left can do that. Who wants to stand around shouting encouragement to enraged boys and girls who are trying to break the bonds of their own blinding victimization by bringing the roof down on all of us?

The same question can be asked about the small minority of young white radicals who are bent on terrorism, although I think it is clear that even the bomb-throwing madmen among them occupy an entirely different and somehow less alarming place in the national conscience than do the Black Panthers. Their motivation, alone, literally is as dissimilar to that of the Panthers as white is to black. The white terrorists are mostly middle-class kids, reasonably well educated, products of affluence, willing beneficiaries of a society that, whatever its faults, encourages the development of critical insights and political action. They seem to have adopted violence itself

as a political ideology, and the wellspring of their motives is as
deep and varied as the human psyche, ranging from genuine
political conviction based on at least some kind of analysis,
to simple-minded romanticism. Somehow we find it easy to
dismiss even murderous, bomb-throwing white revolutionaries
as ill-developed adolescents, turned off by overpermissive or
repressive parents or schools, overreacting to the social problems of a slow-moving, war-sick nation. They pass through
the mind as wild children who at best may grow up to progressive political change after they get over the romance of
contemporary outrage, or, at worst, will blow themselves into
insignificance by their own fumble-fingered handling of bombs
or their hopelessly futile anti-police and anti-institutional
rioting.

But we take the Black Panthers seriously. They cannot as
easily be dismissed, because they are black. Whether we con-
sciously articulate it or not, I think we fear that retribution,
not just radical social change, is their primary goal, and we
know damned well that neither progress nor political wisdom,
but only more tragedy, will grow out of that. We also know
that these enraged boys and girls have come by their common
Samson complex honestly, and that wiping out the Black
Panther Party, as the police and the courts seem intent on
doing, will not remove the wild impulse to retributive suicide
that countless black men and women in this country feel.

Two Negro psychiatrists from San Francisco, William Grier
and Price Cobbs, eloquently expressed what I believe white
Americans fear most in their book *Black Rage*. "As a sapling
bent low stores energy for a violent backswing, blacks bent
double by oppression have stored energy which will be released in the form of rage—black rage, apocalyptic and final,"
they wrote. "The time seems near for the full range of the
black masses to put down the broom and buckle on the
sword."

Unfortunately, that kind of prophecy is dismissed as hyperbole by two many white Americans, even liberals such as

President Nixon's resident sociologist, Daniel Patrick Moynihan, who appears to believe quite seriously that a period of "benign neglect," coupled with such halting and possibly even mean-spirited programs as Republican "Black Capitalism" and a tolerance of *de facto* segregation, will take the sting out of the rage by simply pretending it isn't as threatening as it seems. One is tempted to rub the President's face in the wretched life conditions of America's urban blacks, in the hope that it will penetrate his senses and that he will begin to see and feel with them before it is too late and the hyperbole becomes a fact.

Two years ago, after my first meeting with Eldridge Cleaver and my first exposure to the Black Panther Party, I wrote in *The Saturday Evening Post:*

The tragedy is that understanding [Cleaver] takes an act of spiritual concentration, almost of soul transference, that is beyond the patience of most white people. Sensing a robber in the house, they would rather call the cops than prepare a feast for the prodigal and ask him what personal deprivation led him to his act. To understand Eldridge Cleaver and the Panthers, you must have that patience, literally *feel* the attitudes of a black society diffused throughout a booming white nation that is, in Cleaver's words, "temporizing and compromising over right and wrong, over legality and illegality, over constitutionality and unconstitutionality . . . clashing over . . . what to do with the blacks, and whether or not to start treating us as human beings."

"They were defying the law, weren't they?" he asked, referring to those who debated while he and millions suffered. "I defied the law and they put me in prison. So why not put those dirty mothers in prison, too?"

There is a thirst for retribution in that short passage, written years before Cleaver forsook literature and took his suicidal leap into vengeful revolution. It does not take a great deal of imagination or experience to understand it, but our tragedy is that since the passing of the Kennedys, our political leaders and most of those who mold opinion in America have lacked both. It just isn't popular any more to act against or even to try imagining the wretched conditions that made Watts and Detroit burn, and that are still producing millions of hopelessly frustrated black children whose only recourse to such "benign neglect" will be to lend more force to the violent backswing of the bent sapling Grier and Cobbs envisioned.

The ghetto world, to which at least our imaginations must transport us before we can begin to understand the sources of retributive violence that the Panthers exemplify, was best described, I think, in Eldridge Cleaver's favorite passage from *Seven Storey Mountain,* by the saint-like Thomas Merton. He was writing about Harlem, but his description encompasses all black ghettoes.

Here in this huge, dark, steaming slum, hundreds of thousands of Negroes are herded together like cattle, most of them with nothing to eat and nothing to do. All the senses and imagination and sensibilities and emotions and sorrows and desires and hopes and ideas of a race with vivid feelings and deep emotional reactions are forced in upon themselves, bound inward by an iron ring of frustration: the prejudice that hems them in with its four insurmountable walls. In this huge cauldron, inestimable natural gifts, wisdom, love, music, science, poetry are stamped down and left to boil with the dregs of an elementally corrupted nature, and thousands upon thousands of souls are destroyed by vice and misery and degradation, obliterated, wiped out, washed from the register of the living, dehumanized.

The report of the National Advisory Commission on Civil Disorders—the Kerner Commission—has come and gone and, as the Negro sociopsychologist Kenneth Clark predicted even before it was written, it has been forgotten. Not one American in ten remembers what the Kerner report was about, much less its essential charge: *"What white Americans have never fully understood—but what the Negro can never forget—is that white society is deeply implicated in the ghetto. White*

*institutions created it, white institutions maintain it, and white
society condones it."*

Dr. Milton Eisenhower's national commission on violence
went over some of the same ground, and its dismal report met
the same dusty fate as that of the Kerner Commission. "If the
President and others who have been elected to lead us don't
care," the whites of this nation seem to be saying, "why should
we?"

It seems futile to repeat what the reports, the writers, the
activist clergymen, the thousands of concerned white citizens
who *have* managed a necessary soul transference, the articulate
blacks, the rioters, and even the Black Panthers all have replied to that question, but I will: because elemental human
justice demands that each of us, in his private mind, not only
care but act out of our care to end racism and the injustices
that support it. Perhaps it would be less of an act of futility
to cast the reply in terms of traditional self-interest rather
than simple justice and answer this way: because if white
America does not soon end the conditions of social, economic,
political, and physical deprivation, this "iron ring of frustration" that gave rise to the Black Panther Party, it is certain
that more such suicidally violent black guerrilla armies will
rise up out of the ghettos and in their thirst for vengeance
destroy all that we cherish, including the very lives of many
of us.

That kind of doomsday talk doesn't seem to register, either,
but how else can one express it? The Black Panthers are not
just a passing aberration, sprung upon a jaded public like a
new fad, a colored Hula Hoop briefly and flamboyantly visible
to television viewers and courtroom watchers, to be passed
over and forgotten in another year or two. They are not simply
a black phalanx in the so-called student revolution, either.
They are deeply hurt and outraged boys and girls bent on
organized violence for its own soul-cleansing sake. Professor
Gerald Emanuel Stearn wrote in *The New York Times* Magazine that the Panthers "constitute the sole organized armed

revolutionary tradition of black America." There never has
been such a thing. Nat Turner, Denmark Vesey, and other
leaders of short-lived rebellions were not "organized, armed
revolutionaries," they were slaves acting spontaneously against
insensitive masters. In a figurative sense, so were the dis-
organized ghetto rioters of more recent years. They were
reacting, not acting. But the Panthers are an organized military unit. They are structured as an army, they are armed as
an army, they talk as soldiers do, in mindless slogans, and
they will go on acting as soldiers until all of them are dead or
imprisoned. When they are gone there is not even a shadow
of doubt that others will carry on the military tradition they
have begun, if for no other reason than that at last there is
such a black tradition to grasp and preserve; and so it will
continue until the destruction they seek is wrought or until
American racism is so completely overturned, one way or the
other, that further acts of vengeance on their part become irrelevant.

Recently I visited Muhammad Ali, formerly Cassius Clay,
retired heavyweight champion of the world and certifiably one
of the most effectively violent black men who ever lived. At
a time when the white world was down on him, even trying
to imprison him, I found him deeply involved in nonviolent
pursuits: creating rehabilitation programs for youthful black
drug addicts, raising funds to buy sewing machines for poor
black women, and making plans for an organization of black
athletes that will give demonstration matches and bouts for
the benefit of poverty-stricken Negroes. His programs were
so astonishingly gentle in concept and execution that I tried
to draw a parallel between his approach and that of the Black
Panthers.

"Each of us has got to fight for freedom and go on fightin'
no matter what," he cautioned me. "This is my way. They got
theirs. You got to understand. They're just brothers who want
to be free, *now!* They don't want to wait. Frustration over-
takes a lot of people, and they just don't care no more. Just

don't care. They don't care about dyin'. Life ain't nothin'.
They don't have nothin'. No money. No future. When they cry
protest, nobody hears it. They just don't care no more. So they
got to let the world know they are for real. They got to take a
stand. Pow! Ping! Bang! Shootin' at the police. They got to do
that. Don't you see?"

I do see, now, and the vision is frightening. Curiously, I
thought I saw quite clearly two years ago when I first met some
of the Panthers and believed that I knew and understood their
ideological leader, Eldridge Cleaver. I thought that I understood, as their lawyer Charles Garry understands, the expressed anger of the Panthers, because I talked often with
them and him while he was expounding it during and after
the trial of Huey Newton. I spent hours alone with Cleaver
probing for a better understanding, and continued to probe
when I met him in Algeria after he left the Cuban exile that
followed his flight from the United States. I studied the
miserable city of Oakland, which gave birth to the militant
party. I spent months of private time—one hesitates to use a
word like agony, but that is what it was—intellectualizing
about black despair as it is variously laid out for us in books
such as *Look Out Whitey, Black Power's Gonna Get Your
Momma, Black Rage, Native Son, The Autobiography of
Malcolm X, Soul on Ice, Black Families in White America,
Manchild in the Promised Land,* and so on down a long and
mostly recent black bookshelf. What Muhammad Ali taught
me, I think, is that it is all so much easier to understand if
you don't intellectualize—"When they cry protest, nobody
hear it . . . they got to let the world know they're for real . . .
Pow! Ping! Bang!"

There are other white writers who know Cleaver and the
Black Panthers much more intimately than I do. Paul Jacobs,
the old radical whose ultimate break with Cleaver may be pre-
determined in the fact that he is Jewish, is one of them. Robert
Scheer, the former editor of *Ramparts,* is another. There may
be a few others who are white. But I'm afraid each of them is

bound either by emotion, political conviction, or unfortunate entrapment in an unalterable radical career (where except the *Reader's Digest* or *National Review* can an ex-radical journalist go for professional and political decompression and still earn enough to keep eating?), so that he is not inclined to objective analysis of the Black Panthers, or free to offer insights by relating his experiences with them to those of us who are not so committed.

That is my only reason for presenting this narrative of a deeply disappointing acquaintance. My experience is fragile, but it is unique not only because it is mine, but because I am probably typical of many middle-class white liberals—people whom the Panthers ordinarily would not permit near them—whose consciences have been pinched between a rock and a hard place by the deteriorating relationship of the Panthers and the American judicial system. On the one side we see what Grier and Cobbs called "black rage, apocalyptic and final," and on the other we see what clearly appears to be an unuttered, unwritten police conspiracy to deprive the Panthers of their civil liberties. It has left most of us with the uncomfortable feeling that we no longer have a liberal place to stand, because to defend the Panthers' rights is to hasten their apocalypse and to deny them is to hasten another, the destruction of everyone's liberties.

I think I have located standing room for my own conscience. It may not be valid for others, but it suits me. To explain how I found it requires this rather personal account of how I met the Panthers, and where it led. It was, for me, a quest for Eldridge Cleaver.

D.A.S.
Larchmont, N. Y.
July, 1970

# THE PANTHER PARADOX:
## A Liberal's Dilemma

# CHAPTER 1

## *"Fantasizing about each other . . . making each other up."*

G RAY's *Elegy Written in a Country Churchyard,* "far from the madding crowd's ignoble strife," haunted me when I read it as a Georgia schoolboy because it so aptly described the figuratively dead state of the Negro children we saw occasionally, slapping bare feet down the roads around my half-urban, half-rural school outside of Atlanta. I never knew where the "colored" schools were in Dekalb County at that time, and I doubt if my classmates did, either, but we knew that they were hidden out in the red clay farmland somewhere and that, ever more than our abbreviated eleven-year school, they were intellectual burial grounds.

> *Perhaps in this neglected spot is laid*
> *Some heart once pregnant with celestial fire;*
> *Hands, that the rod of empire might have swayed,*
> *Or waked to ecstasy the living lyre.*
>
> . . . . .
>
> *But knowledge to their eyes her ample page*
> *Rich with the spoils of time did ne'er unroll;*

Eldridge Cleaver, who never read Thomas Gray during his years of self-education in the California prison system, once angrily brushed me aside when I tried to say parts of the poem to him. "I want to pull the trigger," he said, "I don't want to be philosophical about it . . . walking in Gray's *Elegy*." But it remains with me, perhaps too romantic and too lyrical an expression of the guilt that every white Southern child, even a transitory one like me, carries with him to adulthood.

Today I am a 44-year-old, upper-middle-class Northern liberal, immediately descended from poor Norwegian immigrants who built a half-subterranean house of sod and homesteaded barren land in the Great Plains eighty years ago. My family moved to the South when I was a small child, but I left when I graduated from college. Now, I live only slightly discomforted by admitted hypocrisy in a rich New York suburb that, three years ago, made its ritual concession to the temper of our time by admitting to residence one middle-class Negro family with two Ph.D.s. One other black family moved in recently. My other neighbors include a famous theater critic, the presidents of three of the nation's largest corporations, several well-known surgeons, a clutch of wealthy Wall Street lawyers and brokers, a brewery heiress, the editors of two major national magazines, the president of one television network, the advertising man who invented "hard sell," and hundreds of functional millionaires, the latter being all of those whose annual incomes exceed the $50,000 which a conservatively invested million dollars will produce. Like most of them I have developed strong emotional ties to this quiet and genteel life that my immediate ancestors longed for but never knew. I want to preserve it. But I would leave before I would agree that gentility is a product of racial exclusion, which some of my neighbors apparently believe. Even so, I know that the nation's racism is so irrevocably sewn into the high-priced economic fabric of the community that my routine efforts on behalf of fair housing and human rights in this small and very rich village are nothing more than balm to the pained conscience of a hypocrite. So I carry that guilt with me, too.

I have noticed through the years that I am not very different in that respect from most other white liberals I have known.

Before I met Eldridge Cleaver, the only black people with whom I had more than a passing cordial association were a fellow editor whom Time, Inc., employed as its "company Negro"; an elderly dentist and his wife who attended my Unitarian church in Westchester County; three very good black writers; the cook of a U.S. Navy ship on which I served during World War II; and a succession of Negro domestics who have worked for me or for my family. I often brooded about that and told myself that it was an awful reflection on suburban life, on journalism as a profession, and on me. But I did nothing to correct the racial imbalance of my friendships, and as a journalist I even went to some lengths to avoid assignments that would put me in the center of the black conflict, even as an observer. I did not want such a close, one-to-one involvement with the civil rights struggle. Rather, I preferred sending money and encouragement from my calm suburban base and releasing whatever political and emotional energy this generated by "fat mouthing," as Cleaver calls it, at public meetings and liberal cocktail parties. I was afraid.

I'm not very different from most of the white liberals I know in that respect, either.

Thus I was not prepared for my involvement, as some other reporters had been, by gradual editorial immersion through the discernible heat layers of the black revolution that descended for most of them from the tepid legal confrontations of the Urban League and the NAACP, through the warmer but still nonviolent martyrdom of Dr. Martin Luther King's Southern Christian Leadership Conference, into the hot militancy of the Student (formerly Non-Violent) Coordinating Committee, and finally down to the boiling anger of the Black Panther Party. I fell all the way in on my first plunge, and I did so with such fear and naiveté that I blush now to admit it.

I met Cleaver for the first time in the narrow lobby of the offices of *Ramparts* magazine on Beach Street in the North

Beach section of San Francisco, not far from Fishermen's Wharf. At that moment the meeting was almost anticlimactic, following several weeks of futile attempts to contact him by telephone, telegram, and letter. I discovered later that his lack of response was a perfectly natural reflection of his own fear of me. He was, after all, a prison-wise ex-convict who has learned the hard way to avoid welcoming any blind association; there are too many stoolies, narks, agents, unpredictable enemies in and out of prison to risk accepting a stranger unless he is accompanied by a wholly trustworthy recommendation. Even ex-convicts who have spent so many years in straight jobs that their prison experience is all but forgotten retain this understandable suspicion, and Cleaver, in the eyes of the California authorities and the few other white Americans who then had heard of him, was far from straight; he was a self-confessed rapist, just out of prison on a writ of *habeas corpus,* after a gunfight with the Oakland police. To Governor Ronald Reagan, the California Adult (Parole) Authority, and most of the state's conservatives, he was Public Enemy Number One. He also was a candidate for the Presidency of the United States.

The editors of the then moribund and now dead *Saturday Evening Post* had asked me to write a profile of Cleaver for one of their pre-election issues in which they planned to feature this bizarre candidate of the Peace and Freedom Party as the focal point of a special section on Law and Order. I told them they should find a writer who was better acquainted with the radical New Left and with the Negro militants. A black writer, perhaps. I had no acquaintance beyond my own light reading and, furthermore, I did not want to get involved.

"That's why we asked you," one of them said. "We want to see how a middle-class white man reacts to this guy. No one knows him. No other national magazine has published anything about him yet except to review his book, *Soul on Ice.* You don't have to take him seriously. Just find out what he's like."

I contacted Cleaver, finally, through his literary agent,

Cyrilly Abels, who told him only two things about me in
urging him to agree to a meeting: first, that I was honest, and
second, that I was sympathetic. I have never been certain
about the former, but of the latter I did feel a powerful sense
of both sympathy and admiration, based entirely upon reading
*Soul on Ice,* which I viewed, and still do, as a kind of intellectual's *Autobiography of Malcolm X,* a book of forceful
revelation that every literate person in this country should
read. There was the sheer literary power of an extraordinarily
talented writer in Cleaver's prose. The personality that
emerged from his essays, from his imagined sexual-racial
mythology, and from the snippets of letters that made up the
book unwound in concentric circles of complexity, like the
growing rings of a thirsty tree whose roots had probed lovely
springs as well as improbable sewers.

True, much of the writing was overwrought, the word
choices of a man obviously bursting with an eloquence he never
dreamed he possessed, and his concepts of racial conflict—
expressed in metaphorical sex fantasies—were too much affected by the chief preoccupations of a convict: freedom and
women. But the immense critical strength of the man's mind
was inescapable, particularly in one long essay that scathingly
attacked James Baldwin for the distorting effect of homo-
sexuality in his work. Cleaver focused with ruthless accuracy
on the one element essential to an understanding of Baldwin
that white critics, too, had seen but never had dared to analyze.

But above all else there was a romantic element to *Soul on
Ice* that was guaranteed to raise it from merely an unusual
polemic to a contemporary, if sentimental, classic. The book
contained a series of letters that, if not the most lyric cor-
respondence since Elizabeth and Robert Browning, certainly
exposed one of the most improbable love affairs of our time:
Cleaver's impassioned commitment to Mrs. Beverly Axelrod,
a divorced white lawyer who fell in love with him and ultimately got him out of prison.

The letters revealed an almost incredibly romantic relationship between a cultured white woman and a black prisoner trying to guard against "fantasizing about each other . . . making each other up."

"And it is not a fraud, forced out of desperation," Eldridge wrote to Beverly. "We live in a disoriented, deranged social structure, and we have transcended its barriers in our own ways and have stepped psychologically outside its madness and repressions. It is lonely out here. We recognize each other. And, having recognized each other, is it any wonder that our souls hold hands and cling together even while our minds equivocate, hesitate, vacillate, and tremble?"

On that single passage, I think, rested the public popularity of the entire book. Part of its appeal was that it fit all the requirements of the romantic preconditioning most of us brought with us from our conventionally sentimental adolescence. More important, the exposed love affair reinforced other passages in Cleaver's writing that seemed to say he was a universal man without race, a black man with a colorless conscience whose anger was directed, not at whites alone, but at all racism, white and black. It promised a charismatic man, a modern black prince, who by the example of his unaffected love, his unbending honesty, and the angry strength of his intellect could bring the races together.

While I was reading *Soul on Ice,* Dr. Martin Luther King was assassinated—I broke off reading the book to watch on television the mournful procession behind his mule-hauled death wagon. We desperately needed a new black prince.

Still, I was frightened. The book clearly told me I was to meet an extraordinary person, and I already had begun to sentimentalize him, but since writing the passages that had moved me, Cleaver had been involved in the anti-white turbulence generated by Stokely Carmichael and Rap Brown of SNCC in Atlanta and Nashville, Tennessee; he had committed himself to the ominously race-baiting Black Panther Party for Self-Defense (which later dropped the equivocating and dangling modifier); he had been reimprisoned as a parole violater after a shoot-out with the Oakland police in which a teenage boy was killed; and he apparently had forsaken his great love for Mrs. Axelrod, because he had married a black girl named Kathleen Neal. Moreover, his post-prison writing, published in *Ramparts,* for which he worked as a roving editor, lacked the grace, the style, and above all, the authority of *Soul on Ice.*

"The violent phase of the black liberation struggle is here, and it will spread," he wrote after the murder of Dr. King. "From that shot, from that blood, America will be painted red. Dead bodies will litter the streets and the scenes will be reminiscent of the disgusting, terrifying nightmarish news reports coming out of Algeria during the height of the general violence right before the final breakdown of the French colonial regime."

His post-prison writing had none of the lovingness, little of the critical pungency, and even less of the eloquent wisdom he had demonstrated as a lonely convict searching for honor and truth within himself.

A year before the second Kennedy assassination, he wrote of seeing Robert F. Kennedy in San Francisco. "I sat up close and got a good look at his mug. I had seen that face so many times before—hard, bitter, scurvy—all those things. I had seen his face on the bodies of night-time burglars who had been in prison for at least ten years."

He spoke publicly in the obscene patois of the ghetto streets, not with the selectivity and precision of a writer, and he both talked and wrote of "the revolutionary courage to pick up a gun," fondly quoting Mao Tse-tung's dictum that "in order to get rid of the gun it is necessary to pick up the gun."

The prospect of meeting him was scary as hell.

# CHAPTER 2

## *"Cut out that shit, Kathleen!"*

I WAS uncomfortable in the company I shared as I waited for Cleaver to appear in the small lobby of the *Ramparts* offices. They were three young white kids, a lovely but unwashed blonde girl of about 18, and two unkempt boys who appeared to be between 19 and 21 years of age. Both of the boys wore jeans, love beads, and *ruanna*-like shirts from which their necks poked through open slits in coarse cloth. The older of the two, his long dark hair tied back in an Indian headband, was unaccountably gregarious.

"You waiting for Eldridge?" he asked me. "Eldridge Cleaver?"

"Yes. Uh . . ."

"We are, too. We supported him at the Peace and Freedom Convention in Ann Arbor. Beautiful! They're from the Berkeley Commune. I'm from New York. I'm in a group in Greenwich Village called 'Up Against the Wall Motherfucker.' Here's our handbill." He passed me a broadside. The headline was *Kill the Pigs!* "We're getting ourselves together for Chicago." The Democratic Convention in Chicago was two weeks away.

The other boy and the girl drew away from me while their companion rapped on. It was as if I had a disease, and from their point of view, I guess I did. I wore a double-breasted navy blazer, gray slacks and black Italian loafers, and my

8

buttoned-down soft white collar was decorated with the burgeed necktie of the Larchmont Yacht Club. I might as well have had on a blue uniform and a silver badge. The young motherfucker, which is what he said he preferred to be called, was enjoying a small put-on, and his companions had merely disassociated themselves from it.

Behind the sound of his patter, I heard someone mounting the uncarpeted stairs to the *Ramparts* lobby two at a time, so lightly that it was evident he sprang on the balls of his feet, not hitting the stairs with heavy heel and toe. It was Cleaver, hurrying so that he seemed to burst into the small waiting room. The three kids stepped in front of him, all talking at once. He held up both hands, long fingers spread wide, like those of a basketball player or a pianist.

"Wait a minute," he said in a calm voice. "If it's about going to Chicago, I don't think I'll be there. It looks like my parole officer won't let me go."

The kids stood mute, nothing more to say, as Cleaver stepped away from them to shake hands with me. "Hey, man, sorry to keep you waiting," he said. His voice was mid-level and throaty, but he articulated clearly. "Give me a few minutes and we'll go someplace where we can talk." He disappeared inside the rabbit-warren of magazine offices and I was left as mute as the three radical kids who still stood transfixed. It was Cleaver's eyes that had stopped all four of us.

I had forgotten the short passage in his book that recounted the power of his eyes on a fellow Black Muslim who was serving time with him in San Quentin. There was dissent among the Black Muslims of the prison, and in an effort to oust Eldridge X, as he called himself then, from the post of "minister" to the convict congregation, another con tried to lay upon him the Muslim's *mark of the beast*. "Look at his eyes," the brother Muslim said, "he's got the [white] devil's eyes."

Cleaver's eyes are Nordic, Scandinavian; they inspire instant feelings of confidence and warmth when you look into them, like the world-wise eyes of the late Trygve Lie and Dag Hammarskjöld. The lids are hidden beneath the brows by an epicanthic fold of skin, a mongoloid shield evolved among the northmen against bitter arctic wind and blinding glare. But the thing that transfixes you is the startling green irises, as cool and impervious beneath their confident shield as the steel bars of a prison. If there is a physical quality common to people of charisma perhaps it is here, in the eyes, but Cleaver projects an image of strength and internal power in the rest of his makeup, too. He is tall, six feet two inches, and his body is that of a conditioned athlete, finely muscled and tapered like a funnel from his broad shoulders and chest to slim waist and sinuous, lanky legs.

The Panther uniform that he affects adds to the image of power because it accentuates pure blackness, reminds you in the sleek gloss of its tailored, hip-length leather jacket that this is the black leader of a black army, ominous as a black-robed medieval executioner or an ebony-coated cat in the jungle. His gaiter boots were impeccably spit-shined, like those of a soldier, and his slim-legged black worsted trousers creased as if for the parade ground. He wore a pale blue Dacron and cotton turtleneck shirt that seemed to lift his well-formed head like an aristocratic knight's helmet above the black-armored body. In the lobe of his left ear was a gold earbob.

I never saw anyone approach him here or abroad who was not immediately awestruck by his appearance. The man has presence.

"How much time do you need to interview me?" he asked as he stepped back into the lobby. "An hour? If you need more than an hour, you'll have to wait until tomorrow. I've got to go to Oakland this morning." Cleaver is always hurried, always in motion.

"I don't want to interview you," I said. "If I'm going to write about you, I want to know you. I'd like to just follow you around for awhile, go where you go, listen, react to you.

I also want the reactions of other people who know you. If you can't go along with that, then I'll settle for a one-hour interview, I guess, but I doubt if it'll take that long. Frankly, I don't know what to ask."

I expected him to reject this shot in the dark or at least stall for a day or two considering it. He had little to gain from me, and my presence, like a blond, blue-eyed stormtrooper at his side, probably would embarrass him at Black Panther gatherings and on the public streets.

"Man, at least you're different," he said. The stretch of his smile, parenthetically bracketed between the curved whisker lines where his mustache met a truncated vandyke beard, was completely disarming. "Come on, then. We're going to pick up Kathleen and go to Huey's trial."

I was surprised by his unhesitating decision to let me tag along. There was risk in it for him. At the least I could prove to be a hostile writer, storing ammunition through intimate observation for an unpleasant portrait of him; at worst, for all he knew, I could be a police agent sent to spy on him and the Panthers. Two weeks later, when we were far better acquainted, I asked him why he did it.

"I kind of liked you when I saw you, and I knew you weren't a cop because I don't like cops," he explained, simply. Much later, when we were in Algiers, he wasn't so sure any more because his understandable paranoia had broadened in the city's climate of international intrigue to include the Central Intelligence Agency, and he was not as confident that he could spot *their* agents.

As we left the building and started across the street to the parking lot where he kept his car, I watched the first of many scenes that seemed to illustrate a curious link between the Black Panthers, particularly Eldridge Cleaver, and the many well-dressed young and middle-aged white women who appeared regularly at their public demonstrations and, often to the apparent discomfort of the Panthers, seemed to fawn over them, touching, clutching their arms, moving boldly through their ranks apparently seeking physical contact.

An extraordinarily good-looking brunette of about 30 stopped him as we approached the parking lot. Her legs and thighs, which showed beneath a brief skirt almost to the crotch of lace panty-hose, were exquisite. She put one hand lightly on his wrist and with the other caressed the lapel of his leather jacket where he wore a button that proclaimed "Free Huey!" Then she looked up into his face and said something to him that I didn't hear. He nodded, smiled, and replied briefly. Her eyes seemed to mist over and you could almost feel a coital current between them. She stood there and watched him as we walked on to his car.

"Do you know her?" I asked.

"I've seen her around," Cleaver said, dismissing the woman. "We have a lot of white supporters."

The mobile telephone rang as soon as Eldridge turned the ignition key of his new beige, four-door Plymouth Fury. He cradled the radio-phone on his shoulder and talked into it while driving across San Francisco to his three-story frame house on Pine Street in the Filmore district. His wife was waiting.

I held the door as she slipped into the front seat and her black leather mini-skirt rode high on booted legs, revealing the Mediterranean hairiness of her alabaster-pale thighs. She said not a word, but immediately arched her neck forward to get at the back of her coiffure with a can of Pantene spray and a coarse comb. She worked vigorously, pulling the comb, spraying, fluffing until her Natural grew so in size and roundness that it lightly brushed the roof liner of the car. Her hair was auburn in color, and it framed her delicate oval face like the hood of a frizzy parka. She glanced briefly and without expression at me in the back seat, fluffed her hair again, and said,

"Black is beautiful."

Then she turned her eyes to the windshield and began what

sounded like recitation, a set piece to be declaimed for frightening effect in the presence of any white stranger.

"The imperialist pig power structure is uptight because we have the gun. Power grows out of the barrel of the gun. We have picked up the gun. We will redistribute the wealth in this country. We will take the means of production for the people. The colonialist pigs will be swept away . . ."

She spoke in a monotone, softly.

". . . the middle-class pigs in their big suburban houses will . . ."

Suddenly Eldridge interrupted.

"Cut out that shit, Kathleen," he barked. She flicked the car radio to a soul music station, turned it up loud and said no more.

"Do you know who the Motherfuckers are?" he called as we crossed the Bay Bridge.

"I think I just met my first one," I shouted over the sound of music.

"They're good. Doing a good job. Don't mess around with a lot of talk like most of the white groups do. Here, read this." He tossed back the handbill that the kid with the hairband had thrust upon him before we left *Ramparts*. If they were doing a good job, then I was more of a soft-headed liberal laggard than I thought. The handbill called for the random assassination of policemen, beginning NOW!

"There he is, the Oakland pig, the baddest pig in Babylon," said Eldridge as he parked the car in front of a row of rundown buildings a block away from the Alameda County courthouse, where the murder trial of Huey P. Newton, founder and undisputed leader of the Black Panther Party, was under way. He nodded at a city police car cruising past.

Kathleen, obviously still miffed by her husband's rebuke, jumped from the car and waited impatiently for Eldridge to lock it. As we walked by one of the rundown buildings, a boarding house to judge from the gaggle of ill-dressed men and women sitting on the steps, we brushed past a ragged

woman who, like many of the white poor of Oakland, looked
not far removed from Tobacco Road.

"Black trash! You're walkin' with black trash!" she cackled
explosively, apparently speaking to me. I guess the combination of my inane yacht club uniform, the leather-jacketed
Black Panther, and the mini-skirted near-white girl with her
huge, auburn Afro, got to her.

"What'd she say?" asked Kathleen.

"I don't know," Eldridge sighed. He turned to face the old
woman and the group of apparently hostile white men on the
steps of the boarding house. Raising his clenched right fist in
the miiltant salute, he looked steadily at the woman with his
cool green eyes and said, "Black Power!" Hateful eyes glared
back from the group on the steps. It would not be surprising
to find an assassin in such a place. Cleaver turned his back
on them, and we continued to the courthouse steps, where a
snaking line of Panthers and their supporters, mostly teenage
kids, waited patiently for a turn in one of the twelve seats
reserved for the public in the Superior Court room of Judge
Monroe Friedman, where Newton was on trial. Two kids at
the head of the line gave up their places to Eldridge and
Kathleen, who were quickly admitted by uniformed deputy
sheriffs at the taped glass doors, to be escorted to a guarded
elevator and lifted to the oak-paneled seventh-floor courtroom.

"Try to get a press seat," Cleaver called back to me as he
went in the door. I didn't see him again until early afternoon.
Judge Friedman had allotted only three seats in the court to
"out-of-town" press, and they were already occupied by cor-
respondents of *The New York Times, Newsweek,* and *Time.*
I waited in the press room on the sixth floor and some of my
earlier fear returned. I had committed myself to tag along at
the elbow of a controversial black man, yet I was so ill-pre-
pared to deal with him that in the hour-and-a-half we had so
far spent together, I had made no attempt to open a conversation and had asked him only one trivial question. There
was a degree of physical fear, too. Cleaver obviously was

either heroically unconcerned about, or fatalistically resigned to, the possibility of assassination, a fate that a number of people already were predicting for him.

"Cleaver acts sometimes as if he wants to be killed," said a radio news reporter in the press room. "I don't know if it's courage or what it is. It's just like he doesn't care, that's all." In time I learned that Cleaver literally does not care about death. He has lived so long with the threat of it that whatever fear he may have had when he first went to prison has long since been blunted by familiarity with violent killing and a growing conviction that his natural fate is to be martyrdom. At that time, I knew little about him, but he certainly did not appear to be obsessed then by premonitions of death. So far he seemed to me to be only a mildly taciturn, wholly amiable, and slightly impulsive person. I liked him from the moment of his first broad smile, and his seeming unconcern for death did not strike me as suicidal, insane, or even foolhardy. It appeared to grow out of his determination to get on with the struggle, and that seemed courageous.

Not much happened that day in the Newton trial, which dragged on for eight weeks, and the Cleavers rejoined me in the press room after it was recessed. Kathleen stood apart, but Eldridge exchanged a few remarks with a white reporter who asked for, and failed to get, his reactions to the day's proceedings, then he moved to the telephone. For the next thirty minutes we waited while he sat on the top of a desk, legs folded beneath him, and placed phone calls to New York, Omaha, Los Angeles, and his office at *Ramparts*. That evening I finished my abbreviated reflections on the day with these notes:

"As I waited for EC to finish phone calls (he, calmly dialing long distance on the courthouse press phones) I felt a coldness toward me from Kathleen who, I guess, figures I'm just another pig.

"Most of the white press in the room seemed so awed by C that they over-acted a great show of loud camaraderie, like

Southern deputies kissing the ass of a particularly mean sheriff.

"One very chic middle-aged newswoman got close, like the girl this morning, and there were stars in her eyes (I guess she saw herself as a potential rape victim ready to succumb with pleasure). She asked for an autograph for her four-year-old daughter. Four years old? Cleaver wrote his name very slowly, like a man who isn't accustomed to signing things.

"EC rebuffed an elderly white reporter who wanted a ride to SF. ('We have a full car,' he said. Three of us!)

"I sat in the back seat, absolutely unable to strike up a conversation, or to understand what the two of them were saying, like a foreigner in a strange land, losing my own sense of self.

"Although he had been perfectly gentle, polite, pleasant to me, I was relieved to get away. Probably part of the non-communicative nature of this first meeting was due to the frenetic activity that follows the man. When I wanted to talk, the phone would ring, or he'd think of a phone call he had to make. Even so, when I tried a few conversation-opening questions, he responded minimally, and it became a series of strained (on my side) silences. I had the feeling when I left the two of them in front of a garage in SF that they'd really be relieved if I didn't see them again. It was not contempt or hate or scorn on his part, just impassivity, indifference, as if my presence really hadn't registered."

I remember explaining to myself as I made those notes that their reaction to me was perfectly understandable. But I was certain that Eldridge's tough rebuke of Kathleen in the car that morning had been an act of kindness toward me, and that modified my impression of him, at least. He sensed my fear of them and tried to still it. Either Kathleen wasn't conscious of it or she was delighted by my uneasiness and wanted to amplify it if she could. The latter, I think. I wondered if I ever would acquire a real understanding of either of them.

I also remember wondering, quite seriously, if I really *wanted* to understand them, or even to know them. My fear was almost entirely psychic, not the sort one expresses by saying, "Gee, this guy is tough; he and his friends might hurt me." It may have had more to do with my reactions to the sight of the two white women I had observed mentally fondling him that day, because they had expressed a good deal more than my kind of liberal cordiality when they touched him and talked with him. Rather, they seemed to constitute empirical proof of the metaphorical thesis of black-white, male-female relationships that Cleaver had expounded in an essay titled *The Primeval Mitosis* in his book.

In the essay he characterized white ruling class males as *Omnipotent Administrators* who had forsworn their bodies in order to develop their minds. In the process, the white man became weakened and effeminized, while the black man developed conversely. "Virility, strength, and power are associated with the lower classes, the *Supermasculine Menials* (Negro males)," he wrote. Because of the feminizing of the white man, the white woman had to be *Ultrafeminine* "so that the effeminate image of her man can still, by virtue of the sharp contrast in degrees of femininity, be perceived as masculine." This, obviously, robs her of a truly masculine mate. "The psychic core of her sensuality, the male-seeking pole of her Female Principle, the trigger of the mechanism of her orgasm, moves beyond the reach or range of the effeminate clitoris of her man." She confronts a psychic wall of ice, frigidity.

Intuitively, in Cleaver's metaphorical myth, she knows how to break the ice. "Her psychic bridegroom is the *Supermasculine Menial*," he concluded. "At the *n*th degree of the *Ultrafeminine's* scale of psychic lust stands the walking phallus symbol of the *Supermasculine Menial* . . . she is fully convinced that he can fulfill her physical need . . . she is allured and tortured by the secret, intuitive knowledge that he, her psychic bridegroom, can blaze through the wall of her ice, plumb her psychic depths, test the oil of her soul . . ."

The thesis wasn't new when Cleaver wrote it, and in the

context of his own experience as a sexually deprived, imprisoned ex-rapist, it contained a certain amount of personal and racial egotism. But the two women who had seemed to me to be on the verge of falling on their backs beneath him reminded me that the black man-white woman myth is not entirely baseless.

More to the point, however, this speculation, as I made my notes that evening, led me back to another passage in the same essay in *Soul on Ice,* one that seemed particularly relevant to my own fearfulness, if not to the sensuality of two strange women.

"The *Omnipotent Administrators,*" he wrote, "wishing to preserve what they perceive as their superior position and way of life, have, from a class point of view and also on an individual level, a negative reaction toward any influence in the society that tends to increase the number of males qualified to fulfill the functions of administration (intellectual labor). When it comes to anything that will better the lot of those beneath him, the *Omnipotent Administrator* starts with a basic 'anti' reflex. Any liberality he might show is an indication of the extent to which he has suppressed his 'anti' reflex, and is itself a part of his lust for omnipotence. His liberality is, in fact, charity."

I wondered if mine was, in fact, charity, necessarily encrusted with a fear of self-discovery?

# CHAPTER 3

## "No one knows
## who his true enemy is."

I BOARDED United Airlines Flight 294 to Omaha at 6:30, half an hour before it was scheduled to leave San Francisco. Eldridge wasn't there, but I had talked to him just two hours before, and he was confident he would make the plane. As flight time approached I wasn't so sure.

"Eldridge is terribly irresponsible about showing up for scheduled appearances," Eve Crane had told me. "He's chaotic. Maybe it's a reaction against the orderliness of prison life."

Eve is a freelance magazine photographer who worked occasionally for *Ramparts* and had made a personal editorial preserve of the Black Panthers, attending their rallies and photographing Cleaver whenever she could. She was one of the few whites associated with the Panthers who seemed to have retained a semblance of objectivity about them.

"They haven't learned yet to adjust their speech and actions to the audiences they face. I'm not sure they ever will," she said. "No matter where they are, they go on using terms like 'Pigs' and obscene street language. They want support from middle-class people, but they're turning them off with that kind of talk. I really don't know whether the rhetoric is merely a tactic, you know, to polarize people, or whether they're really saying what they mean."

"After listening to Cleaver," I said, "I'd guess it's a tactic. He doesn't talk the same way privately as he does publicly. He's a soft-spoken, obviously literate man. He doesn't even say the same words. He'll use the terms 'cops' and 'police' instead of pigs most of the time. It's almost as if he has to remind himself of the tactical rhetoric when he does use it in conversation."

"But Cleaver is different," she said. "He's a man apart, not like Huey Newton or Bobby Seale or any of the rest. Especially since he got the Peace and Freedom Party nomination. There's so little race consciousness about him that he just doesn't seem like a Panther."

What she said certainly appeared true in the three days I had known him. He had had virtually no contact with other Panther leaders, save his appearance at the Newton trial. His San Francisco house, while usually overrun with a half-dozen kids answering the telephone and helping to prepare Panther broadsides and the party newspaper, *The Black Panther,* was far removed from the "national" headquarters in Oakland, which he had not visited since I arrived. His political meetings so far had been largely white P & F Party affairs, and although he enunciated the usual Panther slogans—"Free Huey or the Sky's the Limit!," "Off the Pigs!," "Power to the People!"—it seemed ritual, as if he felt it was expected of him, not as Presidential candidate but as part-time Minister of Information of the Black Panther Party. I had begun to think of him as an utterly independent man, associated with the Panthers but not really a part of them; a man who, once he cleared away the substantial legal problems that lay in his path, would return to his writing and offer something more than the banalities of his followers in Oakland. Obviously my assumption was wrong, but at the time I thought it was well founded.

Despite my fears concerning our first awkward mid-August day together, he had accepted me as casually as if I were an old friend when we met the next day. He still seemed to be living amid chaos, jumping from office phone to car phone to

home phone, so we found little time alone to talk, but there
was no further evidence of the impassivity or indifference that
I thought I detected before. On the third day he wanted to
closet himself at his *Ramparts* office to write a short piece
about his political candidacy, its value as a platform for the
radical movement. I left him there and called on Paul Jacobs,
veteran of the labor wars of the late Thirties, author of *Is
Curly Jewish?*, and P & F Party candidate for the U.S. Senate
from California. He is short, stocky, and muscular, a radical
intellectual who takes pride in physical and verbal toughness.
Cleaver told me that Paul knew him better, probably, than any
other white man in San Francisco.

Jacobs is a collector of bizarre hats, perhaps because he
likes to accentuate the barrenness of his imposing Yul
Brynner-like skull, and he was sitting at his typewriter wearing
a Moroccan pillbox cap when I arrived at his large and comfortably furnished frame house in an elegant neighborhood on
the corner of Filbert and Scott streets. Around his cluttered
desk, hanging from the walls of the study and propped on the
mantelpiece above the fireplace were yarmulkas, old European military hats, turbans, fezes, pith helmets, and assorted
other headgear, arrayed like toys in a playroom. His wife,
Ruth, a successful San Francisco lawyer, was not at home.
We were attended by a uniformed Negro housekeeper.

"Eldridge and Kathleen stayed as our house guests for quite
a while after they were married," Jacobs said, "and they were
the most perfect guests we've ever had, except that they would
not let the housekeeper do anything at all for them. Ruth and
I noticed and began to get a little embarrassed about it. One
morning I found Eldridge on his hands and knees scrubbing
out the bathtub, and I told him that I hoped it wouldn't embarrass him, but he really should let the housekeeper do that.

"He looked up and said, 'It's not that I'm thinking about
the housekeeper. There's nothing wrong with having a black
woman work for you. I'm down here because of my mother.

My mother taught me to wash out the ring after you've had a bath, no matter where you are.' "

We talked about the Cleavers and their apparent disparity. Eldridge seemed to me to be spiritually calm, however violent his rhetoric, and in his personal relationships with me and others with whom I had observed him he was gentle, almost loving, and thoughtful. Kathleen was the opposite, tense and aggressive, even arrogant in the presence of whites.

"You can't understand Kathleen or Eldridge without understanding one very important thing, and that's SNCC," Paul said. "Every black person who went through the SNCC experience—when whites started taking over the organization and the blacks turned on the whites—was traumatized by it. That's why she has this fantastic hostility and bitterness. Eldridge doesn't, because he never had the experience. While she was being traumatized by the black revolt in SNCC, Cleaver was in jail having different experiences with fellow convicts. He missed all that, so he's free of the hangups."

Jacobs explained that Kathleen was an embittered product of the black bourgeoisie, the only child of a former Howard University professor, Dr. Albert Neal, who had joined the U.S. Foreign Service and served in India, Liberia, and the Philippines. While her mother and father remained abroad, she returned to the United States to begin college. She entered Oberlin, but dropped out after a few months and enrolled at Barnard. After one year she dropped out of the second school and joined the staff of SNCC in Atlanta, not long before the angry black-white confrontation that propelled Stokely Carmichael to national prominence. It left deep wounds on both sides. The rejected whites in SNCC were shocked to be roughly thrust aside by Carmichael's anti-white housecleaning. The blacks, who had chafed at the do-it-all, take-charge attitude of many of the white volunteers, were appalled at how close they thought they had come to being simply another black movement taken over and manipulated by the white liberal establishment. It was a traumatic split, coming as it did after two Northern white youths, Andrew Goodman and Michael Schwerner, lost their lives as SNCC volunteers.

Because of Kathleen's SNCC experiences, Paul thought, Cleaver had found it doubly difficult to push the Black Panther Party into an alliance with the predominantly white groups that made up the radical coalition which became the Peace and Freedom Party. The Panthers still hadn't stopped arguing the merits of the coalition, he said, and only the force of Eldridge's personality had brought them into it; that and his logical insistence that alliance with white radicals need not mean surrender of the black exclusivity of the Panthers.

"He convinced them that the fact that the Panthers already were all black automatically excluded any possible manipulation by whites, as happened at SNCC. Bobby Seale held out, but once Huey agreed, the Panthers went along."

I observed that Cleaver seemed to move with extraordinary ease among all sorts of people, white or black, whether intellectuals, office workers, or laborers; he didn't act like a man who had spent most of his youth and all his adult life in prison, associating exclusively with convicted criminals.

"Don't forget, he had a lot more time for study and for self-examination than most of us ever get," Paul said. "He used it, too. He is extremely well-read, well-informed. He understands himself, so he has confidence in himself. Once he decided to use his prison experience for education, he didn't have to interrupt his studies to worry about making a living. There were no outside distractions.

"Even so, Eldridge is very naive in some ways, understandable ones. I went to New York with him for the publication of *Soul on Ice.* We stayed at the Algonquin, and we were having lunch there on the first day. When the check came, Eldridge started digging in his pockets for cash, and I said, 'Just sign the check and put your room number on it.' He didn't know what I meant. The whole credit economy grew in this country while he was in prison. He tried to rent a car, and the girl at the rent-a-car desk didn't want to take cash. She couldn't believe someone would rent a car without a credit card, and Eldridge didn't know what a credit card was.

"Later on that same day, we were having some drinks with Norman Mailer in a Mexican restaurant. Mailer is a writer Cleaver had respected ever since he first read him. He was impressed with Mailer's concept of 'the white nigger,' alienation of youth in society. Eldridge was sitting there at the table awestruck by Mailer's proximity. I think he would have done anything for Mailer right then, because Norman was one of the few writers who saw Eldridge's stuff while he was still in prison and wrote letters for Beverly Axelrod that helped to get him paroled.

"But Norman is Norman and as we drank, he started to get pugnacious, so I came back at him tough, like we were going to fight, right there. I guess Eldridge thought we were going to mix it up, because he got up and started to reach for Mailer. As much as he adored Norman, he reacted like a con protecting a buddy in the yard from another con; he was going to defend me if Norman threw a punch.

"Mailer held up his hands and said, 'Relax, El. Paul and I are a couple of old club fighters. Believe me, when Jacobs and Mailer get together, nothing happens.' Eldridge sat down, but he didn't know what to make of it. He tries not to show it, but he still has a lot to learn even now about the outside world, little things like credit cards and signing checks, things that the rest of us just take for granted."

"Can he stay out of prison long enough to learn to take anything for granted?" I asked.

"I doubt it," Paul said. "The Adult Authority wants to put him back in prison, and in this state, they have absolute power over any ex-con on parole. He can go on appealing for a few more months, but they'll get him, because the way the law's written, no one can stop them. It's tragic. Here they take the one guy in this country who is saying to the world, 'Look,

blacks and whites can make it together!' and they want to lock
him up."

The doorbell rang. A moment later the housekeeper showed
Eldridge into the room. Smiling, he put an arm around my
shoulder and said hello to Paul. "I hoped I'd catch you here,"
he said to me. "I've got to run right now. It's been bothering
me that we really haven't had any time to talk since you got
here. I'm going to Omaha, Nebraska, tonight. I've got to speak
at a P & F rally there tomorrow afternoon. C'mon and go
with me. We can talk in the plane. It's United at 7 o'clock. I
made a reservation for you. You can buy your ticket at the
airport. Okay?"

As I nodded assent, he waved to Jacobs and left as abruptly
as he had come.

I got up from my seat in the tourist section of the plane
and walked back across the enclosed loading ramp to the
agent's desk just a few minutes before the crew was to close
the doors and start the engines. It looked as if I had been
stood up, but just as the agent urged me for the last time to
get back aboard, Eldridge appeared, with Kathleen, running
down the long hallway. Hurriedly he kissed her and gave the
irritated agent his ticket. The plane door was shut immediately
behind us, and as we took our seats the ship already was
taxiing away from the passenger terminal. I was conscious of
a few apprehensive glances and whisperings from fellow passengers, startled by this bearded last-minute black boarder
with the gold earbob and fitted black leather jacket. Only the
day before, a flight bearing Stokely Carmichael to California
had made an emergency landing in Denver after a bomb scare
that presumably was directed at him. Although far fewer
people knew Cleaver, he was an imposing figure, and he was
black, enough fuel to ignite the imagination of any frightened
air passenger.

While the plane waited in line for its turn to take off, a well-dressed couple in their twenties got up behind us and stepped to our row of seats.

"Aren't you Eldridge Cleaver?" said the young man.

"Yes," said Cleaver, uncertainly turning in his seat and stretching his neck to look up at the standing couple. From their appearance and the sound of his voice, these were well-educated, middle-class people. Like me, they apparently had been deeply impressed by Cleaver's writing.

"We read your book," the young man said, and his wife, or girl friend, held up a hard-covered copy of *Soul on Ice*. "It is a great book. We learned from it. Good luck."

The young woman handed him the book to autograph as the stewardess hurried down the aisle to shoo them back to their seats.

"Here," said Eldridge, "thanks," and passed the book back to them. "Thanks a lot."

The flurry of activity as the stewardess forcefully urged the young couple back to their seats drew more attention, and I could see passengers in the rows ahead rising and turning their heads to see what was going on.

Then the plane began its take-off run. Before releasing the brakes, the pilot pushed the engines of the Boeing 727 to full power, so the machine surged forward when he let it go. Normally the take-off run of a 727 is relatively short. After ten or fifteen seconds the pilot lifts it sharply into a steep climb from the runway.

We rolled for at least ten seconds and I was bracing unconsciously for the sharp lift-off when suddenly the pilot abruptly cut power. He hit his brakes hard. We were thrown forward in our seats as the plane came to a lurching and terrifying halt on the runway.

Now the stuffy cabin atmosphere was electric with fright. I could feel the unspoken question, "bomb scare?" In all of the nearby seats, people turned to stare at Eldridge as if he was explosive.

He looked at me and smiled. I was shaking, but he appeared to be perfectly calm.

"We've stopped to pick up my shadow," he said. "I must have shaken him off on the way to the plane. He didn't have time to buy a ticket. I guess he didn't know we were going to Omaha tonight."

Cleaver often was followed by plainclothes detectives in San Francisco and Oakland, but his shadow tonight, he assumed, would be an FBI man. The day before, as we drove along Pine Street near his house, he had pointed out an unadorned tan Ford sedan parked half a block away. It had a small ultra-high-frequency radio antenna protruding from its roof, and two men wearing Madison Avenue snap brim hats sat in the front seat. "They represent J. Edgar Pig, Adolph Hoover," said Cleaver indifferently.

"How do you know they're FBI?" I asked.

"I've had enough experience. I can tell. I can tell who any cop is just by looking at him."

I was prepared to accept that. But it seemed unlikely to me that even the FBI would stop an airplane during its take-off run simply to put an agent aboard for a tedious flight to Nebraska, where he doubtless would be replaced by another FBI man. I was right. The pilot explained after we had taxied from the runway that one of the baggage doors was loose and had to be refastened. The problem was remedied in a few minutes, and we took off without incident. Our fellow passengers eased back in their seats with only a few more worried glances at Eldridge.

A very young stewardess who had not yet learned to stifle her tension in a crisis sprayed the white gleam of a nervous smile all over the cabin in an effort to reassure us that everything was all right. She stopped by Cleaver's seat and leaned close to his powerful chest to read the two slogan buttons on his jacket. One said "Cleaver for President," and the other cried "FREE HUEY!" I guessed that she thought they were funny buttons and she wanted to try to relax us and herself with a stiff attempt at humor.

"What's a Huey?" she asked.

"It's a man. His name is Huey Newton," Eldridge said.

"Who's Huey Newton?" she asked, now showing such sincerity that I knew it was not a put-on.

Very softly and with a smile that bore no resentment, Cleaver said, "It's a long story . . . a very long story."

She didn't wait to hear it, but the smile reassured her, and her face lost its tension. The encounter was brief, but you could see that she liked Eldridge Cleaver. She certainly was not frightened by him.

I bought two Scotches and water for each of us from her, and we began to talk. I asked Eldridge to tell me about his childhood, his family, his experiences as he grew up. It seemed to me a logical place to begin, but my request annoyed him.

"I'm not sure that's relevant to what's going on in this country, what's going on in the [radical] Movement, you know?" he said. "Right now the primary thing that's happening, the primary thing that is engaging me is *definition*. We have to proceed from a correct analysis of what's happening and redirect the amorphous racial tension in the country, focus it in a useful way. That's what is occupying me, my thoughts. For example, that's why we use the term 'pig' for the police and the establishment. There is confusion in this country. We have been fed lies—black people and white people have been fed lies—for hundreds of years, and no one knows who his true enemy is. After a correct analysis of that situation, the most logical thing is to define a common enemy, an enemy of the people. We could focus on Rockefeller, or L.B.J., but it is ineffective to direct organized enmity at them. We have to start down with that cop, the enemy we see, the enemy we face every day. Focus on him as the pig, and he will lead us to Rockefeller and L.B.J.; it will get them very uptight, you see?"

I was unnerved by this response because it seemed to be the prelude to a bombastic political lecture, and I didn't want to waste the few hours we would have alone together on that.

"I can understand that," I said, "and I'd like to get back to it, later. But right now it doesn't make sense to me to dismiss your own background as irrelevant. You are what your experiences have made you. I think I have to understand them in order to understand what you're talking about."

"Maybe you're right," he said. "I don't know. I've thought a lot about myself, but I've never talked to anyone like you about it. I don't like to talk about myself."

That seemed to end our conversation almost as soon as it began. He leaned back in his seat and closed his eyes as if he meant to sleep away the rest of the journey. Then, to my relief, he began to talk very slowly, unaffectedly, about his past.

# CHAPTER 4

### *"Willing to risk all on the curve of his instincts."*

LEROY ELDRIDGE CLEAVER, as he is identified in the relevant judicial records of the State of California, was born in Wabbeseka, Arkansas, not far from Little Rock, on August 31, 1935, to a couple who were on the verge of a breakthrough into the Southern black middle class. "My father's name is Leroy," said Eldridge. "He was a waiter in a nightclub, and he played the piano. I guess he was a pretty good piano player, not great, but better than average, you know? Mother—her name is Thelma—taught school. It was a 'separate but equal' school, you know? One room, I think. She taught elementary grades. It was rural. Wabbeseka is a rural scene. I don't remember too well because I was very young, but I remember our house, a typical little country house for a black family. It was in the middle of a cotton or corn patch. Very elementary."

When Eldridge was 7 or 8, his father advanced to one of the traditional stepping-stones to the black bourgeoisie. He quit his job in the nightclub to become a dining-car waiter on the Super Chief, then running between Chicago and Los Angeles. It was wartime, which probably made his application for this more profitable work move faster than it would have otherwise, but still it seemed like a big step. At the time Negroes throughout America revered Booker T. Washington and his philosophy of gradual integration through education. Dining-car waiters could afford better homes and more education for their children and, therefore, found more dignity in their jobs. Rural and ghetto kids alike were importuned to finish high school and, if possible, attend college so they could qualify for even more dignified jobs, such as that of Federal clerk or postman. It was a wretched blighting of capability and ambition, but it was all that black people had.

Eldridge wasn't certain why his family picked Phoenix, Arizona, for its next home, but the western city was a railroad layover point for the elder Cleaver and presumably he felt it would be more congenial to a black family than either Chicago or Los Angeles, the Super Chief's terminal points.

"It was about 1944 when we moved to Phoenix," Eldridge said. "That's where I first became conscious of our peculiar relationship to white people, of what white people expected of us because we were Negroes. I guess I was too young to feel it in Arkansas. It happened at a public sports contest, run for us by the white people in a public park. They made a big thing of announcing that there would be prizes for running and jumping and other sports. Prizes are exciting to little kids —you dream about them; surprises, glittery things—and we ran our hearts out. I won my race. *The prize for the winner was a piece of watermelon!* For really the first time, I realized what white people thought of us."

They expected gratitude for the treat of winning a common garden gourd. Cleaver thought that was the beginning of his real anger.

The relationship of black kids to the police shocked him, too. The only means he could devise to earn spending money as a Negro child was shining shoes, so he hustled to avoid paying off the police for the privilege of working on his knees on the sidewalks of Phoenix.

"The police had a kind of racket," he explained. "They owned all the shoeshine boxes. All of them were painted blue, so the cops could spot the unauthorized ones right away.

You had to check out your box from the police station and pay them off. Some of us made our own boxes. I even painted mine blue, like theirs. But the police would catch us shining shoes. They'd take us in and take our boxes away. So I had to hide mine from them, and I had to hide it from my father, too. He thought that shining shoes was undignified."

When the family left Phoenix, Eldridge was about ten years old. He wasn't sure why they were moving, but he knew there was trouble between his mother and father. "I heard a lot of ruckus, but I don't think I want to talk about it," he said. "I'm not sure I even remember it correctly, anyway." They moved briefly to Riverside, California, and then settled in the Rose Hill section of Los Angeles, near South Pasadena. It was predominantly a Mexican-American neighborhood that included a number of blacks and a few whites. While poor, it was not a Negro ghetto, like Watts. This lack of a solid black environment may be what made Cleaver more of a racial moderate than many other militant blacks. It is probable, too, that the absence of his father, who broke with Mrs. Cleaver and moved to Chicago where he still works today as a waiter in a hotel dining room, had a lot to do with Eldridge's subsequent turn toward petty hustling and crime. To support her son and his younger sister, who is now a Los Angeles County social worker, Thelma Cleaver, the former Arkansas elementary school teacher, got a job in the Los Angeles Department of Education. She took the only job they would give her: janitress in the Abraham Lincoln Junior High School. Her work, cleaning out classrooms, kept her until 7 o'clock or later every night, as it still does, and Eldridge, who attended the Huntington Drive Grammar School, was on his own most of the time.

He said he assumed at the time, probably correctly, that there really were only two roads out of the poverty in which his fatherless family lived. One was to excel as a football player at nearby Belmont High School, hoping for local fame and a college scholarship. Cleaver tried to prepare himself for that. "All of us were on the Booker T. Washington kick then," he reflected. "Finish high school. Excel. Get more and more education. Football was the way to do it."

The other road was through hustling drugs and dabbling in varieties of street crime. Eldridge worked at preparing himself for that, too.

"Rose Hill was the marijuana capital of California," he recalled. "It's where everybody came to buy pot. It was everywhere in Rose Hill. When I was in Soledad Prison I wrote a short story about Rose Hill, an autobiographical story that describes what I was doing and how I felt about it. It's hard to remember how you felt about anything when you were a kid, but I tried, and what I put down in that story is true."

Later he gave me the unpublished story. It was called *The Flashlight,* and it described the petty crime into which he led a gang of kids. It also offered a revealing glimpse of Cleaver's view of himself as a man apart. Here is a part of it:

... life was in motion and motion required a direction and Stacey [Eldridge] was young and saw the years stretched out before him as he sprinted down the track of his days ... The others deferred to him as though he were a prince among them with mysterious powers of a higher caliber than theirs, as if somehow he was born with a built-in gun and they with built-in knives ... Had he been less skillful in his choices, less willing to risk all on the curve of his instincts, it would have been their loss as much as his ... [but] Stacey was growing friendlily disgusted with the others, primarily because they seemed content to continue along in the rut of their deeds ...

Only a few weeks ago he could still draw intense delight and deep contentment from the raids they threw in El Sereno, from kicking in a window and ransacking a store, from stripping the hubcaps, wheels and accessories from cars, from stealing the clothing from clotheslines, or from breaking into a restaurant or café after it had closed and eating up as much food as they could hold in their guts ...

When he went on a raid now, it was only because he knew that the others depended upon him and that they would be angry and confused if he refused to go with them.

In the story, Stacey-Eldridge finally drops his gang and, for kicks, begins harassing the *marijuanos,* older Mexican-American boys who peddle and use pot, by shining the beam of a powerful stolen flashlight on them as they conduct their nightly rituals. In the end he joins the Chicano pot smokers

in that underground world, psychologically as far beneath the consciousness of the city's solid citizens as that city's sewerage system is beneath its streets, in the subterranean realms of its vice, inhabited by the narcotics peddlers and users, the marijuana peddlers, the gamblers, pimps, prostitutes, the thugs and the cut-throats, the burglars and robbers, and the police . . .

In another autobiographical story, an incompleted novella that he wrote in prison but that *Ramparts* published only recently (October, 1969) under the title of *The Black Moochie,* Cleaver described how he ran with the Mexican *marijuanos.* "We didn't comb the black circuit, so I was actually absorbing the patterns of the Chicanos," he wrote of his integrated childhood. But in its dismal crime and poverty, its casual indulgence by even small children in promiscuous sex and drugs, and its relationship with the police who were hostile and corrupt Anglo-Saxon outsiders, Rose Hill might as well have been an all-black ghetto.

Cleaver was picked up so many times on well-founded suspicions of vandalism that by the time he was caught in the act of breaking into a store at age 13 it was foreordained that he would be sent to reform school. County juvenile authorities put him in the Fred C. Nelles School for Boys at Whittier, and there was never again a day in his life that he was not either a fugitive, incarcerated, on probation, or on parole.

"That's where my life really changed," he said of his first stretch in reform school. "I made a total breakaway from the rest of society at Whittier. I had always run with a gang; all kids do. But now my total loyalty was to the rebel clique

against the world. The most important thing I learned there—
I mean the most important to *me,* then—was how much
money you could make hustling pot and how to do it. When I
got out, I just had to do it."

Home on probation, Cleaver entered Belmont High School
and went out for football. Afternoon and weekend practice
put a crimp in his activities as a marijuana hustler, but he
managed, by being hurried and a little careless with the latter,
to excel at the former. He was a big boy, strong and fast, and
after the preseason workouts in his first year, he made the cut
for the varsity team. It was his opportunity to excel and,
perhaps, play his way into college. Since Belmont did not
provide its players with football shoes, Eldridge used some
of his marijuana profits to buy his first new pair. He carefully
put them in a drawer in his bedroom a week before the
opening game. He wanted to preserve the new shoes for his
first appearance on the field.

Three days before the opening game he was picked up by
the police as he hurried to sell his daily quota of marijuana.
He was 15 years old. After a quick proceeding in juvenile
court, he was packed off to the Preston School of Industry,
a tougher reform school than the one in Whittier.

"If you see my mother in Los Angeles while you're doing
this story, ask her if my football shoes are still in the drawer,"
he mused. "I'll bet they're still there. I never wore them."

Preston served only to reinforce Cleaver's conviction that
his only possible course in life lay in rebellion against society.
Many of the boys who served there during his two years in the
school were old classmates from the Nelles reform school, and
his loyalty to the rebel clique grew stronger on the basis of
shared experience. As he continued in his career as a California convict, the same faces, most of them black, cropped
up in adjacent cells again and again. All his best friends in
life, like himself, were criminals. Like him, many of them
later became Black Panthers.

He was released at age 18, early in 1954, but his time as a

probationer was limited. In the spring he was caught again, with "a shopping bag full of marijuana." No longer a juvenile, he began his first adult term in prison on June 18. Although he knew he had only himself to blame, if for no other reason than that he allowed himself to get caught, he cursed society blindly and generally for his bad luck. "I became quite personally wired up—alienated from a bad system," he said. "It was like the whole generation of cats who started with me in Whittier were back in prison with me now, and we were all completely alienated, like somebody was after each of us, specifically, because there we were, all of us. I wasn't very sophisticated then, but I had some definite ideas about the system—it was bad, man, bad."

But while he turned society off, he did not turn himself off. He had always done well, with little effort, in his studies. In prison he finished high school and began to read more deeply than the superficial novels which he says captivated him earlier—"junk stuff, like Harold Robbins's novels, you know?" He dabbled at writing, and, as he described it in *Soul on Ice,* he began to formulate a devastating black man-white woman mysticism whose consequences could easily have led him to the gas chamber.

During this period I was concentrating my reading in the field of economics [he wrote]. Having previously dabbled in the theories and writings of Rousseau, Thomas Paine, and Voltaire, I had added a little polish to my iconoclastic stance, without, however, bothering too much to understand their affirmative positions. . . . I began . . . to employ tactics of ruthlessness in my dealings with everyone with whom I came into contact. And I began to look at white America through these new eyes.

Somehow I arrived at the conclusion that, as a matter of principle, it was of paramount importance for me to have an antagonistic, ruthless attitude toward white women. The term *outlaw* appealed to me. I considered myself to be mentally free—I was an "outlaw." I had stepped outside the white man's law, which I repudiated with scorn and self-satisfaction. I became a law unto

myself—my own legislature, my own supreme court, my own executive. At the moment I walked out of the prison gate, my feelings toward white women in general could be summed up in the
following lines:

### To a White Girl

*I love you*
*Because you're white*
*Not because you're charming*
*Or bright.*
*Your whiteness*
*Is a silky thread*
*Snaking through my thoughts*
*In red hot patterns*
*Of lust and desire . . .*

I became a rapist. To refine my technique and *modus operandi,*
I started out by practicing on black girls in the ghetto—in the
black ghetto where dark and vicious deeds appear not as aberra-
tions or deviations from the norm, but as part of the sufficiency of
the Evil of a day—and when I considered myself smooth enough,
I crossed the tracks and sought out white prey. I did this con-
sciously, deliberately, willfully, methodically—though looking back
I see that I was in a frantic, wild and completely abandoned frame
of mind.

He looked upon the white woman as a mystical "Ogre"
and said he was compelled to purge the ogre from his soul.
"Rape was an insurrectionary act. It delighted me that I was
defying and trampling upon the white man's law, upon his
system of values, and that I was defiling his women . . . I felt
I was getting revenge."

But however urgent his vengeful lust seemed when he was
paroled from Soledad Prison after his first three-year adult
term there, he did not rush pell-mell into the orgiastic binge
that he had contemplated. "First I worked out a cool system
of marijuana peddling," he told me on the plane to Omaha.
"I had thought a lot about that in prison, too, and I realized
how stupid I had been to carry the stuff around and deal

openly the way I had. This time I set myself up so I couldn't get caught for selling or for possession, because I didn't make the contacts directly, I stayed in the background, out of sight. It was so cool I think I could have gone on forever without getting caught.

"After seven or eight months, when it was going good, I started to rape."

Cleaver stopped there and reflected for a few moments.

"Can you describe what you did, how you felt when you did it?" I asked. "It must have been something other than the purge you had imagined it would be."

He looked at me quizzically. "I don't think it would serve any purpose to go into any detail," he said. "I wrote about it in my book. I think that's all I really ought to say now. I don't mean the question isn't interesting. It is. I've thought about exploring it more than I have, and one of these days I think I will. I've thought about a novel or a novella about a black rapist. How does *she* respond? How does *he* feel? Is it right? Is it wrong? What goes through his mind? It's not a simple sexual thing, you know?"

For three months, Cleaver said, he went methodically about his two occupations, selling marijuana five days a week and victimizing both black and white women in his spare time, almost as if it was a hobby. "I would spend the weekdays thinking about it, planning it, and I would rape on weekends," he said. In the eleventh month of his freedom from prison, he was caught. He would not describe the final incident in his career as a leisure-time rapist, but the trial and probation records of his last conviction, public documents available at the Los Angeles District Attorney's office and the District Court of Appeals, revealed the following account:

A student nurse at St. Vincent's College of Nursing was sitting in a car near St. Vincent's hospital in the Westlake district of Los Angeles, with her boyfriend, a student at Santa Monica City College. It was 2:30 A.M., November 3, 1957. They testified that a black man with a hat pulled down over his eyes suddenly appeared at the car window. Both later identified the man as Cleaver. They said he brandished a gun and demanded, "Let me in or I'll break in." The frightened college student opened the door. They testified that Cleaver then ordered the girl into the back seat, told the boy to slide over and slipped into the driver's seat. Then he bound the boy's wrists with Scotch tape. (The tape later proved to be the only physical evidence linking Cleaver to the crime. Police found a roll of Scotch tape [but no gun] in Cleaver's own car.)

The young couple said that Cleaver then crawled into the back seat and ordered the girl to take off her clothes. When she refused, she said, he struck her with the gun. She refused again and again, and each time she said he hit her with the pistol.

Her boyfriend, meanwhile, freed his wrists and blew the horn of the car. The victims said that Cleaver, apparently startled, leapt from the car and fled. As the college student started the car to go for help, he and the girl heard shots. They said they could not tell if the shots were aimed at them or where they came from. A young couple parked in a car across the street also heard the shots. A third witness, sitting alone in another car, said he saw a man fire two shots and leap into a light-colored 1949 Ford. The witness, a Standard Oil company salesman, started his own car and chased the fleeing Ford until it rammed another car about six blocks away. He drove on to a filling station and called the police.

When the police converged on the scene, they found Cleaver surveying his damaged Ford and they arrested him. He was charged with five counts of assault with a deadly weapon with intent to commit murder (as police reconstructed the incident, five shots had been fired); one count of assault with intent to commit rape, and three counts of assault with a deadly weapon.

Cleaver pleaded "Not guilty" and testified that he had been parked with his own girlfriend a short distance from the scene of the attempted rape and the gunfire. He said he was fright-

ened because he was on parole from the marijuana conviction, so he started his car and tried to put the scene behind
him. Instead, he said, he crashed into another car. He explained that his girlfriend disappeared in the crowd that
gathered after the crash.

The five-day trial in Los Angeles County Superior Court
began on February 4, 1958, and was conducted by Judge
Leroy Dawson. Cleaver's counsel was Beecher E. Stowe, a
Negro, and the prosecuting Deputy District Attorney was G.
Lenoir, also a Negro. Cleaver was found guilty on two counts
of assault with intent to commit murder and three counts of
assault with a deadly weapon. He was found not guilty of
assault with intent to commit rape.

Judge Dawson received a probation report on March 7,
1958, and sentenced Cleaver to from one to 14 years imprisonment on March 20, 1958. The following are excerpts from the
probation report, prepared by Philip Morentin, Deputy, Central Adult Investigations:

". . . 'The officers feel that the defendant is a potentially
dangerous person whose motivations for present crime seem
to be a sex angle for he was not after money or cars.

" 'All along, the defendant has refused to cooperate and
divulge any explanation of his activities at the time of the
offense.

". . . 'Parole officer believes that the defendant is a cool and
calculating person, not only unscrupulous but vicious . . .

" 'Defendant has feelings of persecution for he thinks he is
being prejudiced because of his race . . .

" 'Defendant vehemently maintains his innocence and con-
sistently protests because of race. There appears in the defendant a feeling of persecution and a distorted sense of
values which give rise to the conclusion that he is a severely
disturbed individual who has become a serious menace to the
community which now must be protected from his predatory
behavior.

" 'He has made little effort to be employed or to accept

any social responsibility. Since he has not profited by experience nor shown any change in his antisocial conduct, it becomes necessary that more stringent measures be applied.

" 'It is, therefore, respectfully recommended that probation be denied.' "

After his return to prison, Cleaver was thankful that his rampage had been stopped when it was.

I know [he wrote] that if I had not been apprehended I would have slit some white throats . . .

After I returned to prison, I took a long look at myself and, for the first time in my life, admitted that I was wrong, that I had gone astray—astray not so much from the white man's law as from being human, civilized—for I could not approve the act of rape. Even though I had some insight into my own motivations, I did not feel justified. I lost my self-respect. My pride as a man dissolved and my whole fragile moral structure seemed to collapse, completely shattered.

That is why I started to write. To save myself.

As we sat in the plane sipping our Scotches, he reflected on his feelings upon returning to prison.

"I didn't really want to be out there selling marijuana," he said. "I didn't really want to be out there raping. What I really wanted to do was to study and to learn, to write, to prepare myself for what I am doing now. In a way, prison is a kind of perverted peace of mind; hours and hours when you know that nothing is going to happen—for years you have no worries about dances, about social life, about girls; you don't even have to take care of your own laundry. You study and learn. You examine yourself."

He said his self-examination and his analysis of the role of black people in America began in earnest not more than a few months after his reimprisonment. He read widely. He wrote. He practiced public speaking and attended prison study courses in subjects ranging from accountancy to philosophy. He joined the Black Muslims and recruited a "congregation." Tossed into solitary confinement for his provocative activities as an agitating Black Muslim minister, he treated the 29-day stretch of idleness as a religious and educational retreat. "They wouldn't let me have anything but the Bible to read when I was in the hole," he recalled. "So I read it over and over. It was a retreat, actually a useful period for me, but there was one moment in the isolation cell that I absolutely could not deal with. That was the moment when they closed the door. *Snap!* I couldn't deal with that.

"The isolation cells and death row at San Quentin are on the same sixth-floor block. Chessman was in there, then. After I got over the first moment of being locked in, it was easy for me to do the twenty-nine days because I couldn't help but think what they were going to do with those others on that block. They were going to kill them."

"Does the fear of death bother you now?" I asked him.

"Death? Violent death?"

"Yes."

"No, it really doesn't. I figure that it will happen. You learn to live with that in prison. In 1960 and 1961, when the Muslims were growing in numbers—the movement was very important in prisons, you know?—there was a lot of racially motivated killing, and I was one of the prime targets. I learned to live with that. Most prisoners do. It becomes a part of your way of life, really. Second nature. For example, two prisoners would never sit the way you and I are sitting now, both leaning back, looking straight ahead."

He leaned forward and turned sharply to face me.

"I'm going to be like this, watching his back while I talk with him, and he's going to be watching mine. We protect each other. But you also know without any doubt that if someone wants to kill you bad enough so he's willing to take a chance or doesn't care if he's caught, there's not much you can do about it. Learn to live with it, that's all."

Eldridge then dismissed his period as a devout Black Muslim in a few brief remarks. "I couldn't relate literally to what Elijah Muhammad said, but I did relate to Muslim dogma symbolically. And I loved Malcolm X. All black prisoners did. It was important for a black man in prison, a source of pride. It got the administrators and the guards uptight, you know? The guards would see me writing, and they would come in my cell and tear up my writing on the grounds that it was Muslim literature or propaganda. That's when I began to disguise my manuscripts as legal documents. Every prisoner becomes an amateur lawyer, constantly preparing writs of *habeas corpus*. That's how I hid my manuscripts so the guards wouldn't tear them up. A prisoner's legal documents are sacred, you know? The guards wouldn't touch them."

It was Cleaver's love of Malcolm X, really, that ultimately settled his course in life and, tangentially, got him out of prison after serving nine years of his maximum 14-year sentence. The Muslim movement was active throughout the U.S. prison system and its convict ministers, such as Eldridge X who was moved from San Quentin to Folsom Prison in a futile attempt by authorities to weaken Muslimism, clashed frequently and bitterly with officials who refused to grant the new movement the customary rights of assembly and worship.

As a tactical measure and in hope of attracting legal support for the Muslim movement, Cleaver began writing random letters to California lawyers whose names cropped up in the newspapers in connection with civil liberties causes. He never expected to gain personal advantage from the letters, but he hoped his campaign would forestall a feared prison system crackdown on the bizarre religious movement. Letters to practicing lawyers cannot legally be censored by prison authorities, Cleaver knew, and he was confident that the officials would shy away from a total crackdown on the Muslims as long as they knew he was in touch with outside legal sources.

"It was a way of keeping prison officials mad but scaring them at the same time, because they never knew when one of the letters would catch."

When Malcolm X broke with Elijah Muhammad, forswore

black racism and began searching for the door to brotherhood between whites and blacks, the Muslim prison congregation was violently split. Despite threats against his life by other convict Muslims, Eldridge X sided with Malcolm. "I have, so to speak, washed my hands in the blood of the martyr, Malcolm X, whose retreat from the precipice of madness (black racism) created new rooms for others to turn about in, and I am now caught up in that tiny space, attempting a maneuver of my own," Cleaver wrote.

The maneuver included a continuation of his legal letter-writing campaign. He mailed one letter a day. By mid-1965, he had almost exhausted his list of lawyers, most of whom failed to respond. The few who did were politely disinterested or kissed him off with snippets of gratuitous legal advice.

At the very end of Cleaver's list was the name of Beverly Axelrod, who had established a solid reputation among civil rights lawyers on the West Coast. He had read about her early in his letter-writing campaign, but he skipped over her name on the assumption that a woman lawyer would not be as sympathetic or as effective as a man.

"One evening I went to my cell, and there was a picture of Beverly in the paper in connection with some case she was involved in. She was a very beautiful woman with a very striking face. All the men had been no help. So I decided to write to her. I wrote her a different kind of letter, a letter that I thought a woman would understand." It worked.

Mrs. Axelrod replied promptly with a promise to visit Cleaver at Folsom Prison within a few days. When she got there, Cleaver was prepared. He had stuffed most of his manuscripts into what looked like a long brief for a writ of *habeas corpus*. In the visitors' room he reassembled his essays and stories and gave them to the comely San Francisco lawyer. She was overwhelmed by the forcefulness of his writing and the evident depth and compassion of his mind. He was overwhelmed by her, and she responded with the total devotion that is evident in the samples of their letters which Eldridge included in *Soul on Ice*. "I feel as though I'm on the edge of a new world," she wrote to him.

"What I feel for you is profound," he replied. "Beverly, there is something happening between us that is way out of the ordinary. Ours is one for the books, for the poets to draw new inspiration from, one to silence the cynics, and one to humble us by reminding us how little we know about human beings, about ourselves . . . We recognize each other. And, having recognized each other, is it any wonder that our souls hold hands and cling together . . ."

Immediately after her return from Folsom to San Francisco, Mrs. Axelrod brought Cleaver's writing to Edward M. Keating, an old friend, who was then the editor-owner of *Ramparts* magazine. Keating, too, was bowled over by the literary qualities of the convict writer. He made copies of the smuggled material and sent them to a number of well-known writers and social critics including Norman Mailer, Norman Podhoretz, Paul Jacobs, Maxwell Geismar, John Howard Griffin, and Leslie Fiedler. All promptly responded with praise and offers of support except Podhoretz, who was busy then writing an autobiographical book called *Making It*.

Cleaver was astonished. He had been writing in an intellectual vacuum, with no adviser, no audience, and no critics against whom to test his style and ideas. He had hardly thought of himself as a writer. Suddenly he was being praised by important literary figures, men whose work he knew and admired.

"I found it hard to handle. Very hard. The extravagance of their comments—things like 'This is great!' I just didn't know what to do with that."

At the same time he was given more than a little hope of freedom by Beverly Axelrod, who turned almost full attention to a campaign to win his parole. Her legal efforts were immeasurably reinforced by the glowing letters from literary figures who had read Cleaver's prose, but they probably were helped the most by Keating's guarantee that he would employ

Cleaver as a *Ramparts* editor if he was released from prison.

Paul Jacobs and David Welsh, who became Eldridge's editor, visited him in prison on Keating's request and began working on what eventually became *Soul on Ice*. "He needed very little editing," said Jacobs, "but he was a real professional about it. He welcomed it. He was so overjoyed to be published." His first published piece was the scathing critique of James Baldwin, printed in *Ramparts* in June, 1966, while he was in Soledad Prison, to which he had been transferred from Folsom while awaiting his parole hearing. Other pieces, published as *Letters from Prison,* followed. Parole authorities were impressed by the fact that he had been promised a job, and in December, 1966, he was paroled to become a senior editor and contributing writer of *Ramparts*.

One of Mrs. Axelrod's close friends recalled to me later the exquisite excitement that the divorcée-lawyer displayed just before Cleaver was released when she knew that her efforts had succeeded.

"She stopped by here the day before he got out of prison, and she was glowing like a bride on the way to church," the friend said. "She was already talking about having his baby. I never saw anyone so obviously and completely in love."

He walked out of prison with Beverly Axelrod in December, 1966. But within a few months the bridal glow apparently faded, for she left San Francisco. Cleaver would not discuss the relationship at all, other than to say, "We began with a great respect for one another, and we still have a great respect for one another."

Another friend of both of them said that "it just didn't work out, that's all. I think he foresaw that even before he got out of prison. In one of his letters to her, he wrote, 'I could arrange (and how easy it would be) to spend the rest of my life in prison, and we could live happily ever after.' The love affair stayed in prison. He didn't."

"I had some very wrong ideas about women," Cleaver mused after his brief reference to Mrs. Axelrod. "I related to them as women only, you know? I didn't relate to them intellectually, as persons, to be respected for their minds. My first introduction to the power of women didn't come until I was in Atlanta, covering Stokely and SNCC for *Ramparts* in 1967. I met a beautiful girl from one of the Ivy League schools. She was a Mississippi girl. A beautiful black girl, working for SNCC. I wanted to sleep with her, you know? She was an artist. When we got to her place, there was a painting she had just finished. It was a painting of a dove, a dove that had been horribly destroyed. A peace symbol. A beautiful painting and one that stirred up ideas. We began to discuss it, and our discussion went on and on over a lot of subjects. The discussion destroyed all thoughts of going to bed; I didn't even think about it. We just sat up all night in that room, talking. It was the first time I realized I could really relate to a woman."

On the same assignment, he met Kathleen Neal. Aside from his commanding presence and charismatic personality, one of the things that most attracted her to him, after her experience in helping to drive the whites out of SNCC, was his membership in the audacious new Black Panther Party of Oakland, California.

After his release from prison, Cleaver had faced a painful dilemma, comparable in an involuted way to his long ago ambivalence toward crime and continued education through the game of football. With the support and critical acclaim already his, he could slip quietly into the literary world, virtually certain of great intellectual and economic rewards as well as sure protection against future entanglements with the law. Important figures in the literary establishment privately lionized him. His prison-written articles in *Ramparts* and *Esquire* magazines had stirred an even wider interest. His first book was being made ready for press by McGraw-Hill Book Company, and those who had read it were confident it would become a bestseller. If he wanted the freedom to write on his own terms with no worries or fears intruding, it was his. He was home free.

"He had a clear choice," said Paul Jacobs. "He could have opted to be the black writer. Everybody was pushing contracts under his nose, urging him."

But the core of all his writing so far had been his desperate need to find an honorable place for the black man in a hostile world. His own ruthless self-analysis demanded action in the front rank of black revolution, and he couldn't feel the action on the keys of a typewriter.

At first, after his release from prison, he tried to satisfy the need by establishing a kind of literary center in San Francisco for militant black writers. It was called Black House. For Cleaver it served as an emotional decompression chamber in which to phase over from prison life to freedom. But it was not much of a battleground for black liberation, and the question of what to do with his life remained.

Huey P. Newton unconsciously resolved Cleaver's dilemma for him. Betty Shabaz, the widow of Malcolm X, was visiting San Francisco. She called on the editors of *Ramparts*. Newton, Bobby Seale, and a few other members of the six-month-old Black Panther Party had appointed themselves her bodyguards and accompanied her to the magazine's offices. They carried shotguns, which was then legal in California, provided they were not concealed. Under the law, an unloaded weapon could be legally "concealed" without permit inside an automobile. Once it was taken out of the car it was considered no longer concealed and legally could be loaded. Newton and his colleagues, who already had begun to provoke the Oakland police with the tactic, made a point of ostentatiously loading their weapons when they stepped from their cars.

After a lifetime of deferring to whites and more than half a life of imprisonment in which he had been conditioned to see weapons only in the hands of his arch-enemies, prison guards and police, Cleaver looked on first with fright, then with genuine awe as Huey Newton strolled the sidewalk in front of *Ramparts* with a loaded shotgun crooked under his arm. Just a few feet away was a group of San Francisco policemen nervously fingering their gun holsters, nonplussed by the brash display.

One of the officers told Newton to stop brandishing his gun. Newton calmly replied that he had a legal right to carry it, a constitutional right. The officer repeated his order. Newton again repeated his constitutional right and his right to arms under the laws of the State of California. The policeman reached for his own gun. Newton shifted his shotgun, ready to raise it. The policeman took his hand from his holster and sighed with frustration. Newton laughed in his face and walked jauntily away.

"It was cool, absolute revolutionary courage," said Cleaver with awe. "Huey never got excited or emotional. He was out of sight, man. The cops just didn't know what to do with that. He stood them down."

Out of admiration for Newton's willingness "to risk all on the curve of his instincts," Cleaver joined the Panthers, whose principal occupation at the time consisted of nightly "justice" patrols in the Oakland ghettos. Newton, Seale, David Hilliard, Charles Bursey, Bobby Hutton, and a few others who made up the membership of the still insignificant militant organization would cruise the streets, armed with guns and law books, watching for what they considered to be unseemly police behavior. When they saw the police accost a Negro, they would stand a legal 15 feet away from the officers to avoid being charged with interference, and read aloud relevant portions of the laws assuring the arrested person his rights. Not surprisingly, these armed interruptions annoyed the police. When Newton and his colleagues began deriding the policemen as "pigs," the seeds of a police vendetta against the new, small, militant group began to germinate.

Somewhat belatedly, the California legislature responded by considering a new gun-control law proposed by an Oakland assemblyman who had become incensed by the Panthers. On

May 2, 1967, while the state assembly was beginning debate
on the firearms legislation, the Panthers assured its passage by
a bumbling, almost comic display of weapons at the State
Capitol in Sacramento that made headlines all over the world.
Much of the action was pure accident, but it was an act of
public relations genius, planned by Newton and carried out
by Bobby Seale, who explained that an audacious armed
invasion of the capitol was necessary to "get the message over
to the people about the fact that we have to arm ourselves
with guns and force against this racist, decadent system, because of what it is doing to us."

A convoy of five Panther cars from Oakland arrived in
Sacramento. Thirty Panthers, including six girls and Eldridge
Cleaver, debarked. Most of them carried guns, which they
made a great show of loading as they left the cars. Cleaver
carried a camera, but whether he was there in his capacity as
a journalist, covering the event for *Ramparts* as he claimed, or
as Minister of Information of the Black Panther Party, as state
officials later charged, was problematical. In either case, he
was there with the advance approval of his parole officer.

The ragtaggle but fierce-looking group entered the building
with Seale in the lead, anxiously calling out, "Where in the
Hell's the Assembly? Anybody in here know where you go in
and observe the Assembly making these laws?" By this time a
crowd of photographers, reporters, and T.V. cameramen had
gathered and were backing down the hall in front of the
Panthers, clicking shutters and grinding film through their
cameras. Unaware of where they were going, the photographers backed directly into the Assembly chamber, which was
not permitted under the rules of the House, and the Panthers
followed in total confusion. In the melee, Seale forgot all
about reading the statement that Huey Newton had drafted.
He remembered it later and read it for the benefit of the press
after the Assembly chamber was cleared. There was no violence, but assemblymen's ears rang with shouts of "Hey, that

motherfucker got my gun . . . bastard, gimme back my gun, I got rights."

Most of the Panthers, including Eldridge, were arrested after leaving the building. For several days, while he was held in jail in Sacramento, it seemed likely that Cleaver would be returned to prison for violation of his parole. But after all the others had been released on bail, Mrs. Axelrod, in what apparently was her last legal favor to Eldridge, successfully argued for his release on grounds that he was a journalist, not a participant in the demonstration.

"It was a beautiful thing, a correct tactic," said Eldridge, recalling the incident. "It focused attention on the Black Panther Party. We made them look like fools."

After that the Panthers were not long out of the news. Numerous minor encounters with the police during the summer and early fall resulted in a few arrests, mostly on technicalities. Then the battle lines between local authorities and the Black Panther Party were drawn in blood by Huey Newton and a 23-year-old Oakland patrolman named John Frey just before dawn on October 28. Frey died of gunshot wounds while attempting to arrest Newton. Another officer named Herbert Heanes was wounded. Newton was shot in the stomach, escaped to a hospital where he sought emergency treatment, and was arrested for the murder of Officer Frey.

Newton's incarceration without bail pending his trial for murder left Cleaver and Seale as the principal leaders-at-large of the Party, but Huey remained more than nominally in charge, sending a steady flow of communiqués and "executive mandates" from his jail cell in Oakland's Alameda County Courthouse. With Newton's active direction from behind bars, the first noteworthy Black Panther legal and fund-raising battle began with the slogan, "Free Huey or the Sky's the Limit!" Recruitment of new members of the Party skyrocketed and new chapters began forming in Los Angeles, New York, Denver, and other cities.

Cleaver, meanwhile, married Kathleen in December, 1967.

After staying for a time as Paul and Ruth Jacobs's houseguests, they moved into a new apartment at 850 Oak Street in San Francisco. One of the local newspapers published a somewhat gushy feature story describing the decor of the newlywed's home, as if the Cleavers were just another prominent, society-oriented Bay City couple. The police followed up on the sweet publicity with an ironic twist of their own. They burst into the apartment at 3:30 one January morning looking for guns. They had no search warrant. The Cleavers had no guns.

Early one February morning, two days after a "Free Huey" fund-raising rally in an Oakland auditorium at which Eldridge introduced as guest speakers Stokely Carmichael, Rap Brown, and James Forman, police officers in nearby Berkeley demanded to be admitted to Bobby Seale's apartment. A patrolman named Edward Coyn said that he stood outside the apartment and heard loud talk and the clicking of automatic weapons. He said there had been a "citizen's complaint" to the effect that voices had been overheard, apparently in the process of planning a murder. Seale and his wife Artie were arrested, as were David Hilliard, two other men, and a woman in the apartment at the time. Their guns were confiscated.

In March the Oakland police issued a statement charging that the Black Panther Party was building up an arsenal of weapons. The police said they had traced a recent purchase of sixty-five 9 mm. Spanish Astra automatic pistols at Skim's Army Goods store in Reno, Nevada, to the Oakland Panthers.

Tension was increasing within both the police department and the black community. The "Free Huey" rally in the Oakland auditorium—at which a short-lived merger of SNCC and the Panthers, as well as the new and surprising alliance with the Peace and Freedom Party were announced—had drawn between 4,000 and 6,000 people, most of them black and obviously sympathetic to the Panthers. As local sympathy for the Panthers grew, the police increased their surveillance of the militants who, under a new state law, no longer were permitted to carry loaded weapons on the streets. A few voices in the black community, notably the Negro newspaper the *Oakland Post,* tried to dampen growing resentment in the ghettos by insisting that Huey would get a fair trial and urging the police to be fair with the Panthers. The tension even extended to the jailhouse, where Newton got into a fight with a white prisoner, identified as a member of Hell's Angels, a motorcycle gang. Both were given three days of solitary confinement after the fracas.

On April 3, Eldridge, David Hilliard, and about a dozen other Panthers gathered at Saint Augustine's Episcopal Church, whose gentle young black priest, Father Earl Neil, was no stranger to violence. He was a veteran of civil rights demonstrations in McComb, Mississippi. The house in which he had stayed there had been bombed and shot at. He had become intrigued by the bizarre Black Panther Party since coming to Oakland and had begun to function as occasional chaplain to its militant members. Neither Cleaver, Hilliard, nor their colleagues in the church were armed. Eldridge left early, without incident. But as the meeting broke up at about 9:30 P.M., there was a commotion at the door. Father Neil hurried downstairs from his second-floor study and pushed through the crowd at the door to confront an Oakland police captain. Behind the officer was a lieutenant, and behind him, at the foot of the steps to the church, was a patrolman pointing a shotgun at the door.

"I introduced myself and told him I was the priest of the church," Father Neil later recounted. "We shook hands. He introduced himself as Captain McCarthy. I asked him why he had come. He said that he and his officers responded to a call on the police radio that someone had been seen outside the church waving a gun, and that there was a crowd of people around. He told me he wanted to come into the church and search the people in the church. I immediately said how disturbed I was over this show of force. To me this seemed very unnecessary, just contributing to what was already a very tense situation . . .

"I refused to let him enter the church . . .

"The only weapons I saw in my church—since I've been here—were the shotgun and pistols of the police officers . . .

"We are now entering a phase of the black liberation struggle where it's going to be the persecution of the Christian churches. If a black group that is trying to do something for the community cannot meet in the sanctuary of a church, where in Heaven's name can they meet?

"It was quite significant that something like this should happen around the Easter season when we begin to meditate upon the events that led up to the arrest, unjust trial, and execution of Jesus Christ. The church is going to be a very vulnerable institution."

There were no arrests at the church, but reports of the incident infuriated all Father Neil's middle-class black parishioners and most of the rest of the black people of Oakland as well.

Easter's grief was just beginning. The next evening Martin Luther King was murdered in Memphis, Tennessee. Oakland, like many other cities, was on the verge of explosion.

The following day, Eldridge, Bobby Seale, David Hilliard, Emory Douglas, Charles Bursey, Bobby Hutton, and other Panther Party members fanned out over the city, walking the streets, visiting junior and senior high schools and talking forebearance with as many young black people as they could. Whether their efforts alone were responsible for saving Oakland from the spontaneous rioting that swept some other American cities is impossible to know. They certainly helped to cool passions that were at the kindling point. But the Panthers made it clear that they did not cool off the ghettos just for the sake of making a peaceful gesture to the city's white establishment.

"The only people who get hurt or killed in that kind of rioting are the black people in the middle of it," Cleaver explained. "We didn't want to see that."

On the very next night, Cleaver himself was in the middle

of what the Panthers called a police riot and the police called a Panther ambush. Along with Hilliard, Bursey, Bobby Hutton, and about fifteen other Panthers in three cars, Eldridge says he was preparing to make calls at the homes of members and supporters, gathering foodstuffs for a Panther-sponsored picnic the next day at Oakland's DeFremery Park.

"I had to have a piss, so we pulled up to the curb and stopped, and the other cars stopped behind us. I shouldn't have done it, you know? Not in the street, but there wasn't any place else, and I had to go, so I got out and stood by the rear fender of the car. It was dark, so it wasn't a question of anybody watching me."

Oakland police officers Richard R. Jensen and Nolan Darnell pulled up nearby in a patrol car. They explained later that they saw a figure "crouching down behind a parked automobile with Florida plates" and got out to investigate. How they so quickly identified the Florida license plates and yet failed to see much of anything else was never explained. Nor was the question of who fired the first shot.

"I was just standing there when all of a sudden the cops fired a shotgun at me," said Cleaver. Within seconds guns were firing from both directions and the Panthers were running for cover. Police reinforcements from central Oakland and nearby Emeryville were on the scene so quickly—the Panthers claimed they arrived within three minutes of the first shot—that their speed created suspicions that the police had planned to provoke an armed clash and had merely been waiting for a target of opportunity when Cleaver's small convoy was discovered.

The Panthers scattered. Cleaver and Bobby Hutton took cover in the dirt half-cellar of a neat, modern frame house at 2818 28th Street, just across from a small manufacturing plant called the Gibson Lounge Chair Company. The police, whose force grew to 100 men before the gunfight ended, crouched behind a low brick façade supporting the plate glass display window of the small plant, which they shattered to open a field of fire at the house. The shoot-out continued from 9:07 until 10:30 P.M.

Bobby Hutton, while not the youngest of the Panthers (14- and 15-year-old boys had joined the Party, and Newton had turned down a number of 12- and 13-year-olds), was the baby of the leadership group. He had begun tagging along with Newton and Seale in 1966 when the two co-founders constituted the entire Party membership, running a radical-baiting con game to raise funds with which to buy guns. The co-founders, according to Seale, had been impressed by the popularity of the sayings of Chairman Mao Tse-tung on the campus of the University of California at Berkeley. They found in Mao's campus popularity a means of raising money for their new organization. Like entrepreneurs moving into a commercial vacuum, they began buying wholesale cases of Mao's *Little Red Book,* in English, at 25 cents a copy and hawking the books on the Berkeley campus for a dollar. It was mid-1966, the beginning of the Black Panther Party, whose formal founding Newton proclaimed in October. Bobby Hutton, then only 15 years old, stuck with them so loyally and handled the money so well that Newton appointed him Party treasurer.

Crouched on the dirt floor of the 28th Street basement as the police poured automatic weapons fire and tear-gas grenades into the building, Hutton showed no panic, according to Eldridge.

"He was cool. I was hit in the leg and bleeding. Bobby was more concerned about me than he was about the bullets. He ripped my pants off so he could see how badly I was hurt."

Hutton was armed. Cleaver was not. As a parolee he had been conspicuously careful to avoid touching any of the Panther guns, because to do so would violate his parole. I find no reason to believe that he is lying when he insists that he did not use a gun on the night of the shoot-out, either.

In any case, a weapon in his hands would have been utterly useless. Cleaver said Hutton got off only one shot before they ducked into the house. There was no window or firing hole in the front wall of the cellar in which they hid. They could have fired obliquely out of the cellar door, but to expose themselves in that way would certainly have brought a rain of counterfire. Moreover, the rate of police fire was so heavy anyway that it is hard to imagine Cleaver and Hutton even rising from the floor, where they were protected by a foot-high concrete retaining curb, much less actively returning shots in the one-sided gunfight.

(Sometime after the incident, while reviewing its details and attempting to shape a coherent picture of the conflicting stories involved, I visited the shattered house with Charles Bursey, a soft-spoken U.S. Navy veteran of 21 who had become a captain in the Panthers. He was hiding in another house around the corner on the night of the shoot-out, so he did not know exactly what took place at the 28th Street house when Eldridge and Bobby Hutton sought refuge there. But it was obvious from the condition of the building—police bulletholes perforating its walls from ground to roof literally like the holes of a vegetable sieve—that anyone who came out of the cellar alive was almost incredibly lucky.)

A tear-gas grenade was fired through a side window and struck Cleaver's shoulder. Another missile, whether a tracer bullet or a gas grenade is uncertain, touched off a fire in the wood timbers of the basement. Hopelessly trapped in a burning building with only one conceivable way to leave it alive, Cleaver and Hutton called out that they were prepared to surrender. Hutton handed his weapon to Cleaver, who threw it out the door.

Cleaver, whose face was swollen beyond recognition by the effects of the tear-gas explosion against his shoulder, had stripped off all his clothes. Most of his friends, including his wife, Kathleen, said he did this because he was a wise old con and knew the police could not confuse the issue of whether or not he was armed if he emerged from the building naked.

"It wasn't that, really," Cleaver told me. "Bobby took off my pants to look at my wound. I took off the rest because of the gas." Hutton kept his clothes on. As they emerged from the bullet-torn, burning building, the wounded and almost blinded Cleaver stumbled. What happened next is clouded in conflicting claims. Cleaver said the police ordered Bobby Hutton to run, then coldly shot him in the back. The police claim they thought Hutton was armed and was trying to escape or go for his weapon. He had moved only a few steps when he fell dead with seven bullets in his head and back. Police who examined his body conceded that he was not armed when he was shot. Cleaver was treated for his wound and immediately imprisoned as a parole violator. Seven other Panthers who had taken refuge in the neighborhood were rounded up. One was released and six were charged with assault with intent to commit murder, as was Cleaver.

On Good Friday, the Black Panther Party, then no more than about 100-strong in Oakland, conducted a memorial service for Bobby Hutton, announced that DeFremery Public Park in Oakland henceforth would be known, to them at least, as Bobby Hutton Memorial Park, demonstrated along with about 100 sympathetic supporters on behalf of "Free Huey or the Sky's the Limit!" at the Alameda County Courthouse, and joined a motorcade to Vacaville State Prison, on the road to Sacramento, in honor of Eldridge who was under guard in the prison medical facility there. It was a busy day, but its only tangible accomplishment was the burial of a 17-year-old boy who had been shot in the back.

Charles Garry, an old-line radical San Francisco lawyer whose skills were respected even by his most politically conservative legal opponents, called the Hutton slaying "pure murder" and demanded that charges be filed against the police. Garry had been retained to defend Newton after the Frey killing, but as each new incident erupted he found his list of Black Panther clients growing rapidly. Now he had seven more and he set about trying to prove that they had been framed, trapped in a police ambush and murderously run to ground.

Police Chief Charles Gain of Oakland, long known as one of the most enlightened police officials in the United States, replied that the Panthers had deliberately ambushed officers Jensen and Darnell and that, because Bobby Hutton's hands were hidden from view, officers assumed he was armed and shot him when he failed to respond to their order to halt his flight. Aside from the police there were few witnesses, because a police barricade of a two-block area prevented the curious from watching the gunfight. One woman who came upon the scene immediately after Hutton was killed said that his body was sprawled face down with his hands reaching straight above his head, as if they had been raised in surrender when he was shot and instantly killed. Cleaver said Hutton's hands were raised. The Grand Jury that considered the case agreed with the police version, as did the subsequent trial juries that, after many delays, began convicting the Black Panther defendants one by one. (After talking with Cleaver, Garry, Bursey, and David Hilliard, and being refused a request of the Oakland Police Department to interview any of the police officers concerned in the shoot-out, I was inclined to side with the Panthers. I remain so inclined. It simply doesn't make sense that Cleaver at that time would risk his freedom by openly carrying a gun, or that the Panthers who only the day before had energetically cooled an incendiary ghetto because they didn't want black people to be hurt, would set a calculated ambush against the police just twenty-four hours later, while the incendiary spark still sputtered.)

Cleaver said that at Vacaville he was far more forlorn than he ever had been during previous imprisonments. This time, he knew, there was not the slightest chance that he would be set free. The conditions of his parole were such that he had five years yet to serve on his old sentence. The Adult Authority, which supervises paroled prisoners, had absolute power to revoke the parole and force service of the remainder of the old sentence. Revocation of parole followed the shoot-out by only a few hours. On top of that, he was afraid of receiving another sentence as a result of his part in the shoot-out, a sentence that probably would include a judicial declaration that he had become a "habitual criminal," thereby making him an unwilling ward of the state for life.

"It was like dying," he said. "I did not expect to be released."

But Garry, a lawmaker's lawyer who had won fame in his profession for successfully arguing through to the Supreme Court the legal concept of diminished responsibility, as well as a man of extraordinary courage who had boldly stood down the House Un-American Activities Committee during one of its witch hunts in San Francisco, thought otherwise. He prepared a brief for a writ of *habeas corpus* on grounds that Cleaver was in effect a political prisoner, being punished arbitrarily in advance of trial because of charges against him concerning which, under the constitution, he had to be considered innocent until proven guilty. Garry argued his case before Judge Raymond Sherwin of the Superior Court of Solano County, California. The Adult Authority, apparently caught off guard by the action, was diffidently represented by the state attorney general's office. The attorney general offered no substantial proof to support the Adult Authority claims that Cleaver had violated his parole by possessing a weapon, associating with people of bad repute, and failing to cooperate with his parole officer.

On June 12, the greying Judge Sherwin, a handsome 52-year-old jurist who had experienced only five reversals of his opinions in twenty years on the bench, quick to smile, hearty, and obviously courageous, delivered his written opinion on the proceedings.

The record here is that though the petitioner was arrested and his parole canceled more than two months ago, hearings before the Adult Authority have not even been scheduled. There is nothing to indicate why it was deemed necessary to cancel his parole before his trial on the pending of criminal charges of which he is presumed innocent . . .

It has to be stressed that the uncontradicted evidence presented to this court indicated that the petitioner had been a model parolee. The peril to his parole status stemmed from no failure of personal rehabilitation, but from his undue eloquence in pursuing political goals, goals which were offensive to many of his contemporaries. Not only was there absence of cause for the cancellation of parole, it was the product of a type of pressure unbecoming, to say the least, to the law enforcement paraphernalia of this state.

The black comedian Godfrey Cambridge, Ed Keating, and a few other concerned friends guaranteed Cleaver's $63,000 bail on the remaining criminal charges stemming from the Oakland shoot-out, and he was set free.

"He [Judge Sherwin] is the first judge I ever encountered who had dignity and the courage to follow the law," said Cleaver as he was released. Returning to San Francisco in Keating's car, Cleaver cried and shouted exultantly, "I can't believe it! I can't believe it!"

Before his two-month imprisonment, Cleaver had successfully led the effort to ally the Black Panther Party with the Peace and Freedom Party, a helter-skelter political grouping of New Left radical organizations ranging from Abbie Hoffman's Yippies to the Maoist Progressive Labor Party and the Independent Socialist Clubs. He had succeeded to the surprise of many who doubted that extremist blacks ever could find common cause with extremist whites. At the Peace and Freedom Party's national convention in Ann Arbor, Michigan, Cleaver overwhelmingly defeated comedian Dick Gregory for the organization's Presidential nomination, even though, at 33 years of age, he was too young to qualify for the office under the Constitution of the United States.

Now he was preparing to make one of his first major campaign speeches in Omaha. At the end of our flight, on an acquaintance of three days, I felt as if I had known him for a long time. I related to him. He was an extraordinarily in-

telligent, deeply emotional, extremely sensitive man, fundamentally honest and gentle in nature, whose past, only partly
by his own choice, had been a wretched combination of oppression against him and by him against others. I wondered
what he would tell a crowd of Midwestern farmers in a Bible
Belt prairie town which I knew could not be receptive to the
political importunings of a radical, black ex-rapist.

# CHAPTER 5

## *"I'm a Presidential candidate. I'm not going to bullshit and lie."*

FONTENELLE PARK in Omaha is an extensive sward that rises along gentle hummocks from a prairie-flat ballfield to a softly rolling public golf course. It is entirely surrounded by undistinguished frame, stucco, and brick bungalows of the kind that spread across lower-middle-class suburban landscapes in the 1920s. Were it not for the existence of countless similar examples of urban dreariness in this country, the neighborhood around Fontenelle Park could easily be proclaimed the world capital of mediocrity. It is one of the "nicest" residential districts in the city of Omaha, which is to say that its residents are conservative and white. It seemed an ideal place for a George Wallace campaign rally.

The crowd that began gathering on the sunbaked ballfield at noon was curiously mixed, as were those at many other Peace and Freedom rallies that political year. Also typically, it was small. Of the 500-or-so who sprawled and sat on the grass before a flat-bed trailer-platform parked just beyond second base, less than a third were black. Some of the white spectators wore their political feelings out front in the form of long hair, hip clothes, and love beads, but most looked as if they could have wandered onto the field from a Lutheran youth group picnic in clean, starched sports shirts, cotton slacks and fresh cotton housedresses. A bewildered elderly couple, who required only a farmhouse and a pitchfork to place themselves in Grant Wood's *American Gothic,* threaded arm in arm through the small crowd, anxiously trying to get it behind them lest they become identified with it. If they were local people, their feelings apparently were shared by most of their neighbors. A few played ball at the far end of the field, away from the small crowd, but most remained visible only in the sanctuaries of their own surrounding yards, cutting the grass or watching remotely as the rally began.

A group of distinctly non-revolutionary teenaged black girls dressed in tight blue shorts and white shirts performed briefly like a sensuous military chorus line, swiveling smoothly, dipping, almost dancing to the Afro rhythms of a small black drum and bugle corps. They were called the John F. Kennedy drill team. It had been only two months since Robert Kennedy was murdered and since *The Black Panther,* temporarily deprived of the imprisoned Eldridge's editorial counsel, published a revolting cartoon that depicted the assassinated U.S. Senator as a dead pig.

There were other anomalies, too. A half-dozen lean men in business suits, all over six feet tall, moved casually around the outer limits of the crowd and behind the speakers' platform. Each carried a briefcase, as if he was on his way to an insurance office or a bank this Saturday noon. They were plainclothes police officers, and I assumed the briefcases contained tape recorders or weapons or both. There were no uniformed men in sight, an apparent act of nonprovocative forebearance on the part of the Omaha police chief.

On the bed of the trailer were a few folding chairs. Eldridge took his place on one next to a grey-haired, red-necked white Christian minister named Rev. Tom Reehorn, who was formally attired in starched white shirt, dark maroon tie, and ill-fitting black suit. He was the Nebraska P & F candidate for U.S. Senator. Eldridge wore his customary powder-blue turtleneck under a black leather jacket that looked tortuously uncomfortable in the hot August sun. Behind his chair, arms folded across their chests, stood two Black Panther captains from Oakland. Their 1960 Ford had broken down in Omaha on the road home from the Peace and Freedom Party convention at Ann Arbor, and they had paused to organize a Black Panther Party chapter in the Nebraska city. Now they stood sentinel behind their leader, shifting their eyes like the Secret Service men around other Presidential candidates, alert for snipers and other possible assassins.

The minister delivered an old-fashioned, stem-winding rural campaign speech, crying out for nonviolent solutions to the nation's troubles and an end to the immoral war in Vietnam. He was a living illustration of the diversity of the radical new political party, a pacifist obviously appalled by the proposals of many of his fellow P & F Party members that guns should become common political weapons in America.

One of these radicals was the next speaker. Ernest Chambers, a fiery local black leader who had made nationwide news by testifying with great force concerning the approaching black apocalypse during the Kerner Commission hearings earlier in the year, stepped to the microphone as a pattering of polite applause terminated the minister's nonviolent appeal.

"A revolution is not something that comes as the result of a peaceful meeting," he cried. "You can't fight with songs. We need guns. Black Power is a well-loaded gun."

There were cheers from the blacks in the audience and a few of the hip white kids joined it, but most of the crowd remained silent.

"The police department is the scum of the earth," Chambers shouted, and the men in business suits looked startled. With an orator's dramatic gestures and a strong, clear voice, Chambers skillfully raised the level of his passion until the entire audience was cheering and clapping enthusiastically. The plainclothesmen began to confer below a corner of the speaker's flatbed platform. They looked concerned. If Cleaver is as fiery, as inflammatory as this, I thought, there will be trouble. Blacks and whites, although small in number, were now together on the ballfield and their emotions were rising. I looked toward the bungalows to see if the neighbors were coming, but they remained unmoved in their yards and on their porches, either unaware of or unconcerned about what was being said.

Cries of "Right on!" "Tell it like it is!" "Black Power!" arose from the audience when Eldridge stood to acknowledge Ernest Chambers's emotional introduction. Two more Black Panthers, teenaged local boys who had joined the new chapter that the Oakland captains were getting together, mounted the trailer-bed platform. Now there were four soldiers standing guard, one at each corner. One of them stood stiffly just above the cluster of plainclothesmen, arms folded and head and eyes shifting rapidly over the crowd, bravado showing only in the fact that he avoided even glancing at the briefcase toters at his feet.

Eldridge took off his jacket. He held up one hand to quiet the crowd, then closed his large open palm into a clenched fist and made the Black Power salute. The crowd erupted with applause and cries. I expected him to boom forth, momentarily, with a loud, clear call for revolution that would heat this small rally beyond the tinder point to which Chambers had fired it. So, apparently, did the plainclothes police. One of them pulled a radio handset from his attaché case and talked urgently into its mouthpiece. Cleaver calmed the crowd with another open-handed supplication. Then in a quiet voice that was almost inaudible, as calm and low-pitched as his auto-biographical monologue to me on the airplane, he began to talk.

"Black power to black people." He paused. "White power to white people." He paused again. "All power to all people."

It was as if he had spread a quenching tranquilizer over the audience and extinguished its emotional fire by the unaffected calm of his quiet voice. People settled back in the grass, leaning against their hands, or relaxing cross-legged in a new mood of patient ease. Those who had stood to cheer Chambers's oratory sat down. Emotions had returned to

normal temperature, and it was clear by his tone that, regardless of the words he used or the inflammatory things he
subsequently said, Eldridge would not bring them back to
tinder point again. It was equally clear that he didn't want to.
Despite the bizarre content of his message, he deliberately
chose to deliver it in a soothing voice.

This was my first introduction to perhaps the most curious
quality of Eldridge Cleaver the campaigner. His speaking style
and tone, conversational, almost chatty, punctuated frequently
with an ironic lift at the ends of his sentences, had such a
soothing, often comic effect upon many of the people who
heard him that the calls to violence in his rhetoric seemed to
become lost in a warm wave of peaceable good will flowing
back to him from the crowd. Circulating among his listeners
at other rallies in the days that followed, I observed the same
paradoxical reaction and felt it myself. It was as if they had
settled back to listen to a quiet comic monologuist who could
draw laughs and audience empathy by gesture and ironic style
alone, while reading the transcript of the Nüremburg Trials.

His platform presence was so much a matter of physical and
oral style that it is literally impossible to convey the truth
of it by recounting his speeches, because the verbal content of
much of his "political" campaigning was so appalling that no
person can read the words in cold print and believe that the
man who uttered them did so in such an inoffensive way that
they seemed not only believable but unprovocative. I know
that many others reacted to this curious conflict of style and
rhetoric as I did, finding the former endearing and dismissing
the latter as so much tactical talk, not to be taken too seriously.

"No white power to white people?" he asked rhetorically.
"No? . . . Yes! Because you haven't had white power in this
country. You've had Pig power."

A tittering from some of the youngest whites in the audience.

"The problems are not going to be dealt with at the ballot
box or over cocktails."

Light laughter.

"The only way to sock it to the pigs is the same way they sock it to us."

More laughter.

"You think I'm a crazy nigger? We're all crazy niggers today."

Light applause.

"They told me it's againt the law to curse in Omaha. I'm a Presidential candidate. I'm not going to bullshit and lie."

Appreciative applause.

"My parole officer must have someone here listening to me. Well . . . fuck my parole officer. Fuck the chief of police. Fuck the mayor. Fuck the governor. Fuck L.B.J. Fuck Hubert Humphrey. To all the pigs of the power structure, I say 'Fuck you!' "

Loud laughter and applause.

"Do you know about the Kerner Commission Report? Somebody called it the white man's confession. It's not your confession, it's your indictment. And we're going to prosecute you. For the murder of the people, you will receive the death sentence . . . death!"

Soft applause.

"I understand this is the Strategic Air Command headquarters here in Omaha. They've got hydrogen bombs here in Omaha. We're going to take some."

Laughter.

"Unless conditions change in this country, we will create new conditions that are so catastrophic that your enemies can walk in here and pick the gold out of your teeth."

Tittering mixed with light applause.

"We're going to create conditions in which if our children don't receive an education that enables them to cope with their environment, then your children aren't going to receive an education, either."

Loud applause.

"To the pig power structure of Babylon: If you brutalize

the people, if you murder the people, then the people have a right to kill you. We want to erase your way of life from the planet earth and create a world in which people can live in peace. Someone asked me what my first act will be if I'm elected President and move into the White House ...."

Laughter.

"I'll burn the motherfucker down."

Loud laughter and heavy clapping.

"I've said again and again that if you're not willing to become a part of the solution, then you are part of the problem. I say this now to you women out there, black women and white women: You have power! Use your power. You can be part of the solution. Make your man become part of the solution. If you want to be part of the solution, you have no business laying up in bed with part of the problem."

Thigh-slapping laughter. Cries of "that's right! He's right!"

"Now listen to this, you women! Power grows out of the lips of the pussy. Can they prosecute me in Omaha for saying that? Pussy Power! Use the power of the pussy until your man becomes part of the solution."

Delighted applause and a buzz of one-line comments from the spectators. "That's true," laughed a teenaged black girl behind me. "They think it's just a joke," said her girl friend.

"Now, all of you! You have to get into the political arena to articulate what's going on here. Power to the people! Pick up the gun. Don't stand in the middle wondering what to do. Be part of the solution!"

Boisterous applause.

"If the pig has his foot on my neck and you're standing there not sure whether you're for him or for me, fuck you and fuck him. You're not doing me any good. You're as bad as he is!"

Cheers, expressed with the kind of fervor that drives fundamentalist penitents down the sawdust trail to cry out their commitment to an evangelical Jesus. But before anyone could

move or the fervor rise, he shifted in the same calm voice to
poetic recitation.

"All I ask is what Ché asked when he wrote:

> *Wherever Death may surprise us*
> *It will be welcome, provided that*
> *This, our battle cry, reach some*
> *Receptive ear; that another hand*
> *Reach out to pick up the gun, that*
> *Other fighting men come forward*
> *To intone our funeral dirge*
> *To the staccato of machine gun fire*
> *And new cries of battle and victory."*

The applause began slowly, then swelled when the spectators realized Cleaver had reached the end of his curious,
disjointed, completely extemporaneous address. It had been
obscene, ironic, and utterly formless, like a monologue in a
streetcorner bull session. It was not a speech at all, really,
yet in a way that I could not fathom, it had done what public
address is supposed to do: communicate the speaker's concepts and generate an enthusiastic response from the audience,
a two-way stream in which questions or demands or ideas flow
out to the crowd and affirmation returns. Robert Scheer, in
observing Eldridge's platform style, once wrote, "Cleaver
was among the few who could draw on the crowd's strength
and then feed the strength back again. That requires taking
chances, thinking out loud; there is the risk of sounding dumb,
but that's a lesser sin than being distant."

The curious thing was that however dumb some of Cleaver's
public speeches—and many of his campaign speeches *were*,
for the most part, either simplistic, facetious, or plain dumb—
the oratorical style with which he calmly and confidently
thought out loud while earnestly shifting his charismatic green
eyes from face to face in the audience somehow embellished
the formlessness and inanity with emotional profundity. It

was as if a dead tree had been ornamented by hallucination to appear bursting with leaves and new life.

The crowd responded with vigor, but you could see the hallucination fade as the volume of applause dimmed and the listeners began shifting their glances toward one another, seeking reassurance that they were reacting as they should. A middle-aged woman with mussed grey hair and wrinkled cotton dress stopped clapping and, with flushed face, leaned toward me. "They never heard nothing like that in Omaha," she said. Cleaver's words, only now, were filtering through to her, but in her mind they would be forever embellished by the style in which they were delivered. If ever she were shown a cold transcript of the speech, I think she would react to it by saying, "But that's not what he said . . . he said, you know, so much more than that."

Occasionally he did say much more, often with the same eloquence and commitment to articulated ideas that he demonstrated when he wrote the essays and letters of *Soul on Ice*. But the purpose behind his speech-making and campaigning remained essentially the same in the eloquent speeches as it was in the frankly simple-minded ones. He tried to get across the concept of black people as oppressed colonial subjects diffused throughout a rich and selfish nation of imperial masters whose time of reckoning had come.

"We say if there's going to be massive death for black people, the best that we can do is get into a position so that there'll be massive death for white people," he told the students of Stanford University not long after the Omaha appearance. "Let us be in a position to lay waste. Let us be in a position to disrupt the economic system, so that the military machine cannot function, so that the enemies of America can come in here and pick the gold out of the teeth of the Babylonians . . .

". . . black people can't do it by themselves. It's going to take white people who recognize the situation that exists in this world today to stand up, yes, to unite with their black brothers and sisters. We're dealing with a situation where people have become antagonistic to each other, they've become estranged from each other, they've become hostile toward each other, and they've painted themselves into their various corners. And we say that this is exactly where the pigs of the power structure want to keep us.

". . . We say that it's necessary to break out of those bags, to take steps, to create room for people to unite together, not on the basis of some phony bleeding-heart liberalism, not on the basis of your looking at me and saying, 'Good luck, we hope that you win'. . ."

Always there was a phrase or two to reinforce the yearning of those who wanted desperately to believe that Cleaver was a man who still retained hope of peaceful change in the United States. But always it was ambiguous, and if you wanted to find the loving, compassionate peacemaker in Cleaver's speeches, as I and many others did, you had to resolve the ambiguity in terms of your own hope.

"We are not nihilists," he said at Stanford. "We don't want to see destruction, so then we have to have an alternative. We're talking these days about an alternative, perhaps the last alternative, the last go-round. We go back to basic principles and we say that in order for this situation to be salvaged, we need sane people in this country; we need sane black people, and we need sane white people . . .

". . . We know that people don't like to be condemned categorically, and we don't like to make our condemnations categorical. We want to leave a loophole for those who recognize that the world has become a death row for everybody, and who want to see a future for the people; who want to see a future for everybody, not just themselves, and who want to see a future where there's freedom; who want to see a future where there's justice, who want to see a future where there's no more restraint upon people by others who exploit them and grow fat while the exploited grow skinny from a lack of all the things that a good society must have. We start with the basic principle that every man, woman, and child on the face of the earth deserves the very highest standard of living that human knowledge and technology is capable of providing."

These agreeable generalities offered little buoyance to keep afloat the hopes of domestic pacifism, but they were seized on by many of us as sufficient evidence that Cleaver still had a capacity to unite blacks and whites in a peaceful movement toward a just society. At a time when cries of "Get Whitey" were ringing through the ghettos, it was deeply gratifying to discover in Cleaver the only genuinely militant black extremist in America who deeply and honestly liked white men and believed that the two races could work together for the good of all. I said as much in the article I later wrote about him. More than a year later, when we met in Algiers, he chided me for it, not because it was untrue or because he had changed, but "because it caused me a lot of trouble in the Movement."

During our return flight to San Francisco from Omaha, I sought to remove the ambiguity. I asked him if he truly hoped that white society would or could change for the better rapidly enough to avoid bloody confrontation.

"Yes, I have hope. Some hope. Some, but not much," he said. "There's always hope. If I can reserve some room for reconciliation based on change, there's no reason it can't happen to others, is there? The key is a new awareness within people which will include a respect for all people and an absence of xenophobia. Man is basically good, you know? I have great faith in man. I am optimistic. But the great danger here is that the power structure will take such kindness for weakness. They're wrong if they do. I will not compromise. We will not fall short of our goals."

This satisfied me, I suppose, because it confirmed what I wanted to believe about Eldridge, what I had observed in him during our few days in San Francisco and our long flight to Omaha: I already had concluded that fundamentally he was a peaceful and kind person, not driven by malice or vengeful anxiety.

It brought me back to the Cleaver I admired the most in
*Soul on Ice,* the man who could put aside his own angry past
and write: "I have been terribly impressed by the youth of
America, black and white. I am proud of them because they
have reaffirmed my faith in humanity. I have come to feel
what must be love for the young people of America and I
want to be part of the good and greatness that they want for
all people . . . There is soul in the air and everywhere I see
beauty."

I recognized, of course, that most of history's revolutionaries
have expressed the same mystically optimistic faith in the
essential goodness of man, that it is this overpowering sense
of righteous optimism, in fact, that has provided the false
moral base for the purges, beheadings, and round-the-clock
firing squads that inevitably follow armed revolution, as if
all revolutionaries adopt the sacrificial religious conviction
that human goodness flowers only when soaked in the blood of
revenge. But, like the red-faced lady in Omaha, I embellished
what Cleaver said with how he said it, and he expressed his
hope and optimism, as he expressed his calls to arms, in such
a soothing, conciliatory manner that dangerous self-righteous-
ness or fanaticism clearly did not seem to be a part of it. "I
detest guns and murder," he said. "The most horrible thing
one man can do is take another man's life."

Only a few minutes after saying this, Cleaver began to
fidget and squirm in his seat on the aisle of the airplane. He
was becoming agitated over the antics of three stocky white
men who obviously had put away more than the two drinks
they were offered in the first-class compartment. Their boister-
ousness appeared to be good-natured, although it had an
arrogant edge in their apparent assumption that the rest of
us would tolerate their misbehavior. It was clearly annoying
one of the plane's stewardesses who frowned and stalked up
the aisle when one of the men slapped her lightly on the
buttocks.

"Change seats with me, quick," Eldridge said. We shifted.

It was the first time I had seen his composure slip. He removed his dark glasses and glared at the man who had touched the stewardess.

"This almost never happens to me any more," he said. "This kind of anger. I could kill that pig."

He spoke with such force that I was certain he meant exactly what he said. For that small moment I had my first glimpse of the other side of Eldridge Cleaver.

# CHAPTER 6

## *"We hold these truths to be self-evident . . ."*

ANOTHER park, another place in the grass, another torrent of forensic obscenities, another crowd warmed but not inflamed by a succession of speakers explicitly demanding the violent overthrow of the Government of the United States. I wonder what would happen to the American political process if there were no public parks where this kind of talk finds a natural muffler in carpets of soothing grass, flowering shrubs, trees, and nostalgic monuments; if instead, it were driven exclusively onto the streets where dirt and social dereliction assault the senses and amplify the revolutionary impulses of frustrated men?

This time it was DeFremery Park in West Oakland, a flat rectangle of about ten acres, fenced off from the dismal city by great, old trees that confine the park's prospect to its own extensive lawn, a quaintly Victorian three-story frame park building and an expanse of unused tennis courts. It is not a tennis neighborhood. DeFremery, renamed after their first martyr by the Panthers, is only six blocks south of the bullet-ruined house on 28th Street where the police summarily terminated the life of teenaged Bobby Hutton. Ten blocks in the opposite direction, Huey Newton was accused of performing the same terminal service upon the life of Officer John Frey.

On this day, Sunday, August 25, there was not the slightest

resemblance to the tidy public park in Omaha, either in the nature of the crowd that gathered or in the purpose of the meeting. This was a Free Huey rally, and the Peace and Freedom Party, although represented by its Presidential candidate, had little to do with it. It was entirely a Black Panther Party affair, the first major one I had attended.

I arrived alone two hours early, and whiled away the time before the crowd began to mass watching two platoons of Black Panthers, each about twenty strong, practice close-order military drill on the netless tennis courts. The drill masters were two Party captains I had seen the previous week standing in line at the Alameda County Courthouse. As local captains in the formal politico-military structure of the Black Panther Party, they also performed a variety of civil functions analogous to those of ward leaders in a conventional political party. Each was responsible for a neighborhood from which he recruited the members of his platoon. He represented the Party to the local residents and merchants, and he was expected to cajole occasional donations from them for the Party treasury. Each also was responsible for maintaining discipline in his ranks by enforcing obedience to the Party's ten rules, which included prohibitions against drunkenness, narcotics and marijuana use while on duty, and discharging firearms "unnecessarily or accidentally." (With the growth of the Party and of its problems, the list of rules to which the membership must adhere has since grown to twenty-six, and now includes such bureaucratic requirements as daily reports from members, written reports from leaders, and strict financial controls.) The leaders also had to see that every member of the organization attended daily "political education classes," which seemed to be largely confined to the rote memorization of Black Panther slogans and "correct responses" to common questions, such as the one most frequently asked of them: "How many Black Panthers are there?" Correct response: "Those who know won't say; those who say don't know." In addition to the indoctrination classes, the leaders themselves had to dem-

onstrate to their superiors that they had spent at least two
hours a day reading "correct" books such as Frantz Fanon's
*Wretched of the Earth,* Malcolm X's *Autobiography* and his
collected speeches, Cleaver's *Soul on Ice,* Mao Tse-tung's
*Little Red Book,* and the Soviet Foreign Ministry's *Dictionary
of Philosophy* which, in addition to providing thumbnail biog-
raphies of noteworthy Communist leaders and theoreticians,
offered "correct" definitions of such second-world political
terms as *revisionist* and *revanchist,* whose meanings were likely
to arouse confusion among semi-literate school dropouts. I
talked about the reading program with one Party leader, a
bright but poorly educated California ex-convict, who said
"I relate to Fanon's book and Eldridge and the Red Book,
but that dictionary gives me a headache. I don't think you
have to know all that stuff to make a revolution." Nevertheless,
he dutifully put in his two hours before going to sleep each
night, reading a little of what he could relate to, then plodding
painfully through the Communist dictionary.

On the tennis courts, the soldiers of what the Panthers call
the Black Liberation Army appeared to range in age from
mid-teens to mid-twenties, with most of them clustered at the
younger end of the scale. Since each had to provide his own
"uniform," there was wide disparity in dress. A few wore ex-
pensive black leather jackets, some had on black plastic
jackets, and the others tried for uniformity by wearing black
sweaters or dyed Eisenhower jackets from Army surplus
stores. All but a few wore black berets.

As each platoon lined up in columns of ten, the captains
made a half-hearted effort to distribute their troopers according to height. There was no horseplay in the ranks, but there
was little military formality, either. The captains, neither apparently well versed in close-order drill himself, issued com-
mands in quiet voices. Occasionally one halted his double
column to rebuke a lagging marcher: "Brother, stay in line
and keep up. Keep up." There was none of the snap and
precision that makes Army and Marine Corps drill sergeants

beam with pride, but it was clear enough, from the dogged willingness of the troops to obey and keep marching, that the purpose of the drill was as well served here as it ever has been at Parris Island or Fort Dix. The soldiers were being indoctrinated, in the classic Spartan fashion, to accept orders without question and to perform willingly, even eagerly, no matter how hot the noontime sun or monotonous the repetition of the same column turns and flank movements during their two hours on the makeshift parade ground. It did not matter to the captains that each man marched to his own rhythm or that the turns and flanks were ragged and, to an observer, comical. What mattered is that the boys were learning to drill together and to do what they were told. (Fidel Castro's guerrilla army acquired its spit and polish *after* Havana fell, not during the war when their orders were not to march smartly, but to terrorize and kill.)

The Black Panthers I saw on the tennis courts, and others I saw drilling in subsequent months, wasted little time or effort on the niceties of military bearing; response to command was sufficient evidence to the leaders that discipline existed. It was far more important that minds, not feet, be indoctrinated to stay in step. Thus the leadership, whose ideological program chairman still was Huey Newton even though he was in jail, emphasized daily "study classes" (indoctrination sessions, that is, not forums for questing, critical minds), constantly reminded the new recruits and the old hands as well that serious infractions of the rules meant immediate purge, with the offender's picture reproduced prominently over the terrifying demand, "Wanted," in *The Black Panther,* and exhorted them by scrawled poster and through the party newspaper to memorize the party's ten-point program.

Paul Jacobs, whose insights into the Panthers seemed more sharply defined to me than those of any other of their white supporters, observed one day that "Dick Nixon has practically got the Panthers' ten-point program himself." Jacobs said that "if you subtract the notion of guns, armed self-

defense, and the release of all black prisoners from jail, practically everybody in the United States supports the Panther
program." There is at least some truth in that. The Party
"platform and program," as it always is titled, was written by
Huey Newton, in collaboration with Bobby Seale, with the
editorial assistance of Eldridge Cleaver. It states:

1.  We want freedom. We want power to determine the destiny
of our Black Community.
2.  We want full employment for our people.
3.  We want an end to the robbery by the CAPITALISTS of
our Black Community.
4.  We want decent housing, fit for shelter of human beings.
5.  We want education for our people that exposes the true
nature of this decadent American society. We want education that
teaches us our true history and our role in the present-day society.
6.  We want all black men to be exempt from military service.
7.  We want an immediate end to POLICE BRUTALITY and
MURDER of black people.
8.  We want freedom for all black men held in federal, state,
county, and city prisons and jails.
9.  We want all black people when brought to trial to be tried
in court by a jury of their peer group or people from their black
communities, as defined by the Constitution of the United States.
10.  We want land, bread, housing, education, clothing, justice
and peace. And as our major political objective, A United Nations-
supervised plebiscite to be held throughout the black colony in
which only black colonial subjects will be allowed to participate,
for the purpose of determining the will of black people as to their
national destiny.

One might quibble over the semantic confusion of terms
like "CAPITALIST," "decadent," "POLICE BRUTALITY
and MURDER," or "peer group ... as defined by the Constitution of the United States." And the question of black self-
determination by United Nations-supervised plebiscite certainly would raise the prickles of sovereignty on any traditionalist's back. But in its essence as the last rational plea of

desperate young men, the Black Panther Party platform and program is neither insensitive nor un-American. Basically, it is no more than an affirmation of the Declaration of Independence and the 14th Amendment to the Constitution of the United States. "All men are created equal," the Panther program says. "All persons born or naturalized in the United States and subject to the jurisdiction thereof," it says, "are citizens of the United States and of the state wherein they reside. No state shall make or enforce any law which shall abridge the privileges or immunities of citizens of the United States, nor shall any state deprive any person of life, liberty or property, without due process of law; nor deny to any person within its jurisdiction the equal protection of the laws."

The Panther platform states those honored American truths in spirit, at least, just as the Declaration and Constitution, in spirit, say that there are no acceptable grounds for excluding any citizen, regardless of race or creed, from his rights of citizenship. Equal opportunity is the philosophical basis of the ten-point program.

By the time I first encountered it, I think my acquaintance with Eldridge already had brought me to the point of "soul transference" about which I later wrote. I doubt if any white man can fully succeed in encasing his imagination in black skin, but I found no difficulty whatever in adopting, as an exercise in empathy if nothing else, Cleaver's view of American society, the view of a black man who already had been through much of the worst that we have to offer in his country, but who I thought retained a shining vision of what America could be.

As I sat on the grass in DeFremery Park, the physical and social ambience of Oakland, California, certainly made that soul transference much easier for me than it would have been in Omaha or even in New York, whose slum-ghetto, Harlem, evoked the almost sobbing description of black blight in Thomas Merton's book.

I don't know how to describe Oakland other than as a

depressing industrial slum on the eastern shore of San Francisco Bay. Thousands of its white residents will reply that it is a
progressive "business" city, brimful of well-landscaped, "nice"
neighborhoods. And so, by their lights, it is; but to see it
that way they must ignore the dreariness and the degrading
life conditions of most of downtown Oakland, as my neighbors
and I are inclined to ignore much of the Bronx, Harlem, and
Bedford-Stuyvesant from our comfortable base outside of New
York City.

Oakland is a city on the skids and I saw little hope there
that it ever will rescue itself from decline. Whether experienced
through the senses of sight, touch, and smell, as one can
experience it from DeFremery/Hutton Park, or through the
statistical portraits of the discouraged sociologists who have
studied it, the decay is instantly apparent. It is a discouraging
place to visit, a wretched place to live, and a rotten place to
look for the virtues of an egalitarian society. Gertrude Stein
was born there and left at an early age. "The trouble with
Oakland," she is said to have observed, "is that there's no
*there* there." Kay Boyle, another distinguished lady of letters,
called it "less a city than a shocking state of affairs."

It is run by a small white power elite that, like the power
structures of many American cities, sees itself as progressive,
democratic, and totally free of racial prejudice. This handful
of businessmen and politicians is presided over by the patrician
former U.S. Senator William F. Knowland, who owns and
publishes the *Oakland Tribune*. He is a right-winger, too far
gone even for Richard Nixon's tastes, who once hoped to
extend his power to the governorship of California, for which
he was defeated, and the Presidency of the United States,
which was *his* dream, unshared by many even on the right.

On the surface it is the kind of city that the nation used
to be proud of. Oakland was applauded by *Look* magazine
in 1955 as an "All-American City," and a plaque attesting this
honor still hangs in City Hall. Its public buildings are models
of modern official architecture, crisply glassed in, delightfully

landscaped, elegantly marbled. Four major automobile freeways slice through it like fire lanes laid down to stem an expected conflagration. They are elevated and cast a shadow of
affluent indifference over mile after mile of slum blocks which
crowd three sides of Oakland's downtown business area. These
massive concrete highways, the public buildings, and a lovely
park that surrounds Lake Merritt near the center of town are
the only evidences of public planning visible on its pock-
marked face. Examples of profitable private planning are
more numerous. Kaiser Industries' international corporate
headquarters is the cleanest of them. It towers over Lake
Merritt in a curved glass and aluminum building, a modern
rival to the needle-topped, baroque *Tribune* tower downtown,
where Mr. Knowland, the local baron, presides. But most of
the city reveals its "business is the business of America" history
in ugly sprawl; functional industrial sites grow helter-skelter
like mushrooms amid dark neighborhoods of deteriorating
turn-of-the-century bungalows, emitting their varicolored flatu-
lence from small and large smokestacks that continually feed
a yellowish bank of low-lying smog that seems to flow glacially
up the Sacramento River toward the state capital.

In 1967 and 1968 an urban researcher named Dr. Floyd
Hunter of the Social Science Research and Development
Corporation studied Oakland and its power structure under
contract to the U.S. Department of Commerce's Economic
Development Administration. His report is a rare document,
because it was suppressed by the Department of Commerce
at the urging of Oakland's city fathers. As far as I know, the
people of Oakland still have not had an opportunity to see
this mostly dispassionate picture of what and who make their
hometown tick.

Hunter noted that "commercial and industrial establish-
ments have been able to encroach with impunity on living
areas, so that the resulting smoke, grime and industrial stink
have become characteristic of the community." By its open-
arms policies toward unrestricted business and industrial de-

velopment, he said, Oakland has "welcomed the destruction of human values."

"The whole can only be described as organized greed," he concluded.

Dr. Hunter, a serious social scientist who is not given to glossing over the problems he examines nor to fortifying Chamber of Commerce promotional ambitions, systematically delineated Oakland's power structure, naming the small group of men who run the city and assessing the power of each of them over social, political, and economic decision-making in both the public and private sectors. Hunter devised a scientifically constructed pecking order that rated the leaders according to how powerful they themselves and other "leader types" in the community felt them to be. Four men emerged with at least twice the power of the remaining 63 who were identified as decision-makers. At the top of the list, not surprisingly, was the city's mayor, a local businessman named John Redding, followed closely by William Knowland and Edgar Kaiser. Almost all the others were corporation executives. This business leadership, Hunter noted, "remains, on the surface, heartily optimistic. Like a number of other American cities, Oakland, 'The All American City,' has embarked upon an ambitious plan to redevelop its ceremonial buildings . . .

"The power structure of Oakland must close their eyes a thousand times a day to the aging litter of decay—even as they speak in Rotary of the new image."

Hunter's report proved both statistically and by representative interviews that the one-third of the population unfortunate enough to be black, red, or brown—underhoused, underemployed, underpaid, and unconsulted—was systematically excluded from the benefits of the city's business expansion. The blacks of Oakland emerged from the report as grossly misused and downtrodden, economically, socially, politically, and geographically, as if they were a herd of drowning turtles, submerged in Lake Merritt, with the white population standing on their backs greedily keeping their own heads nicely above water at a level where they could see only the pretty foliage at lakeside.

"The status quo in Oakland is vigorously maintained by those in power," wrote Dr. Hunter. "The power structure controls the city's capital, maintains and directs its police force, *enforces its racism* [italics mine] ... In Oakland, the decisions relating to both wide-ranged community matters and specific economic development are made by a few men. These few decision makers have a limited field of vision and leave many problems untouched, or at best, superficially touched. This fact is a major community problem."

I could go on for chapters, documenting good and sufficient reasons for finding the place detestable, a feeling I share with most of the people I know who have visited it and at least a third of the people who live there. Beginning with this day in DeFremery Park, I spent more than two months crisscrossing its streets and alleyways on foot and by car, and talked to many of its citizens on both sides of the chasm that separates its two societies, one white and pretty well off, the other black and poor. I found that, at best, the city is dreary and dull, a sort of lackluster Birmingham. At worst it is the most dismal and repressive major city in the United States. Except for Oakland's hillside residential areas, which climb above the mess along the foothills of the coastal mountain range, and a spread of sparsely integrated middle-class neighborhoods far outside the downtown area, it is one vast industrial and residential slum.

Oakland's greatest distinctions as I write this, dubious grounds for pride, are that it has not yet suffered from a major race riot among the bottom third of its diminishing population of 360,000, and that it is the birthplace of the Black Panther Party. I concluded that Dr. Hunter's observations on the racist nature of power in Oakland, the absence of widespread black rioting, and the birth of the Black Panthers are related. Specifically, the power elite that has been so abysmally deficient in preserving human values with its rush toward ever-greater industrial growth has been extraordinarily efficient in policing the three large ghetto areas of West, East, and North Oakland; which is to say that the Oakland police have been so unrelenting in their pressure that instead of igniting riots as a loosely controlled or ill-trained police force sometimes can do, they have scared the wits out of the city's black citizens. I heard many reports that both Oakland and the Alameda County sheriff's office had gone as far afield as Mississippi, Alabama, and Georgia to recruit rural white youths for their forces. I don't know if those reports are true. However, it is significant evidence of the people's deep fear that the stories persist.

In that setting, I did not find it at all difficult to view the rest of American society with more than a little empathy for the Panthers. When one does this, I discovered, one begins to see not objectively nor even humanely, but with the same baleful wonderment, clenching slowly like a fist into pure rage, of an increasing number of black men exemplified by Cleaver and his comrades. Looking out at the institutions from the misery of Oakland's ghettos one sees a different vision, and it is not surprising that the conditions of this wretched city led the Black Panthers to formulate such devastating concepts as these:

*The Negro in America:* A subjugated, colonial people diffused through the land which 360 years ago enslaved them; lacking, as colonials always lack, the power to order their own lives, their economy, their schools, their business institutions, their "foreign" relations (with colonialist white society) or even their own criminals; at war, as colonials always remain at war, with their conquerors.

*The Police:* An Army of Occupation, recruited from the lowest segments of the imperial white society, deployed throughout the fragmented black colony, not to provide public safety and security within the ghetto but to keep the lid on it, to protect the affluent white colonialists outside of the ghetto from the poor blacks within it.

*Jails and Prisons:* Detention centers where devious white criminals are given precedence over black *prisoners of war* whose crimes, even heinous crimes against humanity, are not fundamentally malicious but are a natural and forgivable result of colonialist oppression.

*The Churches and the Mass Media:* Propaganda instruments of the white colonialist establishment that have indoctrinated the black colonials with standards of white theology (God is white) and culture, thus automatically demoting blacks to inferior status; robbing them even of their standards of beauty; emasculating black men and defeminizing black women; enticing black men to lust after what Eldridge Cleaver called the "ultrafeminine" white doll, and suffering black women to accept rape at the hands of white and black men alike.

*Firearms:* The instrument of power, the phallus with which the emasculated black man will regain his manhood and throw off the colonialist masters.

*Established Political Parties:* Manipulative instruments of the white colonialist establishment, elaborately constructed to give the appearance of equal representation, but in fact allowing neither representation nor power to anyone outside the white power structure.

One can go on and on with this kind of empathetic examination and reach perfectly predictable conclusions about almost anything in our society. As I noted above, the conclusions will be neither objective nor humane. They will be brutal, angry, and, to most Americans, *almost* totally false. But from the perspective of a black man trapped in the city of Oakland or within the imprisoning color walls of any dehumanizing ghetto, such concepts can shine with truth as bright as a laser beam.

I think that it is only when viewed in this way that one can begin to understand black rage and the Panthers, and I have projected that view here, within the context of Oakland, not only because that is where I first saw it clearly, but because the oppressive conditions of that city are what gave birth to the Black Panther Party to begin with.

The Party's ten-point program was conceived within the intellectual limits of these concepts. To make them even more explicit, Newton, Seale, and Cleaver added, in an awkwardly phrased codicil to the platform and program, their proposed solutions to the problems raised by colonialist society as they saw it. Whereas each of the party's ten points began with the phrase "we want," each of the ten subparagraphs began with "we believe" or its equivalent.

1. We believe that black people will not be free until we are able to determine our destiny.

2. We believe that the federal government is responsible and obligated to give every man employment or a guaranteed income. We believe that if the white American businessmen will not give full employment, then the means of production should be taken from the businessmen and placed in the community so that the people of the community can organize and employ all of its people and give a high standard of living.

3. We believe that this racist government has robbed us and now we are demanding the overdue debt of forty acres and two mules. Forty acres and two mules was promised 100 years ago as restitution for slave labor and mass murder of black people. We will accept the payment in currency which will be distributed to our many communities. The Germans are now aiding the Jews in Israel for the genocide of the Jewish people. The Germans murdered six million Jews. The American racist has taken part in the slaughter of over fifty million black people; therefore we feel that this is a modest demand that we make.

4. We believe that if the white landlords will not give decent housing to our black community, then the housing and the land should be made into cooperatives so that our community, with government aid, can build and make decent housing for its people.

5. We believe in an educational system that will give to our people a knowledge of self. If a man does not have knowledge

of himself and his position in society and the world, then he has little chance to relate to anything else.

6. We believe that black people should not be forced to fight in the military service to defend a racist government that does not protect us. We will not fight and kill other people of color in the world who, like black people, are being victimized by the white racist government of America. We will protect ourselves from the force and violence of the racist police and the racist military, by whatever means necessary.

7. We believe we can end police brutality in our black community by organizing black self-defense groups that are dedicated to defending our black community from racist police oppression and brutality. The Second Amendment to the Constitution of the United States gives a right to bear arms. We therefore believe that all black people should arm themselves for self-defense.

8. We believe that all black people should be released from the many jails and prisons because they have not received a fair and impartial trial.

9. We believe that the courts should follow the United States Constitution so that black people will receive fair trials. The 14th Amendment of the U.S. Constitution gives a man a right to be tried by his peer group. A peer is a person from a similar economic, social, religious, geographical, environmental, historical, and racial background. To do this the court will be forced to select a jury from the black community from which the black defendant came. We have been, and are being tried by all-white juries that have no understanding of the "average reasoning man" of the black community.

10. When in the course of human events, it becomes necessary for one people to dissolve the political bands which have connected them with another, and to assume, among the powers of the earth, the separate and equal station to which the laws of nature and nature's God entitle them, a decent respect to the opinions of mankind requires that they should declare the causes which impel them to the separation.

We hold these truths to be self-evident, that all men are created equal; that they are endowed by their Creator with certain unalienable rights; that among these are life, liberty, and the pursuit of happiness. That to secure these rights, governments are instituted among men, deriving their just powers from the consent of the governed; that whenever any form of government becomes destructive of these ends, it is the right of the people to alter or to abolish it, and to institute a new government, laying its foundation on such principles and organizing its powers in such form, as to them shall seem most likely to effect their safety and happiness. Prudence, indeed, will dictate that governments long established should not be changed for light and transient causes; and accordingly, all experience hath shown, that mankind are more disposed to suffer while evils are sufferable, than to right themselves by abolishing the forms to which they are accustomed. But when a long train of abuses and usurpations, pursuing invariably the same object, evinces a design to reduce them under absolute despotism, it is their right, it is their duty, to throw off such government and to provide new guards for their future security.

After its final, lengthy extract from the Declaration of Independence, an ominous graphic signature always is used to conclude printed copies of the platform and program. It is a carefully-drawn sketch of a short-barreled submachine gun, with bullet clip attached. It was put there, one of the Panthers told me, "to show that we're for real; we're not foolin' around. You see the gun. We mean pick up the gun."

There were no guns in evidence here in DeFremery/Hutton Park on this sunny Sunday afternoon, but evidence of the impact that the Black Panther Party was having upon the Negroes of Oakland as well as upon sympathetic whites was all around me. By the time a five-piece combo—guitars, drum, saxophone, and soul singer—mounted a temporary platform to begin the rally, more than 5,000 people had gathered. It was as if I was viewing the Omaha rally at Fontenelle Park through a magnifying mirror: two-thirds of the huge crowd were well-dressed blacks, many gathered on the grass in family groups. The remaining whites were mostly solid-looking middle-class people. While the combo performed, a dozen young Black Panther girls, all wearing at least one piece of black clothing, circulated in the audience with petitions calling for a public referendum in Oakland on the Panther's proposal to give the black community autonomous control over its own police force. Another group of boys and girls passed cigar and shoe boxes in which to place donations for the "Free Huey" legal fund.

The two captains who had worked their platoons into a sweat on the tennis courts marched them now, in a long single file, to a position in front of the speakers' platform. They all stood quietly there, at parade rest, facing the audience for solemn effect and forming a defensive shield, like a police line, against any rash attempt by anyone to advance toward the microphones. It was a far more impressive demonstration of protectiveness than the thin bravado shown by Eldridge's four Panther bodyguards on the platform in Omaha.

There was another striking difference, too. Despite the peaceful petition and legal fund-raising campaign that was taking place among the spectators, none of the half-dozen speakers who followed the soul combo on the platform even remotely approached the notion of nonviolent solutions to either local or national problems. Only two of the speakers were authentic Black Panthers. The first man at the microphones was a slight young student from Teheran by way of the University of California at Berkeley. His features were Levantine and his accent was Arabic, but his command of English came straight out of the Free Speech Movement. His name was Haaji, and he said he had come to express the solidarity of international students with the Black Panthers' demand to "Free Huey" and to "kill the oppressors in this motherfucking imperialist country." His pronounciation of the modifying adjective got so tangled around the consonants that it came out sounding like "mollar-pooking" and not many people were sure of what he meant.

A large, middle-aged black lady, whose pendulous breasts and rotund cheeks evoked images of benign mammies in the Old South, followed Haaji and delicately avoided his functional vocabulary. But she was every bit as inflamed in her revolutionary anger. She urged a city-wide boycott of white-owned stores in the interest of applying pressure to "Free Huey." Then she escalated to a boycott of all national holidays as a measure to bring down the capitalistic economic system. "We'll jes' tell 'em there ain't gonna be no profit-making Christmas this year nor any year fom now on!" Finally, she asked all of the black women in the audience to take jobs as domestic servants in white households in the interest of armed revolution against the government. She paused as most of her listeners looked back in uncomprehending surprise. Then she explained. "Go to work for the Man. Get inside that big house on the hill. Make the beds. Tidy up the drawers. It won't be long before you find what you're lookin' for. The Man got a gun in there somewhere. Under his pillow. Under the mattress. In the drawer. In the closet. You'll find it. You just liberate that gun, then you don't have to go back to work for him no more. If you afraid to carry it down to the brothers of the Black Panther Party, why you just drop that piece in a trash basket on your way home. Don't you worry. The brothers'll find it there. Get the Man's gun!"

A frizzy-haired white youth representing Up Against the Wall Motherfucker appeared next and exhorted the crowd to begin killing policemen. "But don't give your life for just one of theirs. That shit's no good. Your life is worth more than the pig's." He suggested that pigs should be killed only when there was little risk of being killed in return, and that ideally they should be ambushed in groups so that several dead policemen would make the risk to the ambusher acceptable. "Jesus, that kid's crazy," said a black woman sitting near me. No one seemed to be taking the exhortation seriously.

Eldridge was next. Like any other Presidential candidate faced with the demand to speak one or more times a day, he rambled extemporaneously through more or less the same things he had said before, and the responding laughter and applause flowed back to him with the same enthusiasm. I noted that very few people in the audience seemed bothered by Eldridge's or any other speaker's obscenities, which splattered across their oratory like unpredictable raindrops. The younger listeners clearly appreciated the creative flexibility of the four-letter words, listening with the same rapt attention that a buff will give to a jazz group as the soloists slide to surprising new combinations of old themes and old sounds. Among the older people and the middle-class whites, most seemed to dismiss the talk condescendingly, as if it were intended only for the young blacks in the audience and not for them. In all-white gatherings, such as a white San Francisco lawyers' club where Cleaver spoke even more obscenely than he did in the open-air meetings, the language clearly was a tactical weapon, meant to polarize the audience. Those few who were with him, he reasoned, would overlook or understand the language of the streets; those who rejected it probably belonged on the other side, and by his reasoning it was better to have them clearly against him than standing in the middle wondering which side of the revolution to join.

I talked about this with Father Earl Neil, the Panthers' black Episcopalian chaplain, a handsome and studious man in his early thirties who moved to black militancy from Carlton College in Northfield, Minnesota, and Seabury Western Theological Seminary in Evanston, Illinois. Father Neil became involved with the Panthers not long after accepting the pastorate of St. Augustine's Church in Oakland, whose congregation, like those of most churches, is middle-income and aging.

"I'm one hundred percent with Eldridge when he says *fuck* or *motherfucker* because these words have very special meaning in the black ghetto. They are syllabic words with some thrust to them. *Motherfucker* is a contemptuous word, and we think of it in the same way we think of the slavemasters who fucked our mothers.

"The phrases that infuriate me—the true obscenities of our language—that the white church and white people generally use are *justifiable homicide, easy credit no money down,*

*you're different, these things take time, boy.* These things are
obscenities to me, much more so than simple functional words
like fuck or shit or whatever. The acceptable obscenities of
this society are far more deadly than these functional words,
because they are a part of the official language and therefore
the official policy this country employs to subjugate and de-
humanize people. We simply don't view these words in a
profane way in the ghetto. When white people react with
horror to them, it merely underlines the great gap of understanding. Black kids see their reaction and say, 'If the man
don't like it, it must be good.' "

Cleaver was followed by the featured speaker of the day.

His eyes were shaded by heavy dark glasses that, like
mirrors, picked up and reflected the bright reds and yellows
of his collarless, loose-fitting African shirt. It was Stokely
Carmichael, ceremonially identified as "Prime Minister of the
Black Panther Party," the sole remaining relic of the Panthers'
brief amalgamation with SNCC, which Carmichael once
headed. The alliance had lasted only from March until July,
when a delegation of Panthers in New York reportedly
brought SNCC's international affairs chairman, James Forman, to the point of nervous collapse by dramatically threatening his life. The Panthers were said to have entered Forman's
office and flashed pistols. One of them reportedly put the
barrel of his gun in Forman's mouth and pulled the trigger
three times. The gun was unloaded, but the hostile intent of
the Panthers clearly was not. Shortly after the incident, SNCC
expelled Carmichael and broke with the Panthers for good.
Now Stokely divided his time between traveling with his wife,
the South African singer Miriam Makeba, lecturing, and ap-
pearing only occasionally at Black Panther Party affairs. He
never became an active, authentic Panther.

After becoming mildly turned-on by the inflammatory rhetoric that preceded Carmichael, the crowd appeared ready
for a final push from this internationally known figure who
had been crying since 1966 for blacks to arm themselves as

urban guerrillas and "fight to the death." He was a woeful disappointment. I timed his speech at one hour and forty minutes, during which about a third of the audience left the rally. Carmichael spoke in flat, unemotional tones, droning his deliverance of an academic lecture on the "correct definitions of revolutionary terms." It was as if he was reading aloud from pages *Ab* through *Re* of the Soviet *Dictionary of Philosophy*.

Near the end of his tedious talk I walked toward the platform. Eldridge was standing below it amid a cluster of black jackets, quietly but heatedly saying something to Bobby Seale, whom I had not yet met. As I approached, two Panthers stepped from the phalanx of guards in front of the speaker and blocked my way. Neither said a word; they just stood silently between me and the group surrounding Eldridge and Seale. I could not hear Cleaver but he was quite clearly angry, and his anger appeared to be directed at Seale alone. I guessed that perhaps he was rebuking Seale in advance for something he planned to say when Carmichael finally wound down, but that guess was based only on a growing awareness that Seale's unpredictability represented something of a thorn in Cleaver's side. I had heard Eldridge speak unflatteringly of Seale to Kathleen one day as we drove across San Francisco. "Bobby just doesn't think before he talks," Eldridge said, then fell quiet when Kathleen frowned and motioned toward me. Other people who knew both men had told me that Eldridge's relationship with Seale was often quarrelsome. "Bobby just isn't very bright," said Keating, "and it irritates Eldridge when he spouts off."

Not long before, Seale had created a major crisis within the Party by blurting, "We hate you white people!" to a gathering of white youth in New York. "And the next time one of you paddies comes up here and accuses me of hating you because of the color of your skin," he added, "I will kick you in your ass. We started out hating you because of the color of your skin . . ." Word of Seale's intemperate outburst spread quickly

among whites of the Peace and Freedom Party, and led many
to conclude that the Panthers were simply reverse racists, a
charge that Cleaver had vociferously and successfully dis-
pelled then he brought the Panthers into the largely white
political movement. Forswearing any kind of racism, black
or white, in fact, had become a major element of Panther
doctrine, and Seale's slip of the tongue, if that is what it was,
shook the entire organization.

Seale seemed chagrined, but apparently he was not angered
enough to respond to what Eldridge was saying to him, because he shifted his attention to Carmichael when Cleaver's
tirade ended and looked anxiously at his watch; the harassed
program chairman clearly was more unhappy over the pace
of the rally than he was over Eldridge's remarks to him.
Cleaver looked up and saw me standing uncertainly before
the two silent Panther soldiers. He stepped between them
and shook my hand, then led me to Seale and introduced us.
"This is Bobby Seale, Party Chairman," he said. Seale acknowledged the introduction with a nod, glanced at his watch
again, then ducked behind the platform.

Carmichael's mind-deadening lecture finished, finally, and
the 3,500-or-so people who remained in the park were clearly
ready to go home when Seale jumped onto the platform. He
wore a black leather jacket, but its military effect was canceled
out, somehow, by an open-necked, soft-collared, button-down
shirt underneath. "Who's that?" I heard a white in the audience ask. "I think it's Bobby Seale, but I'm not sure," someone
replied. He did not possess the commanding public presence of
Cleaver or even of the young madmen who had exhorted the
crowd before Carmichael spoke. But he was the only speaker
of the day who addressed himself exclusively to the purpose
of the rally, which was to raise funds for Huey Newton's legal
defense and to reiterate the Party's categorical assertions that
Huey was the innocent victim of an official conspiracy. His
speech was short and pointed, and it drew little response until

the end, when he cried, "Let's hear it from everybody! Three times for Huey!" He paused a moment, then led the crowd in a loud cheer: "FREE HUEY! THE SKY'S THE LIMIT! . . . FREE HUEY! THE SKY'S THE LIMIT! . . . FREE HUEY! THE SKY'S THE LIMIT!" The voice of the crowd could be heard halfway across Oakland.

# CHAPTER 7

## "... a Gestapo policeman has been executed ..."

HUEY NEWTON remains an enigma to me, as he must to those who know him only by reputation as the founder and Defense Minister of the Black Panther Party, imprisoned throughout most of his Party's history. He is just as enigmatic to most of his followers. Only a tiny group of Panthers in Oakland, probably fewer than fifty of the Party's members, had met him before he was jailed, and many of those, including his closest comrade in the movement, Bobby Seale, were subsequently imprisoned, too. To the others he was and remains an icon, a stern-faced young man in black, glowering from tens of thousands of Panther posters that depict him sitting regally in a high-backed reed chair, flanked by African tribal shields, a rifle in one hand, a spear in the other, feet firmly planted on a zebra hide rug. Except for the incongruous throne, which looks as if it was borrowed from the back table of a Polynesian restaurant, the picture shows a modern-day African chieftan ready for war. In another poster he stands defiantly with black beret almost covering one eyebrow, holding a riot shotgun at ready arms, and wearing a cartridge belt of extra shells looped dramatically across chest and shoulder.

In the pantheon of the Panthers he is the chief god, an almost literal Christ who offered his life for their sins of acquiescence to the white pharisees. That he was not, in the end, crucified does not sully their image of him as the black messiah; on the contrary, it fortifies it, because he lives on, resurrected from an execution-bent courtroom in Oakland, as the god-man who has arisen from the living death of prison to send fresh sets of revelations and admonitions to his followers in Babylon. Of the living saints in his company, Bobby is Peter, Eldridge is Paul; the martyrs, most of them elevated to sainthood by police bullets, according to the Panthers, are Bobby Hutton, killed in Oakland in 1968, Fred Hampton and Mark Clark, killed in Chicago in late 1969, John Huggins and Alprentice Carter, killed early in 1969 in Los Angeles (allegedly by other blacks from an organization called US which is led by black nationalist Ron Karenga), and two dozen other Party members whose deaths were less dramatic. (In his most recent annual report to the House Committee on Appropriations, J. Edgar Hoover said, "the BPP was hard pressed to identify even 20 of the members which it claimed were 'killed in cold blood' by police. Of the 20 named, four had been killed by members of a rival black extremist group on the West Coast; one died of barbiturate intoxication; one was shot and killed by a store owner during a robbery attempt; one was killed by his wife over a love affair he was having with a female Black Panther; and another is alleged to have been tortured and killed by BPP members, 14 of whom, including Chairman Bobby Seale, have been indicted in connection with this member's death.")

In the company of the saints and martyrs are more than 300 Party leaders and ordinary members who have been arrested and in many cases charged with crimes ranging from simple assault to murder. To the party faithful, as to the true believers of a religious cult, all the persecuted, martyred, and sainted are innocent victims of an evil conspiracy. They are innocent, even when circumstances strain one's faith, as, for example, when eight Panthers driving a *Black Panther—Black Community News Service* pickup truck were halted almost

immediately after allegedly robbing a San Francisco gas station, then unsuccessfully shot it out with policemen in broad
daylight a half-block from the city's Hall of Justice. All eight
were captured unharmed. Three policemen were wounded,
two of them seriously. The Panthers claimed they were framed,
and the party faithful throughout the country accepted the
claim without question, as an act of faith. The fact that the
aggrieved filling station attendant identified the truck, both
by its *Black Panther* markings and license number, when he
raised the alarm minutes before the shoot-out, made the story
of a frame-up hard to believe, unless you assumed with the
Panther faithful that the victim was a police provocateur, a
favorite Panther device for explaining away any crime of
which its members are accused.

The innocent above all innocent Panthers, of course, is the
Christ-figure himself. And the killing for which Huey Newton,
then only 25 years old, was imprisoned took place under
circumstances just cloudy enough, both in time and the
recollections of witnesses, to make his innocence believable
not only to the adherents of his true faith, but to many other
blacks and whites as well. This is why Seale was able to
raise such a rousing chorus in his cries of "FREE HUEY!
THE SKY'S THE LIMIT!" The chorus became so strident
and so insistent, in fact, that it literally was heard halfway
across Oakland in the courtroom where Newton's fate was
being decided.

Newton's Gethsemane began on Friday, October 27, 1967,
only two weeks after the first anniversary of the formation of
the Black Panther Party. It was a rare night for him. He had
decided not to go out after the "pigs." Normally Newton took
nightly turns on "justice" patrol with others of the then less
than fifty members of his Party, cruising the streets to confront
policemen whom they found harassing Negroes. On this
night he took a holiday. Three years before, almost to the day,
he had been convicted of stabbing a fellow guest at a buffet
dinner, after a brief altercation over the use of the term

"Afro-American." He admitted nicking his antagonist in the chin and on the hand with a steak knife. Newton received a probationary sentence of three years, the first six months of which were served in the Alameda County jail. His probation was to end at midnight on October 27, and Newton decided to celebrate because he had looked forward to the occasion for a long time. For one thing he would now be free to operate without official supervision by probation officers, an annoying inhibition that had forced him to refrain from leading his troops on such Panther forays as the armed invasion of the state capitol the previous May. Another provision of his probation forbade his possession of hand guns, although he was legally free to carry a rifle or a shotgun. That restriction, too, would end at midnight.

Huey testified at his trial that he wanted his fiancée, Laverne Williams, to join him that night, but she was ill, so he borrowed her 1958 Volkswagen and went out alone. His first stop, at 10 P.M., was the Bosun's Locker, a bar where he drank one rum and coke "Cuba Libre" and cheerfully announced the end of his probation to an acquaintance he met there. Half an hour later, he drove to a nearby Congregational Church, where he occasionally lectured African history classes, and joined a black youth group which was having a Friday night dance in the church's social hall. He said he spent a few hours there, most of the time circulating among people he knew. "I was talking to people and socializing in that manner because I hate to admit that I don't know how to dance," he explained. One of the people he saw at the church social was Gene McKinney, an old friend, who unwittingly joined Huey in Gethsemane when he agreed to go along to another party in a nearby private home that Newton wanted to attend. It was now 2 A.M. Saturday. The second party, Newton testified, was like the first: "Some people were dancing, some people were playing cards, and some people were talking . . . I stayed there until the party broke up." As a witness in his own defense, Newton was asked by his lawyer, Charles Garry, what happened next.

*Newton:* "Gene . . . was hungry . . . (and) asked me to leave and take him on 7th Street because we both knew that there are a couple of after-hours eating places there . . . It must have been about quarter after four . . .

*Garry:* ". . . did you have anything more to drink in the way of alcoholic beverages other than the Cuba Libre that you already have spoken of . . . ?"

*Newton:* "No, there was nothing else, only the one drink . . ."

*Garry:* "All right . . . Pick it up from there."

*Newton:* "I started to drive down to 7th Street . . . I made a left turn at 7th and Willow and as I made the turn, I noticed a red light in my rear window. I pulled over to the curb and came to a stop. The police officer (Patrolman John Frey) got out of—stayed in the car a minute, maybe, got out of his car, walked over to mine and said, 'Well, well, well, what do we have. The great, great Huey P. Newton.' He was—he had his head almost in my window, maybe six inches to a foot from my face . . . He asked me then for my driver's license, which I gave to him. Then he asked me who did the car belong to, and I said it belonged to Laverne Williams, and as I said this I took the registration out of the window and handed it to him. At this time he gave me my driver's license back, and he went to his car with the registration. It might have been about two to three minutes . . . another officer (Patrolman Herbert Heanes) pulled up behind the first officer, so there's two officers there now . . ."

Frey was a tough young cop who, at 23 with less than two years on the force, already had ruffled the feelings of some blacks in the ghetto area he patrolled. A few of them testified that he had cursed and unjustly hassled them and that he often used the term "nigger" and threw his weight around. He once denigrated blacks and referred to them as niggers in a lecture on police work he delivered to a group of white children at his old high school. He was five feet ten and a half inches tall, weighed 200 pounds, and worked out regularly to keep himself in shape. In high school, where he was a mediocre student of apparently limited ability, he was on the varsity football, wrestling, and track teams. He was a bachelor.

Heanes, a far more mild-mannered man who also had been on the force less than two years, was patrolling an adjacent radio car beat when he received a call to "cover" Frey at 7th and Willow. He already had heard Frey ask on his radio for a "quick rolling check" on the license number of the car Newton was driving and, when the radio dispatcher acknowledged by saying "we have got some information coming out on that," Frey had radioed: "Check. It's a known Black Panther vehicle." So Heanes was alert when he stopped. Both he and Frey had been briefed at regular police lineups to use caution when dealing with the Panthers, and they had been shown photographs of all known Panthers, including Newton.

When Heanes arrived, Frey was sitting in his squad car, apparently completing the first blank spaces of a traffic ticket. The incompleted ticket was found later, made out not to Huey Newton, but to "Lavern Williams." Strangely, the ticket bore Newton's address, not that of Miss Williams, as if Frey had taken some of his information from Newton's driver's license and the name identification from Miss Williams's automobile registration. This anomaly led the Newton defense to suspect that Frey had been interrupted in the act of attempting to frame Newton on a charge of false identification.

*Newton continued:* "I had never heard (of) or seen either of the officers, but it was a common thing that I would be stopped. It is unusual that I drive and I am not stopped ... The second officer paused at the first officer's car for a second and then walked up to my car and asked me, and I quote, 'Mr. Williams, do you have any further identification?' And I said, 'What do you mean, Mr. Williams? My name is Huey P. Newton and I have already shown my driver's license to the first officer.' The second officer then just looked at me and said, "Yes, I know who you are.' . . . It was a total of about ten minutes. The first officer was still in his car. The first officer then got out of his car, came over to my door and ordered me out of my car. As I got out of the car, I picked up my law book which was in between the seats . . ."

*Garry:* "Just a minute, Mr. Newton. I show you here People's Exhibit Number Thirteen and ask you if you have ever seen this book before?"

*Newton:* "Yes, this is my book. This is the book that I took out of the car . . . my criminal evidence book which covers search and seizure and reasonable cause to arrest . . . I had both courses at Merritt College and the Assistant District Attorney, Mr. [Jack] Meehan taught me evidence . . .

"I got out of the car with the book in my right hand and I didn't open up the door . . . the first policeman opened up the door. He opened up the door and I got out of the car with the book in my right hand, and I asked him if I was under arrest. He [Frey] said no, I wasn't under arrest, but 'just lean on the car,' so I had the book in my hand and I leaned on the car with my hands on top of the book . . . and the officer made a frisk in a very degrading fashion. He took my shirt tail out and made a complete search of my body. At this time, four of us are in the street. The second officer (Heanes) has come around to the street side with the passenger, Gene McKinney . . ."

When Heanes testified, he did not disagree with Newton in many significant respects, but he did deny that Frey ordered Newton to lean against the car or that Frey searched him. Newton insisted, however, that he was thoroughly frisked.

"Right after I was searched," he continued his testimony, "the first officer told me to go back to his car, he wanted to talk to me. So, I took a couple of steps going back, and he got on the side of me . . . and took my left arm with his right, and we started to walk back to the car. Actually, he was kind of pushing me, because he was walking at a pretty rapid rate . . . We stopped at the back door [of the police car].

"At this time ... I opened the book up and I said, 'You have no reasonable cause to arrest me.' And at this time he [Frey] said, 'You can take that book and stick it up your ass, nigger,' and as he says this, he gives me a straight arm, or a smear in the face ... hooked me in the face ... I stumbled backwards ... maybe four or five feet, and I was dazed. I went down to one knee.

"I think I still have my book in my hand, and as I was getting up off my knee, I saw the first officer draw a service revolver and then I felt like it was a sensation like hot soup had been—boiling hot soup had been—boiling hot soup had been spilled on my stomach, and then I remember hearing a sound, a loud sound or volley of shots, or it was like an explosion to me.

"I didn't know what it was. It was coming—it seemed as if it was coming all around me, and I can vaguely remember crawling on the ground or moving or being moved, but I can vaguely remember being on my hands and knees and things were spinning. And I don't know whether someone was carrying me or something, but I had a moving sensation and—or being propelled.

"After this I don't know what happened. The next thing that I remember is that I am at the entrance of Kaiser Hospital ..."

Up to the point at which Newton claimed Frey struck him in the face, there was only the one significant disagreement between his testimony and that of Officer Heanes, but from that point on, none of the public witnesses to the incident agreed with Newton. The only one who might have corroborated his story, Gene McKinney, claimed his Fifth Amendment privilege against self-incrimination after answering two innocuous questions. He was jailed for contempt. The two remaining witnesses were Heanes and an Oakland bus driver.

Heanes said that Newton whirled on Frey, rather than the other way around as Newton claimed. The city bus driver,

Henry Grier, a 20-year Negro Navy veteran who drove his vehicle to within yards of the two police cars and the Volkswagen just at the moment Newton was being walked to the rear car, confirmed Heanes' version. He said Newton, not Frey, was the aggressor.

But there were inconsistencies in Grier's testimony and at least one glaring and crucial change in two versions of the incident that he recounted. In the first account that he gave to police interrogators within hours of the tragedy, he described Frey's killer as a "sort of pee-wee type fellow," about "five feet" tall, wearing a "light tan color jacket" and a "dark colored hat," not a cap or beret. But when police showed him a photograph of Newton's face, he identified the five-feet ten-inch Black Panther as Frey's assailant. In court he insisted his identification of Newton was accurate, although he appeared to be confused over the question of whether his bus was only a few feet or many yards away from the scene when the shooting took place. On one observation he remained firm. He said he saw Newton reach inside his jacket or shirt and pull out a pistol.

Heanes admitted that he never actually saw Newton holding a gun in his hand. Heanes said he drew his own revolver, heard one shot and realized he had been struck in the right arm. After that, he said his memory of the event was hazy, although he remembered watching Newton and Frey tussling on the trunk lid of the police car. He also remembered shifting his revolver to his left hand and firing once at Newton's mid-section.

Grier said Newton fired the first shot as Frey struggled for the gun. At that point, Grier claims that he shifted his attention to the two-way radio in his bus to call for help. When he looked back, he said, Newton was pumping bullets into the falling figure of Frey.

An autopsy later in the day showed that Frey had been struck by five bullets, four of which entered his body. Only one bullet was recovered. Two of the shots, at least one of them fired by his own police .38, entered his back. He rapidly bled to death from one of the latter. It was clear that Frey's assailant, whether previously armed or not, had disarmed the officer and shot him at least once with his own weapon. Heanes's wound also proved to have been inflicted by Frey's weapon.

Grier said he saw Newton and another man, presumably McKinney, run from the scene immediately after the gunfire. Heanes crawled into Frey's radio car and called for help. Within minutes all freeways in the area were alerted and all available elements of the Oakland police force began a manhunt, looking at first for a small, unshaven Negro man ("a pee-wee type" Grier called him) who was wearing a dark hat and a tan jacket. A few minutes later all units were alerted to the fact that one of the two escapees was Huey Newton, because Heanes by then had identified him. "He's a light-skinned Negro and he has his hair piled up pretty high on his head," said the police radio dispatcher. A voice came back to the dispatcher from one of the radio cars: "It's real fuzzy and soft, but not piled up high. Just a lot of hair." "Check," the dispatcher corrected his description, "it's one of those fuzzy hairdos. The latest style." The voice came on the air again. "No grease," it said. "Check, original style hair," said the dispatcher. "African style," said the voice.

A witness then told the police of seeing the two hunted men commandeer a car. The police seemed to become almost panicky in their chase. "Attention all units," called the dispatcher. "Attention all units in the City of Oakland. Be on the lookout for two male Negroes of any type riding in any vehicles."

As the radio cars screamed around Oakland on the lookout for Newton and McKinney, other officers at the scene of the shooting examined Laverne Williams's Volkswagen. They claimed they found an unfired 9-mm. shell and a matchbox of marijuana in the car, and two expended 9-mm. shell casings outside of it.

Newton and his companion, meanwhile, allegedly forced a black man named Dell Ross at gunpoint to drive Newton to Kaiser Hospital. As a result, Newton was later charged not only with murder but with kidnapping, but when Ross refused to testify against Newton, the charge was dropped. In any case, Newton arrived at the hospital with a bullet wound that entered his gut near the navel, perforated several loops of intestine, and exited near his spine. And the Oakland police were hard on his trail.

His testimony continued: ". . . I was experiencing excruciating pain [from the stomach wound] . . . I walked in and I asked for medical attention . . . It seemed a long period [subsequent testimony showed that the emergency room nurse made Newton wait almost half an hour before attending to him], like someone was aggravating me because they wouldn't give me the doctor . . . finally someone helped me into this room and helped me up on to a gurney . . .

"I was on the gurney for a short length of time and then the police stormed into the room using much profanity, calling me son of a bitches and all sorts of profane names, and they rushed over to me and put the handcuffs on me with my arms stretched over my head . . . they closed the handcuffs very tight . . . they were beating on the handcuffs and the pain . . . was more severe than the pain in my stomach . . .

"I started to scream to the doctor who was watching them to tell the police to loose the handcuffs, and the doctor then told me to shut up . . .

"The police then struck me on my face or head. They were all around the gurney . . . they started to make statements like, 'You killed a policeman and—or maybe two, and you are going to die for this. If you don't die in the gas chamber, then if you are sent to prison, we are going to have you killed in prison, and if you are acquitted, that—we will kill you in the streets!'. . .

*Garry:* "Mr. Newton, would you please tell us how you were dressed on that evening."

*Newton:* "I had on a black beret, a black leather jacket, white shirt and black trousers, black shoes and black socks." (Shirt, pants and jacket subsequently were admitted as un-contested evidence; the police claimed there were fragments of marijuana in the trouser pockets.)

*Garry:* "Mr. Newton, did you have any knowledge that there were fragments of marijuana in any one of your trouser pockets?"

*Newton:* "No. I had no knowledge of any marijuana what-soever. As a matter of fact, I haven't ever seen any marijuana other than in my physical and mental hygiene class, pictures of it in school, when I was in school."

*Garry:* "Have you at any time ever used marijuana?"

*Newton:* "No. It is strictly against the rules of the Black Panther Party to use any narcotic whatsoever ... I personally think that it is not good physically, and the second reason is that Black Panthers are stopped daily, and if they have any contraband in the car they are asking to be put in jail, so we obey the law to the letter. Caesar's wife must be held beyond reproach."

Garry's implication in the relatively insignificant matter of the marijuana was that the police had planted evidence as a part of the broader scheme to frame Newton for the murder of Frey. Newton, he claimed, had blacked out after the first shot, therefore could not have assaulted Frey. A "little pee-wee" wearing a tan jacket, matching Grier's original descrip-tion to the police, killed Frey, not Newton. Garry maintained that Newton was as pure as Caesar's wife.

The prosecutor, an assistant district attorney named Lowell Jensen who had announced at the outset of the trial that he would seek the death penalty for Newton, worked doggedly at destroying the young defendant's "Caesar's wife" image of himself. He pressed his belief that Newton was armed with a P-38 pistol at the time of the fateful pre-dawn encounter with Frey and Heanes. Newton denied it. When asked if McKinney, whom Newton said was not a Black Panther, was armed,

Newton replied, "I don't know one way or another." Bearing
down on the question of weapons and what he said was Newton's avowed intention to kill policemen, Jensen produced a
paper.

"Let me show you something here. Would you look at this?
This is a Xerox copy of *The Black Panther* . . . there is an
insert here which indicated 'By Minister of Defense Huey P.
Newton,' something in reference to guns."

"Oh yes, this is a poem that I wrote," said Newton.

"All right. And would you read the poem for us?"

"It says:

> *Guns, Baby, guns;*
> *Army .45 will stop all jive*

("I am not a very good poet here)

> *Buckshots will down the cops;*
> *P-38 will open prison gates.*
> *The carbine will stop the war machine*
> *A .357 will win us heaven*
> *And if you don't believe in lead*
> *You are already dead."*

Later in the cross-examination, however, Newton denied
that he had ever urged the killing of anyone or that the Black
Panther Party favored guerrilla raids against the police. He
said he merely had been predicting these events, not advocating them. Jensen reminded him of a published interview
in which he had been quoted as saying he would be willing to
kill a cop when the time comes, "that it wouldn't be just a
couple of cops when the time comes, it will be part of a whole,
national coordinated effort . . ."

Newton denied that he was that specific in his remarks to
the interviewer. "I told him that there was a possibility, even
a probability, of a physical conflict between the occupying
army in the black ghettos, and the ghetto dwellers, because
of the objective and subjective conditions of the ghetto, and

I predicted that there would be an uprising and people would be killed."

"What did you say about the role of the Black Panther Party as far as that is concerned?" Jensen asked.

"The role of the Black Panther Party is to attempt to curtail this violence, to stop it," said Newton.

"... try to stop violence .. ?" Jensen asked in an incredulous voice.

"Yes, that is true, by negotiating with the authorities and hoping that the army of occupation in the ghetto would withdraw from our community, and we would set up our own security force as well as control the other institutions in our community. We feel that this is absolutely essential in order to have peace in America."

Jensen then reminded him of even stronger language in an article in *The Black Panther* that Newton admitted writing only three months before the death of Officer Frey. At Jensen's request, Newton read the article aloud to the court.

"... When the vanguard party destroys the machinery of the oppressor by dealing with him in small groups of threes and fours, then escaping the might of the oppressor, the masses will be overjoyed and will adhere to the correct strategy. When the masses hear that a Gestapo policeman has been executed while sipping coffee at a counter and the revolutionary executioners fled without being traced, the masses will see the validity of this type of approach to resistance ..."

But Newton calmly disowned the statement even while admitting its authorship. "As a matter of fact," he said, "after this was published there were many intervening variables came into play, and we no longer abide by this statement that I did write."

When Garry returned to the witness for re-direct examination, he tried to soften Newton's image by asking if he felt "any personal antagonism just because a person is a police officer?"

"No. The way the Black Panther views the police," Newton replied, "... They are the fall guys of the power structure.

They go in and do the dirty work of the exploiters and they do it so that they can meet the notes on the house and take care of the kiddies, and they only take orders. But the real brutality is not police brutality but social brutality, political brutality and economic brutality. The police are in the community to see that the power structure persists . . . But as far as hating the police, we don't hate the police."

In his testimony Newton ranged widely over African history and the possibilities of peaceful solutions in which he said he still believed. In an apparent attempt to strengthen his portrait of Newton as a downtrodden ghetto youth who had been ill-treated by society, Garry asked whether or not he was functionally illiterate when he graduated from Oakland Technical High School.

"Now, because of this inability to be able to read and write," Garry asked, "did you take any tests where your mentality was graded?"

"Yes . . . One time I was on the Stanford-Benet intelligence test. I scored fifty, which is on the idiot level, I believe, and another time I scored seventy-five, which is a dull normal."

"And this was because of your inability to be able to read; is that correct?"

"Yes."

". . . Was this humiliating to you?"

"Yes. If it had been discovered it would have been very humiliating."

"You say there were other blacks in the class in the same category as yourself?"

". . . About eighty-five percent, I would predict, getting out of the various high schools, are not able to read or write."

Judge Monroe Friedman, a 72-year-old former Federal jurist who scarcely concealed his impatience with Newton and his attorneys, interrupted. "Can they read or write at all?" he asked, querulously. "Can most of the blacks read or write when they get out of high school? Can they read or write at all; not semi-illiterate," he inquired, as if to distinguish between illiteracy and semi-illiteracy.

"Most of them are illiterate or semi-illiterate," Newton replied.

"... Now what was there, Mr. Newton, that converted you from an outward—almost an idiot from the intelligence test to a person who started learning?" Garry asked. "What converted you? What was the trigger point after you finished high school?"

"After I finished high school, that—all the way through high school the instructors were telling me that I couldn't go to college. About the last year I was telling them I was going to college and they said, 'No, you can't go to college because you are not college material,' and it was the part of showing them that I could do anything I wanted to.

"And besides that, the first book that I learned to read was the *Republic* of Plato and it was the cave allegory in the book that impressed me and the stories about cave prisoners ... hypothetical thing where the prisoners are in the cave and finally one is freed and he sees the outside world and he returns to the cave to tell the cave prisoners that they are only seeing symbols or they are seeing reflections on this wall because of a fire at the mouth of the cave and they are not really viewing reality. And many of them told him that he was crazy that he had gone mad, and he couldn't convince any of them ...

"And all of this is symbolic of learning the truth of a situation or gaining wisdom or knowledge. You go into a whole new world and you are able to distinguish between reality and things that are falsified."

"And you would say that this was a trigger point in your life?"

"Yes. This was a real trigger point because after I finally succeeded in reading this book, that I sort of gobbled up everything I could get that I would attempt to read other books, and I could understand them. And I found that even with my limited ability to read from the start, that I would grasp the essential point in the book, and it was a gratifying experience."

Newton's confident performance as witness and defendant was superb. Dressed neatly each day in an immaculately fitted pale grey suit and dark turtleneck shirt, he looked clean-cut, handsome, and self-assured. He smiled frequently, spoke crisply and with calm authority, and appeared to enjoy the testy ripostes of his defense attorney and Judge Friedman who frequently let his displeasure over Garry's questions and Newton's discursive testimony show.

I sat in on some sessions of the eight-week trial and found myself drawn to the defendant despite the seeming weakness of his case. He did not look or act like a cop killer. And there were enough soft spots in the prosecution's testimony to leave considerable room for doubt about who killed Officer Frey, or even about the possibility that Newton may have killed him in self-defense.

Heanes said that he did not see a gun in Newton's hand and that, except for firing one shot himself, he remembered very little of the detail of the incident because he blacked out momentarily after he was hit in the arm.

Newton stoutly maintained that he, too, had "blacked out," lost consciousness after his own wound, and therefore could not have pumped the fatal bullets into Frey.

McKinney, when called to the stand, said that he was with Huey in the car. He said he could not remember how he was dressed at the time. Then Garry asked him, "Now, Mr. McKinney, at the time and place on that morning at approximately 5:00 o'clock in the morning did you by chance, or otherwise, shoot at Officer John Frey?"

"I refuse to answer on the ground that it may tend to incriminate me," McKinney replied. Because he already had begun testifying about the incident, the judge ruled that he could not apply the Fifth Amendment selectively to subsequent questions involving the same incident, so he jailed McKinney for contempt. But doubt had been raised in my mind at least by McKinney's brief and enigmatic appearance on the stand.

Grier, the bus driver, had originally described the killer as a "pee-wee," about five feet tall, wearing a dark hat, not a beret, and a tan jacket. Newton was five feet ten inches tall, weighed about 155, and wore a black jacket and a black beret, not a hat. Grier's description in the courtroom differed from his earlier testimony. Now, he said, he was positive of his identification of Newton as the killer, yet he showed great confusion over whether his bus was only a few feet or many yards from the scene of the shooting. He was not a strong witness.

There was doubt over weapons used and bullets fired, too. Heanes's police .38 was the only weapon involved in the shooting that remained on the scene. Frey's gun, which fired a special ball-powder bullet of great power, was missing, and if another weapon was used in the shooting, it, too, was never found, although two expended 9-mm. cartridges and one intact one were discovered at the scene. Moreover, both Frey and Heanes were hit by bullets propelled by the kind of ball powder that Frey, alone on the Oakland police force, used. It seemed possible that Frey could have shot Heanes by error, lost his gun in a struggle, and died from his own powerful bullets, and that a third weapon, the 9 mm., also was fired by one of the participants.

On the surface, it looked to me as if Newton may have struggled with Frey, grabbed his gun and started shooting, but there was enough doubt to make me wonder if he was not as innocent as Seale, Cleaver, and the others claimed that he was. Filled with doubt, I went to see Ed Keating, who was serving as an unpaid volunteer attorney, helping Charles Garry with Newton's defense.

Keating is an amiable and talented man of enormous good will and deep sentiment, a modern-day reformer who, like Don Quixote, seems never to have gotten a firm grip on either

his saddle or his lance. He is a lawyer by training, but until
the Newton case, he had spent very little of his life in the
practice of law. His fortune, which probably amounted at one
time to more than a million dollars, was in real estate. While
he enjoyed the comfortable accouterments of upper-middle-
class life and lived on a mildly elegant scale not far from
Shirley Temple Black in Atherton, south of San Francisco,
he had an overwhelming desire to reform every tradition-
bound institution he encountered, beginning with the Catholic
Church and ranging thereafter from American racism to hide-
bound local, state, and national governments. The vehicle for
his tilt at the windmills of the American Establishment was a
small Catholic lay quarterly called *Ramparts,* which he
bought in 1962. Under his editorship, the magazine became
an outstanding liberal Catholic periodical, crusading against
a restrictive church hierarchy and reaching far afield to
espouse liberal causes throughout America. Gradually, its
editorial realm broadened; it became a monthly, and finally
it evolved into the first slick, radical, general magazine in the
United States.

During the period when Keating was devoting a great deal
of personal effort to Beverly Axelrod's campaign to win Eldridge Cleaver's release from prison, the owner-editor himself
was gradually becoming imprisoned in an untenable kind
of editorial solitude on his own magazine. With the expansion
of *Ramparts,* Keating had welcomed outside help in meeting
capital needs, and he no longer owned outright the property
that he had developed. To his dismay, a group of young and
more radical editors, led by an eye-patched youth named
Warren Hinckle who had been Keating's promotion manager,
gained the backing of *Ramparts*'s outside investors and
shouldered Keating aside. By 1968, he was frozen out of his
own magazine. Although he had lost a reported $800,000
bringing *Ramparts* from Catholic orthodoxy to political radicalism, he was philosophical about his loss. "If all that

*Ramparts* ever accomplished was to get Eldridge Cleaver out of prison, it was worth it," he told me.

We sat in his paneled study one Sunday afternoon during the Newton trial, and I reviewed my doubts about the case with him. I said that despite the softness of both defense and prosecution cases (Newton said he blacked out after feeling the "boiling hot soup" of his stomach wounds; Heanes, too, said he blacked out; Grier appeared confused; and at least one of Frey's wounds appeared to have come from his own pistol), it seemed reasonable to believe that Newton had shot Frey during a struggle, perhaps to defend himself from unprovoked attack by the police officer.

"I don't believe Huey fired a shot," said Keating firmly. "I don't think McKinney could have killed Frey, either. He was standing too far away, beside Heanes. I doubt if Garry can prove it, but I'm convinced there was a mysterious third person involved."

Keating said that Heanes, Grier, and McKinney were not the only witnesses to the shooting. For one, he said, a group of black prostitutes had seen it, as had an unknown number of bystanders on the street at that early hour. A few of them had been traced by both police and defense investigators, he said. While none of their stories jibed with any of the others, Keating said they supported his belief that there were three civilians involved in the fatal gunfight, not two. "None of those witnesses are credible either from the defense point of view or from Jensen's," Keating said. "That's why none of them are being called to the stand by either side—they're just too disreputable to make believable. But I'm positive there was a third person and that Huey is the innocent victim."

At that moment, I decided to stay on in the Oakland area and try to get to the bottom of what clearly seemed to me to be a mystery story of major proportions. I had almost finished writing my profile of Eldridge Cleaver, an article that made clear my unabashed admiration for the subject if not the black militant army with which he was affiliated. In the course of doing that article, I had developed a strong empathy for Cleaver, the fundamentally raceless radical intellectual, as well as for some of the bizarre points of view of the Black Panther Party. Now, it seemed, there was a strong possibility that these young men, ill-served and mistreated in a society that condemned them by the color of their skin to permanently blighted lives, were acting out their own fateful parts in a contemporary passion play; but it wasn't a stage performance. Huey Newton's life was at stake. Cleaver's continued freedom to speak and act against the system that wanted to reimprison him was drawing to a close under what clearly appeared to be official state persecution. And the small militant political party itself was being systematically destroyed by the police, the Oakland establishment, and the authorities of the State of California. Moreover, Federal authorities had begun to play a role, if Cleaver was correct in identifying the FBI agents who had staked out his house, and I had no reason to doubt him. No one who became acquainted with Cleaver and his colleagues or followed the Newton trial at that time doubted that J. Edgar Hoover had joined the Oakland police on the trail of the Black Panther Party. Hoover, himself, made no bones about it a few months later when in his annual report to Congress he cited the Party as a significant threat to the internal security of the nation.

At the same time, the very tactics that the authorities and the police were using in their attempts to stamp out the Party, like the oppressive measures of the Romans against the early Christians, were serving only to enhance it as an explosive political force in the ghettos of many American cities. An ambitious Panther recruitment campaign accompanied the loud outcry over the Newton case, and new chapters of the militant party already had formed in San Francisco, Los Angeles, Denver, New York, Omaha, Baltimore, and half-dozen other American cities. What had begun as a local anti-police party of a few kids led by Huey Newton and Bobby Seale had now become a national revolutionary organization

with branches spreading everywhere and a membership up
from no more than fifty when Newton encountered Officer
Frey, to at least a thousand, if not more.

I was convinced when I left Ed Keating's house that Sunday
evening that by using my growing friendship with Cleaver
as a starting point, I could penetrate the Party apparatus to
learn just how large it was, how it was structured, and how
widely its influence was spreading. At the same time, I saw
the possibility of a gripping and meaningful mystery story
emerging from the Newton case itself, if only I could locate
the witnesses who, Keating said, placed a third man at the
scene as the killer. By now I had lost all the personal fear I
brought with me to my first meeting with Eldridge. I had
become emotionally involved as a person, not simply as
journalist-observer. The self-generated fear I had previously
carried as a crust to disguise sentimental charity—"his liberality is, in fact, charity"—had been replaced by zeal, but its
source, I think, remained as sentimental as it had been at the
beginning. Also, I remained as woefully naive as ever.

# CHAPTER 8

## "We can't even trust the local fishwrap . . ."

Two of my hundreds of conversations in Oakland stand out now as the quintessence of my failure to get to the bottom of anything. One of them was with a police lieutenant named Larry McKee, an Oakland native, ex-merchant sea-man, 21-year veteran on the force and director, at the time, of police Community Relations. It was a job, he explained, that he was ordered by Chief Gain to accept, even though he de-tested it. "My forte is auto theft," he grumbled. "I'm really good at it." The other was with Mrs. Armelia Newton, now 63, the mother of seven children including her youngest, Huey, and wife of the Rev. Walter Newton, an Oakland street cleaner who preached from time to time in various churches. Each typified, in his and her own way, the obstacles to objectivity faced by any white reporter, no matter how deeply and per-sonally involved, on a black story.

I had attempted without success to contact Officer Heanes and a half-dozen other policemen who had testified in the course of the Newton trial, and I was not surprised when none of them responded. As witnesses in a murder trial, I knew they had been cautioned not to discuss the case, any-way. I also tried chatting informally with random police officers on the street, but in each case the officer's eyes nar-rowed and informal conversation ceased when I mentioned

that I planned to write about the Newton case and the Black
Panther Party. The most voluble of them said, "The only
police officer who can make any statement about that is the
chief. You won't find a cop who will talk about it unless the
chief tells them to."

When I called the police department to arrange to see Chief
Gain, I was directed to Lieutenant McKee. Community Relations, it seemed, also encompassed press relations. "There's
nothing I can do for you," he said. "Chief Gain is the only
person in the department who can make a statement about
that."

"That's why I called," I said. "I want to talk to Chief Gain."

"He's away."

"Can I reach him by telephone?"

"No, you can't. Absolutely not. The reason he is away is so
that he won't be nagged by people like you."

"When will he be back?"

"I don't know."

"Next week? The week after?"

"I don't know. Maybe next week. Maybe the week after."

"Well, until he gets here, I have some other requests and
perhaps you can help me. I'd like to ride on night patrol with
a police car in one of the ghettos, and I'd like to . . ."

"You can't do that. I can't help you."

"Well, one thing I need to do is to ascertain the chronology
of events with respect to the police department and the Black
Panthers—you know, just list from police records when each
arrest took place, the charges, that sort of thing."

"I'm not going to cooperate with you in that."

"May I come in to headquarters and see you? I'm sure that
if we could talk, if I could explain what I'm doing . . ."

"You can come in. I'm here. But I'm not going to help you."
He hung up without saying goodbye.

The next morning I went to McKee's office in the modern
police headquarters building at 7th and Broadway, about a
mile and a half from the place where Frey was killed. I had

long since given up the blue blazer and the yacht club tie as counterproductive, but for this occasion I donned straight clothes—a suit and vest—and even had my rather shaggy hair cut. McKee was utterly unimpressed.

He greeted me coldly and told me to expect no cooperation of any kind from the Oakland police department.

"Why?" I asked. "You don't know me or anything about me. You don't know whether I'm pro or con on the Newton case, whether I hate the Panthers or sympathize with them. All you know about me is that I write for *The Saturday Evening Post*." My first highly favorable article about Cleaver had not yet appeared on the newsstands.

"Just knowing you write for anybody is enough for me," he said. "You ding dongs take even the simplest things we say and turn it around. For example, if I said 'we have a problem here in Oakland,' you could do something with that, couldn't you? You wouldn't explain what I mean by that, you'd just turn it around. We can't even trust the local fishwrap," he growled, pointing out of his window to the nearby tower building of Mr. Knowland's conservative *Oakland Tribune*.

"Lieutenant McKee, I haven't even talked with you yet and you already are assuming that I'm out to cut your throat or something . . ."

"I don't trust any reporters," he shot back. "Even the boys upstairs (the regular police reporters from the local paper), some of them are friends of mine, but their editors take this stuff and jazz it up."

I sat there, dumbfounded, as he delivered a long and bitter monologue in which he characterized the press and the police as hostile power groups. The police, he said, were merely exercising their rightful power to protect themselves and the public from criminal elements in the community, while the press was abusing its power, using it as a weapon to diminish the power of the police. I have known quite a few policemen in my life, but never had I heard one characterize the police in this country as an autonomous power group that must struggle to maintain its strength in the fact of hostile power groups. McKee's was a kind of Balkanized view of society at its most fundamental level. No wonder Oakland police public relations were deteriorating. I listened for almost half an hour, then exploded.

"You make me sore as hell," I shouted. "You don't even know me, yet you've decided in advance that because I'm a reporter I represent some kind of insidious threat to police power. With cops who talk like you do, it's a goddam good thing the press *is* trying to diminish your power, if that's what they're doing here."

I don't know whether it was my outburst that took him back or whether he simply faced the fact that I wouldn't go away and decided, therefore, to mollify me, but his belligerence eased somewhat.

"Let's not get mad at each other," he said. "Have a cup of coffee and tell me about your background. I don't think I can help you, but who knows? Maybe we can work something out."

He took my name and home address in Larchmont, N.Y., asked how long I had lived there, and copied the serial number of my New York driver's license, which seemed a strange approach to probing a professional journalist's background. I started to hand him my old White House press pass, left over from assignment in Washington during the Eisenhower and Kennedy Administrations, but he waved it away. "Cards don't mean anything to me," he said. "You're probably legitimate, what you say you are. But anyone can walk right in here off the street, you know."

"What are you going to do? Run a police check on me in Larchmont, New York?" I asked incredulously.

"We have our ways," he said, cryptically, and smiled.

"Then look me up in *Who's Who*," I said. "You'll find more there than you'll get on a police wire." The whole encounter was becoming unreal.

"No kidding? You in *Who's Who*?"

"Yes," I said. "But maybe you'd better get a copy right now and check it. I could be lying, you know, just walking in off the street and all that."

Now all was changed. It was as if the lieutenant had suddenly discovered that I was no longer a threat but an ally. I had establishment credits. I told him that until the year before I had been editor-in-chief of *Holiday* ("That's a pretty magazine; I always liked it"), Managing Editor of the *Post* ("I don't see it much anymore since they changed"), a Washington correspondent for *Life* ("They do pretty good, especially on pictures"), a war correspondent in Korea ("I sailed in Asia; I'd like to go back"), a foreign correspondent writing from most parts of the world ("When we've got more time, I'd like to tell you about my stretch in the merchant marine; I really got around"), but that until now I had virtually no experience in reporting about black people.

"That's where it is," he said, as if picking up a cue, "that's where our real problems are. It's terrible, but everybody thinks that just because we're cops, we're racists or something. If only they would understand. We're not racists. Far from it. If only they knew all of the things we do, the little unsung things to make better race relations, instead of blowing all out of proportion a few incidents and turning them upside down against us. There's absolutely no racism in this police department."

"That's a pretty broad statement to make," I said. "How do you know?"

"I know it, that's all. I been here twenty-one years. I know that I don't have any racial prejudice and I know that the other guys on the force don't have any either. For example, you see that nice little gray-haired officer in the next room?"

I looked across the glass partition which enclosed McKee's office and saw a nice-little-gray-haired-officer in civilian clothes sitting at a desk in the next room.

"Look at him. He was a great policeman on the street. They brought him inside, and he's in charge of missing persons now. He's the kindest, most gentle person you ever saw. You know, *those* people (it was clear that he meant blacks) abandon their children all of the time, a lot more than *other* people do. He gets a lot of these cases. Why, he had one in there with him just before you came in. I wish you'd seen her. Cute little three-year-old pickaninny. He was bouncing that little pickaninny on his knee. It warmed your heart to see it."

After several weeks of parrying, during which all but one of my requests were denied, Lieutenant McKee succeeded in getting an interview for me with Chief Gain. But after McKee, the rational police chief was pure anticlimax. Gain was the image of the modern, progressive, well-educated police leader, obviously sincerely concerned about relations between the races and about the spot on which the Black Panthers had put his own police force. "They're nothing but a black vigilante group," he said, "and I don't see how anyone can sympathize with that. I don't condemn or decry militancy by itself. When people are on the bottom, they've got to publicize their plight. But to accomplish anything, they've got to focus on good programs, well supported. The Black Panther program is based in large part on undocumented and irrational charges. To become known, they've found the easiest way to do it is focus on the police. It gets to be a pretty irrational thing. I'd like to meet with them, to talk with them, but they won't meet."

Gain, who acted as a consultant to the Kerner Commission, echoed the Commission's findings. "My main concern about what has to take place in this country is recognition that we have a white problem; not just black, white. The whites either have to face the problem or flee it. Unfortunately, too many are fleeing. We must have a national commitment for change. Either change it or the races will get farther and farther apart."

Gain lamented the fact that his own force was almost totally white; of roughly 800 officers, only 27 were black and only one of them had achieved the rank of captain. I asked him if it was true that the Oakland police department made a policy of recruiting officers from the rural South. He scowled and, without replying directly to my question, said that it was becoming increasingly difficult for police forces anywhere to recruit qualified young men. "We are thirty men short right now and we're having trouble filling all those positions."

I suggested to him a favorite idea of my own. "Wouldn't it make sense to apply Selective Service to the police, to give young men two or three years of police work as an alternative to military service?" I explained that I believed such a constant infusion of non-police-minded civilians on urban forces would be a healthy influence on the police themselves, while at the same time the young recruits would benefit by contact with a much broader spectrum of society than army experience provides. For one thing, I suggested, it would solve both his recruitment problems and the problem of racial imbalance on his force.

"You can't force men to do police work," he said, dismissing the idea in a sentence.

I concluded the interview by asking him if he believed all the officers on his police force were as committed to stamping out racism as he obviously was.

"I am sure that they are," he said.

For all I know, Gain could be right about many of his policemen, but if he is, their commitment to racial justice is well concealed, or at least it was to me. During two months of wandering around Oakland, I made at least some effort every day to befriend a cop and talk with him. All of them were amiable enough until I mentioned racial problems or the Black Panthers. Then they shut up. I found only one man on the entire police force who would talk freely. He was black and worked in Community Relations, with undisguised loathing for Lieutenant McKee. "I'm so low on this police force now that the only promotion they could give me is out," he said. But aside from the fact that he had once met Huey

Newton and found him to be a bright and thoughtful young man, he knew virtually nothing about official police policies concerning the Black Panthers. Except for the one black policeman who held the rank of captain, none of the handful of blacks on the force ever had been assigned to duty sensitive enough to bring them into contact with the Panthers, he said.

My investigative efforts fared little better in unofficial Oakland than they did in the police department. Charles Garry generously gave me a carte blanche to his own files, and I spent a great deal of time in his San Francisco office analyzing and copying the Newton trial transcript, but I had no luck whatever in turning up additional witnesses to the killing who might support Keating's third-man theory.

Garry himself had earlier questioned two purported witnesses to the death of Officer Frey. One of them was a black man named Johnny Jones, who told Garry that he saw "ten whores standing on the corner" watching Heanes, Frey, Newton, and McKinney just before the shooting. Garry had lost track of the man. Looking for someone named John Jones in any city is a formidable job. I spent three fruitless days trying to relocate him in the hope that he could lead me to the ladies who he said had observed the killing. I found several people named Jones and one named Johnny Jones, but all disclaimed any knowledge of the Newton incident.

Garry's other unused witness was a woman, but in deference to her sex and her professional status, I will omit her name. She was washing up after entertaining a customer in a rooming house near the scene of the murder when she saw the action on the street unfold, she had told Garry. After the shooting, "I saw three fellows run from the area of the police car," she had said, thereby reinforcing Keating's theory; but, she had added, "it looked like he (Huey) got the policeman's gun away from him," which seemed to make Keating's theory academic at best. I guess I will never fit the image of the bulldog reporter who relentlessly pursues his sources, however long it may take to find them. I spent only one day searching for her, because it simply became too awkward for me to continue. A middle-aged white man looking for a black whore in West Oakland is apt to be received coolly by anyone who hears out his inquiries. After a day of maladroit explanations, I was afraid to go back to the neighborhood.

Keating's third-man theory of the killing had raised an exciting journalistic possibility: there seemed to be no doubt that there were other persons on the street at that hour, and it was altogether possible that an unknown bystander had joined in the struggle in which Newton was wounded, grabbed Frey's gun, shot him and melted away in the pre-dawn darkness. But now, as far as I was concerned, the theory was as dead as Officer Frey. I knew I would never find evidence to prove it. Even if I were less fastidious about pursuing possible sources, the elusive witnesses had been too unstable even for Newton's defense attorney to put on the stand. And no matter what I discovered, by the time of my uncertain investigative efforts the Newton jury already had settled on my initial hypothesis that Newton did not kill Frey in cold blood, but may have shot him during a struggle.

After hearing a charge (to which Garry objected on grounds that Judge Friedman had failed to properly instruct them), the five jurymen and seven jurywomen, led by a black bank official named David Harper whom they had elected foreman, brought in a verdict of voluntary manslaughter, not first-degree murder as the state had charged. On a second charge of "assault with a deadly weapon upon a peace officer" (Heanes), the jury found Newton not guilty. Garry's last plea in the eight-week trial was that Newton be freed on bail pending appeal. He estimated that the appeals process would take two years and that it simply was not fair to make the defendant serve that much more "dead time" (he already had been held without bail for almost a year). Garry was confident he would win a reversal. The final page of the transcript of the trial of Huey Newton reads as follows:

THE COURT: Anything further, gentlemen?

MR. GARRY: No, Your Honor.

THE COURT: Motion for bail is denied. Please take the defendant upstairs.

THE DEFENDANT: Power!

VOICES: Free Huey. God bless Huey. Free Huey now.

THE COURT: There will be order in this courtroom. Recess. (Whereupon at 9:35 o'clock A.M., an adjournment was taken *sine die*.)

Newton was sentenced to two to fifteen years and sent to Vacaville prison for initial processing. Later he was moved to the model Men's Colony at Los Padres, near San Luis Obispo. A year and eight months after sentencing, the California Court of Appeal reversed his conviction on grounds that Judge Friedman failed, as Garry had claimed, to instruct the jury properly. Garry had asked the judge to include in his instruction the admonition that if the jurymen believed Newton's story of losing consciousness after he was shot, they should find him not guilty. Had Judge Friedman done so, it is doubtful that the jury's verdict would have been any different, because it was clear that most of them did not believe Newton's story. Although the jurymen did not publicly discuss their deliberations, I received descriptions of them from a third party whom I believe to be reliable. Several of the panel reportedly wanted to convict Newton of first-degree murder, but only one sought outright acquittal. Their ultimate decision, according to my informant, was not so much a plain compromise of these diametrically opposite views, as it was political. Outright acquittal appeared to be out of the question in view of the feelings of most of the jurymen. On the other hand, one of the jurors was said to have communicated to them his own deep fear that a first-degree murder conviction might ignite the entire black community of Oakland, a spontaneous fire under the Panthers' banner of "The Sky's the Limit." Thus the jury reportedly settled for the ambiguity of "voluntary manslaughter." In essence, therefore, it was a political verdict, meant to cool

passions that had been aroused by the Panthers' strident cries.
"FREE HUEY! THE SKY'S THE LIMIT!" had been heard
halfway across Oakland. The only act of violence that came
in the wake of the verdict was utterly unexpected, and it was
against, not from, the black community. Two white Oakland
policemen, uniformed and on duty in their patrol car, drove
up to the storefront headquarters of the Black Panther Party
late one night and riddled its plate glass windows with shotgun
pellets and bullets from their police guns. Their apparent targets were posters of Huey and Eldridge that had been affixed
to the front of the building and to the office walls inside. The
posters were torn to shreds, but no one was injured. Both policemen were found to have been drinking on duty and were
suspended from the force.

I was anxious to talk with Newton. Other journalists, including representatives of the so-called "underground press,"
had been allowed to interview him in jail. The California Department of Corrections thought he would be permitted at
least a few interviews at Vacaville, too, so I sent in my own
request. Before seeing him, however, I wanted to meet all
the members of his family and learn as much about his personal background as I could. With Ed Keating's kind assistance, I began with Huey's older brother, Mel, then 30, a
studious and mild-mannered sociologist who had earned a
master's degree and hoped to go on to his Ph.D. He was supervisor in the Alameda County Welfare Department and was
teaching, part-time, at Merritt College as well. Mel Newton is
almost self-effacing in his quiet good manners. He has none
of the flamboyant "willingness to risk all" of his younger
brother, and he thought the difference in personality came
from their utterly different approaches to ghetto life when
they were small children.

"Huey was always moving," Mel said, "always going somewhere, doing things. He had a bicycle and he was constantly
exploring Oakland and having experiences. I was in the library

or at home in our room, reading and studying. I spent very little time with anyone outside of our family group, so I was really not conscious of ghetto conditions, or of cops harassing people. Huey was. My experiences were very limited because I avoided outside contact, but he would tell me about his. I think his sense of injustice began in elementary school when he was playing in a sandbox. He took his shoe off to empty the sand into the teacher's wastebasket, and for some reason she hit him on the head with a book. He threw the shoe at her. He always reacted to injustice. I just sort of accepted it. For example, in a junior high school social science class we were supposed to do a report on 'the land of our ancestors.' That put the black kids in the class in a hell of a spot, because none of us knew where we came from. It was embarrasing, but I didn't protest. I just picked Ethiopia, because I knew there were black people there."

Mel said the Newton family, contrary to Daniel Patrick Moynihan's then current and dire observations of black family life as essentially matriarchal, was a strict patriarchy. He described for me what he remembered and what he had heard of the family's beginnings in Oak Grove, Louisiana.

It was a place of dirt roads and tired earth, he said, a somnolent cotton town, in the extreme northeast corner of the state where the cultural patterns are one with those of neighboring Mississippi and Arkansas; the kind of rural Southern community in which all male Negroes, from the youngest to the most respected elders and clergymen, are called "boy" by their white fellow citizens. The Reverend Walter Newton, who felt "the call" and became a self-ordained Baptist minister when he was in his teens, was comforted by the Christian promise of a glorious life after death, but he was just as religiously fed up with the lack of promise of real life in Louisiana. So when the U.S. Government in 1944 advertised wartime jobs for unskilled laborers in Oakland, California, he moved. Newton told his children in later years that if he had stayed in Oak Grove, he would have been killed, but he never explained to them whether a specific incident had created that fear, or whether he simply concluded that what Mel called "his overwhelming need to assert his manhood and independence" would inevitably lead to his death.

In either case, he made it clear to them that Christian hope for a better life in the hereafter had been replaced in his mind by the certain conviction that he and his race deserved far better than the marginal living and the subhuman caste they were accorded in Oak Grove. His feelings may even have solidified as a result of the populist promises of the late Senator Huey Pierce Long, the demagogic former governor of Louisiana who was gunned down by an assassin in 1935. Long's dream to make "every man a king" had stirred the imaginations of as many Negroes as whites in that dismal countryside, and Walter Newton's strong conviction that he was the equal of any white man was reinforced by it. When his seventh and last child was born in Oak Grove in February, 1942, Reverend Newton chose a symbolic name for him: Huey Pierce Newton. From the beginning, the family was uncertain of the correct pronunciation of the Kingfish's middle name, so when it was used at all in the noteworthy life of Huey P. Newton, it was spelled and pronounced Percy.

At the time they migrated to Oakland, the Newton children already spanned an entire generation. Huey was 2, Mel was 6, Doris was 13, Walter was 16, Leola was 17, Myrtle was 19, and Leander, the oldest son, was 21.

"We were a close family," Mel said, "but each of us was very different from the other. My father raised us to be different from one another. Everyone had a role to play and he demanded that we play it. Certain things were expected of certain individuals. Huey was the baby who could do no wrong, and he wasn't supposed to lose. My father disciplined him very harshly when he came in crying from a fight. Lee was the big brother, and all of us had to give him respect. Walter was the ladies' man. Once these roles were assumed, however they got started, they were expected of us, and we had to live up to them. My father always told me that I would be the scholar of the family, and perhaps that is why I became what I am.

"He was a very proud man, and he insisted on protecting his family. He would never let mother work for white people; in fact, he never let her work at all—her place was in the home. He worked very hard in order to spare us from hardship. We never suffered. There was always enough when we needed it. Father always told us, 'You get an education and make something of yourself; that's the way you solve these social and economic problems.' He was very firm about that, but school was hard for everyone because of the way we were treated. It didn't bother me too much, because I just withdrew from it and studied. But it made Huey angry all the time. Like the gym teacher at Woodrow Wilson school, who would always shout, 'the last one in the shower is a nigger baby,' to Huey's class. They made it very clear to black kids what they thought of you. Most of them were shunted off into shop courses, automobile mechanics, things of that sort; and they didn't even provide automobiles to work on."

Not surprisingly, brother Leander and sister Myrtle, who had grown to maturity in Louisiana, got the least education. Neither finished high school. But Doris and Leola graduated, married well, and became middle-class housewives. Walter graduated from high school, too, and became an airplane mechanic and a painting contractor. Mel worked his way through collage at Merritt, San Jose State, and Berkeley. Huey finished high school, worked at casual jobs in, among other places, the Oakland street department and a cannery, and intermittently attended Merritt College over a period of about six years, during which he earned a junior college certificate. At one point he enrolled in San Francisco Law School for one course, but dropped out before the year ended.

Mel said that when Huey began cruising the streets of Oakland, armed for informal legal confrontations with the police, the elder Newtons were appalled, not because they thought he was wrong, but because they were certain he would be killed. "All of us tried to talk him out of it," Mel said, "but we couldn't dissuade him. He was determined, and we were afraid for him. My mother and father were the most upset, and their arguments with him got pretty heated."

Huey's sister, Mrs. Leola Carr, said, "we were all afraid of the Black Panther thing when Huey started it. He felt that this is what's wrong with everything and the important thing that he had to do was bring to light the police department problem. He always felt that someone needed to speak out; no matter what happened, he had to be heard."

I spoke to her in the tastefully furnished living room of her two-story brick house in a well landscaped, integrated neighborhood on the outskirts of Oakland. Like her brother, Mel, she was quiet and reserved. And, like Mel, her attitudes toward the Black Panther Party had changed substantially since Huey was wounded and charged with murder. In the beginning the organization frightened her. Now, on the mantelpiece above the fireplace, amid a collection of tiny china figurines, was the large and gleaming glass figure of a black panther, crouched as if backed into a corner and pre-pared to fight. She was very much in favor of the Party now, she said, "but I think they need more educated leaders, a little older than some of them are now."

Her brother, Mel, apparently was what she had in mind. My first meeting with Mel was over dinner with his wife, Joyce, who had left their three-year-old son, Gregory, with Leola for the evening. He wore a soft tweed sports jacket and looked as professorial as he was. When we parted, he told me that he hoped to win a foundation research grant that would permit him to travel to East Africa to study black family life there. It never even occurred to me to ask him then if he was a Black Panther. Our second meeting, a few days later, was at the San Francisco airport. Ed Keating and I joined him there for a flight to Los Angeles, where he and Keating were to speak at a Unitarian church in which a "Free Huey—Free Eldridge" fund-raising and petition campaign was to be organized. For this occasion he wore a black leather jacket, black slacks, a turtle-neck shirt, and a beret. He seemed embarrassed by the Panther uniform, as if, somehow, it didn't fit. Mel told me then that he had become acting Minister of Finance of the Party, but he made it clear that if Huey had not been jailed, he probably would never have become involved in the organization.

"The people that have been ripped off—Huey, Eldridge, and the others who are under indictment for one thing or another—offered a very brilliant kind of leadership, and you can't duplicate that," he said. "But I feel that I have to try, to at least offer myself now that Huey is gone. Fortunately, much of what he stands for has been committed to writing. The importantant thing is not what the organization does, but what the community does as a result of their own learning. Look around. Now, for the first time there's an identity in the black community, people identifying with their own community. The Panthers have had an influence there. I think the main objective of the Panthers has been to lend some kind of a structure of understanding to the black community on social and political problems that the people confront daily. I think all observers would admit now that there's no turning back. Black people will be reckoned with, and they will have their dignity, otherwise there'll be continued unrest and battling to get it."

He seemed such a mild-mannered man that I asked him if he honestly went along with the Panthers' emphasis on guns and their scarcely concealed goal of armed revolution.

"I don't believe in guns or in killing, no matter who does it," he said. "I hope it never comes down to armed conflict. I don't think it will."

In Los Angeles we were met by a heavyset, graying white man, who drove us to the organizing meeting. He said there were a number of liberal groups represented at the meeting and that he hoped that at least some Black Panthers from the

Los Angeles chapter would come. "We invited the Communist Party, and they'll have a few people there," he said, "but for God's sake don't mention it when you talk. It turns off a lot of these liberals, you know."

There were four Black Panthers in the small group of about forty people at the meeting. Mel knew only one of them by name. He introduced me. It was John J. Huggins, who was killed three months later during a dispute with other dissident blacks at U.C.L.A. Huggins and his three colleagues sat apart from the mostly white audience and seemed impassive as Keating and Mel spoke of their firm beliefs that Huey was innocent. The jury's verdict, Keating said, "was a spineless, mean, petty admission of their own guilt." Since it was an organizing meeting, entertaining ideas for conducting fund-raising in the Los Angeles area, Mel injected two fresh notions he said he had been pursuing but had not yet checked out with Bobby Seale and other members of the Panther leadership. "I want to organize two new groups to help the movement," he said. "One of them we will call 'Uncle Toms for Huey,' to mobilize all the black people who are afraid to join the Panthers, and the other we will call 'Racist Liberals for Huey,' to get more white liberal support." Huggins and his Panther colleagues stared at Mel in disbelief and grimaced as if with pain. A few days later Mel told me that Bobby Seale had vetoed the idea. "I still think 'Toms for Huey' was a good idea," he complained, "but they're afraid of it."

I spent many days hanging around the Panthers' new headquarters on Shattuck Street in Berkeley, just across the city line from Oakland, but I never saw Mel there. He was busy with his casework in the Alameda County Welfare Department, as well as with his classes at Merritt College. But I also had the feeling that even though he was the founder's older brother, he felt no more comfortable among the Black Panthers than I did. After thirty years of sidestepping racial confrontation and striving to make it within the limits that white society permitted, he seemed to have moved too deeply into the integrated middle class to manage such an abrupt turnabout. It was clear, also, that he abhorred violence, and no matter how disarming the happy-go-lucky, barracks-room atmosphere of Panther headquarters, where dozens of pretty, miniskirted, teenage girls cheerfully turned out mimeograph stencils and talked in the banalities of ordinary office workers as they bundled copies of *The Black Panther* for street sale, the place sustained a deliberate atmosphere of violence. Lists of recommended weapons, pictures of rifles and machineguns, stark drawings of armed children and cartoons depicting dead pigs in police uniforms surrounded huge posters of the armed Huey and an angry Eldridge on the walls. Although I never saw Mel there, we did meet a few more times, and he seemed firm in his commitment to the organization. At our last meeting, he gave me a small brass tiepin that he said John Huggins had given to him. It was a crudely carved brass hand on whose palm was etched a snarling black panther.

The other members of the Newton family were not as generous with their time as Mel and Leola. When I called on Huey's oldest sister, Mrs. Myrtle Seymour, Walter, the entrepreneur and ladies' man of the family, was with her. They were cordial, but like the Oakland police, they were not willing to discuss Huey or the Black Panther Party. "We just don't think we should talk about Huey to anyone unless Momma tells us it's all right," Myrtle explained. "Mel told us he thought we ought to talk to you," said Walter, "but our mother hasn't made up her mind yet, and until she does, we're just not going to say anything." I had been trying, with Mel's help, to arrange a meeting with the Reverend and Mrs. Newton, and he had cautioned me, "My father won't talk to you, but give her time —I think she'll come around," so I had not pressed for an appointment. But I was becoming worried now that I would get no further background on Huey before I interviewed him at Vacaville, and all I knew about him was the little that Mel and Leola had told me. I telephoned Mrs. Newton. "Mel told me about you," she said. "I don't think I want to tell you anything, but I ain't decided yet. You call me back next week."

The same day Ed Keating called to tell me I had been cleared by the prison authorities to interview Huey in the visitor's room at Vacaville at 11 o'clock on the following morning. As one of Huey's defense attorneys, he said, he would accompany me. I wondered why the word came from Keating instead of from the Department of Corrections, but assumed that the authorities screened applications for interviews with the prisoner's attorneys, so it seemed reasonable that Keating would be alerted to the appointment before I would. Unhappily, I was wrong. When we arrived at Vacaville shortly before the 11 o'clock appointment, Associate Superintendant James A. Kane told me I would have to wait at least a month, until Huey was transferred to San Luis Obispo, and even then it was doubtful that I would be permitted to see him. He knew nothing about my request for an interview.

In his own eagerness to help me, it seemed, Ed Keating had gone outside of official channels and made arrangements for my interview with one of the sergeants inside the prison. The sergeant was not on hand, but the associate superintendent was, and his word was final. Kane smiled and told Keating that as one of Huey's attorneys he could talk with the prisoner if he wished, but I would have to wait in the prison reception room. I knew Keating had a tape recorder in his briefcase, and that even though it was officially frowned upon, he probably would be permitted to use it in the visitors' room. Hastily I asked him to conduct the interview by proxy. There was no time to prepare a list of questions for him. I waited for an hour and a half while Ed and Huey talked.

The real purpose of the interview, to meet Huey Newton face to face and make a personal assessment based upon all of the subtleties of direct communication, was lost, but I hoped that something, at least, would come of the proxy conversation. Unfortunately, Keating had only the vaguest idea of the kind of information I wanted. Assuming that I already knew as much as I wanted to know about Huey's case and the origin

and goals of the Black Panther Party, he skipped those subjects altogether and asked Huey what kind of ideal society
he envisaged for the future. Normally, the Black Panthers
view that kind of question as "counterrevolutionary." Eldridge
once explained to me that the Panthers see themselves as "part
of the process" of achieving a socialist society; their task is
that of revolution itself, not that of conceiving and building a
new society. "The contours of the new society we can save for
others, whose duty that would be," he said.

Surprisingly, Newton did not react as Cleaver had to the
question about the future, but rambled along for most of the
interview elaborating upon a vaguely conceived socialist government that would be based upon ethnic rather than class
or geographic representation. "Every ethnic national group
would have a seat in the ruling body or the administrative
body of the country," he said. In addition, there would be a
Ministry of Culture whose prime role would be to perpetuate
individual ethnic and religious cultures: Afro-American culture, Jewish culture, Irish culture, Chinese culture, and so on.
In time the various cultural groups would form their own
exclusive physical communities so that ethnic representation
would, in effect, become geographic representation as well.
At the same time there would be free cultural mobility, so
that any individual could identify with and adopt any ethnic
culture he wanted to. "Now people become converted Jews,
people become converted Catholics, but what I am propos-
ing," he said, "is that in the future we will be able to become
converted Afro-Americans, converted Chinese and take on
the whole cultural pattern of the people, simply because of
the beauty of this particular pattern, and this will be through
conscious choice." He didn't mention the possibility of anyone
wanting to convert to Wasp.

Within Newton's ethnic agglomeration, he said, "we're
going to have a socialized country, a socialist country where
the national enterprises will be operated and owned by the
people ... national monopolies. General Motors, Standard

Oil, Bell Telephone, General Electric, these will be nationalized. Each ethnic group will be represented there. By the same token, local enterprise also will be socialized and controlled strictly on a localized basis. Profit will no longer go into private hands, but it will go back into the many national, ethnic communities. It will discourage privately owned business, period. Usually if a person goes into business, it's to gain a profit and to own a bigger business some day. It's like the peasant—the peasant owns a small plot and hopes someday to own a larger plot, and there's no real difference between the small peasant and the big peasant. The small peasant wants to be the big peasant. So there will be no private enterprise whatever."

Newton did not foresee a process of Balkanization occurring within his society of many cultures. "You'd truly have a nation of nations, and these nations would grow and also would influence the whole foreign policy," he said, "because then the people would be taught to live with people at multiculture levels instead of trying to suppress and rob them of their cultures. I can see not only the blacks accepting and whites adopting the Afro-American culture, I can see the blacks and whites will adapt to other cultures, because the whole thing then will be that you will adopt a culture strictly from the esthetic value, and all cultures are beautiful, so it will be simply a subjective thing when you make a choice, similar to the religious experience.

"I think that after we achieve this, while we're achieving this, we'll work for the elimination of the material incentive, which is the real evil. The people will work then from the moral incentive, similar to what the Cuban government is trying to establish. There will be certain goods that the country will turn out and certain needs that each local community will demand and the people will work in the national factories and the local institutions, creating these goods for the use of the many communities, and they will be distributed throughout the country."

"Suppose for a moment that this ideal society has been realized," Keating interjected. "What would you like to do, where would your role be, how would you live in this state of freedom?"

"I like to be with people, and I like to communicate," Newton replied. "As long as there are people, there are going to be contradictions, disagreements, and people are going to misunderstand each other. Communication will be a problem on a national and international level. Because of the pleasure and the self-fulfillment I get out of working with people, I think that I would like to have some position where my communication will be expanded.

"I read this one book that was very interesting by B. F. Skinner, called *Walden Two*. Walden Two was Utopia, there was no money and no competition in Walden Two. But they had a board of sociologists or psychologists; anyone could get on the board, and they would do experiments and they would try to solve certain problems, such as improving the human being's desire to create, and they would do these actual, simple experiments, and they would try them out on themselves and introduce them to the community, and the community would attempt to implement them, and if it didn't work they would just tell the board, 'Well, it didn't work,' and they would work on this. So, I wouldn't know exactly what position I want to have, but it would be some place like this, dealing directly with the people instead of, say, in physical science or something."

Whether Huey Newton, the idealist, had given any more thought than that to his vision of "human engineering" and socialism in America, he didn't say. The tone of his taped discourse sounded as if the ideas were emerging by free association, on the spur of the moment. But they did underscore what always has struck me as the most significant ambivalence in the organization and attitudes of the Black Panthers: their inability to decide firmly whether they are engaged in a revolt of race or of class, and their concomitant incapacity to structure their plans for the future clearly around one or the other premise. Huey's longing for the independence of varieties of ethnic and cultural groups under a single socialist government, whatever it lacks in political sophistication, represents a deep yearning for black autonomy, a kind of black nationalism. The political programs of the Black Panther Party, all originally promulgated by Huey, reinforce this. Black community control of all businesses and institutions, including the police, in the black community; black liberation schools; free breakfasts for black children; free medical clinics in the black community; universal pardons for blacks in jails and prisons; blanket exemptions for blacks from military service; black juries for black men. The organization itself is exclusively black, and while it welcomes alliances with action-minded, white revolutionary groups such as the Weathermen, the Yippies, and Up Against the Wall, it does so always with the understanding that the Black Panther Party follows no one's counsel but its own and always remains free to go its own way regardless of the feelings of its nonblack allies. Yet, as if they sense the futility of revolt by a single color minority, the Panthers vociferously and, I think, sincerely deny that they are either black nationalists or reverse racists; their goal, they say, is not simply to get The Man off their back in the black community. On the contrary, they look upon themselves as the "vanguard party" in an ideological war against "the system" that is run by a small, mostly Waspish, capitalist ruling class. Their strategy in waging this holy war demands as its most essential element that through their alliances and their actions, including the vital act of provoking their own persecution, they will change the attitudes of white, middle-class people who will become radicalized and bring about the system's downfall. Cleaver, Newton, Seale, Hilliard, and all the other Panthers who have been able to articulate the Party's philosophy have insisted again and again that theirs is a revolution of class, not of color. In a political sense, they scorn black exclusivity as "cultural nationalism." Yet the party's membership, its platform and program, its few ongoing social activities such as the breakfast program, its publications, and even its dreams, if Huey's vision is the guiding one, are as exclusively monochromatic as are those of the Ku Klux Klan. It is a kind of organizational and philosophical schizophrenia.

Probably the most damaging result of this ambivalence is an only partly buried *fear* of theorizing about the future, expressed in Cleaver's attitude that such projections are counterrevolutionary because they distract minds and energies from the process of revolution.

Cleaver quotes Bakunin and Nechayev's *Catechism of the Revolutionist* to justify his stand. Before beginning his career as rapist, he says he took the Catechism "for my bible." The only revolutionary salvation, according to Bakunin, lies in utter "root and branch" destruction. Cleaver reinforces this fragile intellectual base with Ché's and Regis Debray's romantic notions that violence is a sufficient end in itself, because order and beauty will follow of their own volition *after* the destruction has been wrought.

This kind of political romanticism serves as an efficient substitute for ideology among the preponderance of Panthers (and other revolutionaries) who are not well-enough educated or sophisticated enough to grasp a rational philosophy. But Cleaver is both educated and sophisticated, and I think his dogged determination to avoid peering beyond the process of revolution itself reflects fear more than romanticism. Thus, anyone who asks him the obvious question, "What kind of system will you supplant this system with?" will be told that a "Yankee Doodle Dandy kind of socialism" will arise, like the flowering plant of a long dormant seed, but that to attempt to describe it, shape it or define it is counterrevolutionary, and all such questions must be rejected out of hand. Beneath his rejection, I think, is not just romanticism, as many young people seem willing to believe, like the mystical faith that Newton illustrated in his prison interview, but fear: fear that no matter what the form of government, whether Maoist Com-

munism, Russian Communism or a yet to be devised indigenous American socialism, blacks will remain an oppressed
minority because forms of government cannot by themselves
eliminate racism among either the governors or the governed;
and a mystical faith that with hope alone, this damnable fear
will be swept away once the present system is overturned.
Those whose duty, in Eldridge's mind, will be to establish
"the contours of the new society" will somehow come up with
a governmental form so perfect that all ethnic groups will
exist in harmony with equal power over the whole and total
power over their own communities and cultural patterns.

It is as if the articulate Panthers are afraid to think beyond
the destruction of the present system to the construction of
a new system, because no matter what new system they are
able to conceive, the old problem that gave birth to the organization to begin with—racism—remains. Thus, to satisfy their
own crying demand for dignity, manhood, freedom, and
power, the Party must at one and the same time be an exclusively black liberation army and the vanguard of a mystic
revolution in which racial exclusivity somehow will become
irrelevant. It is necessary for them to believe that in the
process of destroying the society that currently exists, the
hearts and minds of men in that society will undergo a mirac-
ulous change that will permit them, in Huey's vision, to live
peacefully and prosperously as a "nation of nations."

Back in Charles Garry's office in San Francisco, I listened
to the tape of Huey's optimistic hopes and felt my enthusiasm
for this whole self-generated exploration of the Panthers wind-
ing down like the spring of an untended clock. My interest
in their origins and the conditions that led to their accelerat-
ing growth remained unabated, but the frustration of my
hoped-for meeting with Newton, following as it did the un-
cooperativeness of the police and my laughably inept attempts
to investigate the slaying of Officer Frey, somehow struck me
as a watershed. Moreover, I was making very little progress
in ingratiating myself with other members of the Black Pan-

ther Party whom I met in the course of my research. Only Eldridge and Mel Newton had accepted me on open and equal terms, but neither had been able to extend his influence on my behalf to other members of the Party.

During the many afternoons that I sat in the outer office of the Panthers' fake Tudor-style building in Berkeley, I found most of the young black members who passed to and fro to be cordial and even friendly. Many of them had seen me with Eldridge, and that, evidently, had removed any cause for overt hostility or suspicion. But when it came to discussing Party affairs, they were as negative as Lieutenant McKee.

"Those who say don't know; those who know won't say," was the standard response to most of the questions I tried obliquely to slip into casual conversations. Questions that did not fit the all-purpose reply were shunted aside with, "Ask David or Bobby about that; they're the only ones who are authorized to talk about that." I saw David Hilliard and questioned him about the shoot-out in which Bobby Hutton was killed. But after that we never got beyond an exchange of amenities because he was too much in a hurry to stop and talk. Bobby Seale barely acknowledged my presence until one day, at Eldridge's urging, he invited me in to his small, bare office in the back of the building and delivered a brief, set-piece lecture on the Party's ten-point platform and program. I tried to interrupt to tell him that I was familiar with the program, but he went on, like a beginning piano student playing a piece from memory and afraid to hit a wrong note or stop because that would mean he would have to go back to the beginning again to pick up the thread of his melody.

At the end of the Declaration of Independence, he said, "We advocate the abolition of war—pick up the gun to get rid of the gun."

We talked desultorily for about fifteen minutes. I asked him about the free breakfast program for ghetto children, which was only then getting started in Father Neil's Oakland church. It has since spread to all the organization's thirty-five to forty chapters around the country, and the Panthers claim they are feeding hot breakfasts and political lectures to 50,000 children each morning. Already there had been a few complaints from black businessmen, passed along to me by a worried black lawyer in Oakland, that the Panthers were extorting food and donations for the program by running what amounted to an old-fashioned mob-style protection racket. "That's nonsense," said Seale, "our donations from the black business community are freely given and gratefully received."

I asked him if it was true that children who came to the church for breakfast were subjected to political indoctrination and asked to recite Panther slogans such as "Off the Pigs" along with their grits and bacon. "A lot of kids begin at an early age to relate to black history," he said. "We try to help them. Of course we help them to relate to the Black Panther Party."

I asked him about the Party's growth. In the month or so since Huey's conviction, he said, the number of chapters had almost doubled, from eighteen to thirty-five. With the rapid expansion, there were problems, but he thought he could cope with them. What sort of problems, I asked, police infiltrators, undisciplined new Party members? "Maybe some of both," he said, and dismissed the subject. Inevitably, I asked how many members there were. "No one knows," he said. "It's a political party, not a club. Who knows how many people follow any political party at any given time?"

A lithe young secretary of about 17 interrupted to tell Seale that he was wanted on the telephone, although I had not heard the instrument in his office ring, nor had any of its several plastic extension buttons lighted to signal an incoming call. He lifted the receiver and waved me out of the room. That was the end of it.

Mrs. Armelia Newton received me in the modestly furnished living room of her small frame house the next day. She is a blunt and plainspoken woman who looks a little bit like the black comedienne Moms Mabley. Without a word she brought a straight-backed chair from the adjoining dining room and put it down in front of an aging, overstuffed lounge chair. Politely she asked me to sit down in the stuffed chair, then she sat facing me in the other one. While my interest in hearing family reminiscences about Huey Newton had become considerably less urgent than it was when I thought I was to interview him, I remained interested and still wanted to talk with her. But our conversation took only a few minutes. Before saying a word about her son, she said she wanted a legal contract from me guaranteeing her no less than $5,000 for her cooperation. I excused myself and shook hands. She smiled understandingly and waved before closing the door behind me.

# CHAPTER 9

## *"I'll never go back to prison."*

ELDRIDGE stalked exuberantly into Black Panther
Party headquarters on the afternoon of my last day in Berkeley
and Oakland, and I shook his hand for what I was certain
would be the last time. The Court of Appeal had overturned
the writ of *habeas corpus* by which Judge Sherwin had set him
free after the Panther-police shoot-out in April. Garry was
appealing the new ruling but he had little hope of upsetting it.
Cleaver was due to return to prison on November 27, less
than four weeks away. I was going home, professionally
starved after two months of nibbling without nourishment at
the edges of the Newton case and the Black Panther Party,
discouraged over having wasted so much time on a story that
remained buried in police intransigence, black reticence, and
my own investigative failures. If there was a hidden mystery
in the fatal Newton-Frey encounter, I had not revealed it, and
if there was journalism of value to be found in going beneath
the surface of the Black Panther Party, I had failed to penetrate it. If the experience had any value to me at all, I thought,
it was metaphorical, like Plato's cave allegory that had so
impressed the pre-literate Newton. I had perhaps seen some
of the light that was casting shadows on the walls, but it was
only a glimmer and I was not sure that even the glimmer was
real. I thought I had learned enough to cast a shadow of doubt
on Newton's guilt, and I could see flickers of hope in Cleaver's

remarkable power to lead, a power I thought could be diverted
to peaceful change if only he could shake himself free of the
law and of the stultifying limitations of Panther sloganeering.
I felt as if I understood and sympathized at least with what
the Panthers were about, but concerning how they intended
to accomplish their goal of a just society, I hadn't a clue. There
were explanations enough, to be sure, and I had heard and
read all of them: interminable statements by Huey, lengthy
rhetorical responses to my own questions to Eldridge, public
utterances by Seale and Hilliard, and statements of intent in
*The Black Panther,* many of which pointed quite specifically
toward armed revolution, urban guerrilla warfare with bullets and bombs. But, like the well-meaning white liberals at
DeFremery Park who condescendingly dismissed the speakers'
obscenities as merely street talk intended for the black kids
who appreciated it, I dismissed the widening stream of violent
threats and cries of revolution as if they were the babbling of
a brook passing over some rapids on its way to a peaceful
river downstream. I'm still not certain why I sought comfort
in such poetic sublimation, although on reflection I think that
my personal admiration for Eldridge Cleaver and my naive
unwillingness to believe that any sane person seriously would
encourage blood-letting by Americans in America were largely
responsible for it. But the fact is that I quite deliberately put
aside almost every threatening word that the Panthers said as
just a lot of big talk by mostly small kids, immature remarks
to be heard condescendingly and then forgotten. Frankly, I'm
still not sure that I was wrong, because as I look back, the
threatening talk of killing policemen, burning the White House,
and overturning the system by violence was not the *leitmotif*
that Cleaver's speeches and most of the Panthers' public meetings made it appear to be. Most of the rhetoric, the Party's
rules, the more strident sections of the ten-point program were
fundamentally defensive in nature. "Pick up the gun to get rid
of the gun" could be argued quite convincingly, as it was to
me by a young Panther in the Shattuck Street building one

day, as simply a call for self-defense that meant no more than "keep a gun in your house, ready for use in case you are illegally attacked." Not very different, really, from the precautionary arms many Americans maintain at bedside for protection against lawless intruders.

Another phrase from the Party platform that the Panthers used like an exclamation point at the end of any cry for power, freedom, or justice was "by any means necessary." It had an ominous ring until it was put to the test. The phrase was used almost as often as "The Sky's the Limit" to emphasize demands to "Free Huey," and in concert with other demonstrative cries from the Panthers it led the entire city of Oakland to expect conflagration. As only one example, male and female Panther demonstrators had chanted outside of the courthouse as the Newton trial began:

*Females*: It's time to pick up your gun!"

*Males*: "Use it!"

*Females*: "All our brothers in jail; pigs are gonna catch hell!"

*Males*: "Off the pigs!"

*Females*: "Off the pigs! And make sure they're dead!"

*All together*: "FREE HUEY! By any means necessary!"

Mayor John Redding expressed the city's common fear when he lamented not long after that demonstration: "If Huey Newton is found guilty of murdering the Oakland policeman, I look for the Black Panthers to try every type of disturbance or riot to force another showdown with the police. The police and the city administration are prepared for it."

But when it came down to the crunch, "any means necessary" turned out to mean "any legal means." Huey sent word from his jail cell that the Panthers would exhaust all legal means before doing anything rash, and Bobby Seale dutifully explained that the founder was certain his conviction would be overturned on appeal, as indeed it was.

It was not too difficult to accept the Panthers' explanations of their seemingly threatening slogans. If Huey doted on guns, they were for armed self-defense, not for ambushing police-men; and if the Party called, in Huey's words, for "complete destruction of this decadent system," it did so in recognition of the Kerner Commission's findings that the system is racist and that it could be changed without civil war.

Eldridge was eloquent, if somewhat contradictory, in ex-pressing his own hopes for peaceful change to me one after-noon. I had seen him only infrequently during the previous two months until we met one day in the second-floor sitting room of Paul Jacobs's house, overlooking a sunbathed San Francisco Bay. I had long since finished my article about him, so I made no notes on our conversation, but I remember the earnestness with which he reiterated something he had told me before. "I hate guns and I hate violence. The most horrible thing you can do is take another man's life." He said that civil war could be considered only as an absolute last resort, when all other means of effecting change had been exhausted, and he drew a careful distinction between forecasting guerrilla warfare in America and advocating it as something to "get together right now." He told me that he thought there was still time—how much he didn't try to guess—in which to effect the changes necessary to forestall bloody revolution. And, although he felt that the only acceptable changes would have to conform to the unrealistic ten-point platform and program of the Panthers, he was almost eager in his willingness to con-tradict himself and his Party in that respect. "If all people in this country can show a true respect for the American prin-ciples of liberty and justice for all," he said, "we can dissolve the Black Panther Party right now and live decent lives as free men. I don't want to live like this, in constant danger, you know. I want to go home and write, have a drink in the eve-ning with my wife, raise some children." Then he repeated something he had said to me before, when we were flying back to San Francisco from Omaha. "If I can reserve some room for reconciliation based on change, there's no reason to think it can't happen to others, is there?"

The November 5 election was only a few days away, and Eldridge laughed over the impossibility of his own candidacy, yet he hoped for a vote large enough in the few states where he was listed on the ballot to indicate a substantial sympathetic interest in radical change. But even more significant than his own candidacy, he felt, were the local races in which the imprisoned Huey Newton was running for Congress, Bobby Seale was running for the state assembly from his Oakland district, and Kathleen Cleaver was running for assembly from San Francisco. None of them would win, either, he knew, but all were anxious to analyze voting patterns in their districts to determine how great an impression they had made on older, uncommitted Negro voters in the two cities. They hoped to attract substantial numbers of older followers in ghetto districts. As it turned out, they were disappointed on all local fronts, and Eldridge, the Peace and Freedom Party's only national candidate, drew less than 200,000 votes nationwide. Nevertheless, the earnestness with which they pursued the electoral campaign belied fears that the Panthers had given up totally on an orderly approach to political action.

Eldridge campaigned vigorously, with the active and generous support of his parole officer, a slight, mild-mannered man named Stan Carter who was more social worker than penal official. When we met that day in Jacobs's house he had just returned from a swing through the northeastern United States that Carter had eagerly approved. I told him that my wife had attended one of his speeches at Iona College in New Rochelle, N.Y.

"I wish she had introduced herself to me," he said. "I like to have someone in the audience I can relate to, talk directly to, and I could have talked to her because I know you. I remember that speech. I didn't know anyone in the audience. It would have been more effective if I'd known she was there."

It was kind of him to say so, but somehow I was just as happy that she had not made herself known and thereby become the direct recipient of some of Eldridge's more intimate notions of anatomical power.

His speech-making and a wave of international publicity that was generated at the same time by an unthinking Governor Ronald Reagan and the California Board of Regents, coupled with a certain suspense over whether he would have to return to prison, had brought Cleaver from relative national obscurity when I had first met him three months before, to a position of prominence or notoriety, depending upon one's point of view. His name and a vague understanding of his forensic style were known everywhere. *Newsweek* had devoted most of a full page to the text of one of his more obscene speeches, substituting blanks for the offending words. There were more blanks than punctuation marks in the text. *Life* sent a black reporter-photographer team to follow him and the Oakland Panthers around, but their story didn't appear until long after the election, and it, too, delicately avoided his more colorful remarks. The *Post* scrubbed my own profile of him clean of verbal offense, and *Look,* in what is known in the trade as a "one-stop" piece based on a single interview, referred euphemistically to his more common obscenities as "defiant black words." The television news shows that focused on his appearances delicately "bleeped" out the routine obscenities. So that while it was known to all who read about him or saw him on television that Eldridge "talked dirty," very few Americans ever got a first-hand feeling for a platform style that, at the very least, could have provided them with a sharply cutting contrast to the measured dreariness of Richard Nixon's prose or the babbling timidity of Hubert Humphrey. George Wallace and Curtis Lemay were the only national candidates who offered Eldridge any hyperbolic competition.

Despite the fact that he invariably called out "Fuck my parole officer" whenever he stood on a platform, Eldridge ungrudgingly admitted to a fondness for Stan Carter. "He has good instincts and he tries to do right," he said, "but he's a tool of the pig power structure and he has to do what he's told. He can't help it."

Carter, an assistant supervisor in the California Department of Corrections, was fond of Eldridge, too. I had called on him one day, and he willingly volunteered his warm feeling for his most prominent parolee. Far from putting roadblocks in Eldridge's bizarre Presidential campaign, Carter said he was encouraging the ex-convict's political activity as an unusual but effective exercise in rehabilitation. "I think he comes across much harsher in the newspapers than he does in person," Carter said when I asked him how he reacted to Cleaver's repeated reference to the sexual act that should be performed upon his parole officer. Carter mused about it a moment and added, "He has a good sense of humor."

"I'm not personally worried about Cleaver starting or inciting any violence," he said. "I think he would want to stay away from any violent situation. He's got so much going for him now that I doubt if he wants to screw things up."

Carter said that he was pleased with Cleaver's progress as a parolee, despite the fact that he had been involved in a fatal shoot-out with the Oakland police, was presently conducting an escalating verbal duel with the governor and university regents of California, and was probably about to be reimprisoned for the second time for violation of his parole. "I think he's a changed person," said Carter. "He's taken an interest in politics, in writing, and in social reform. I try not to interfere with his civil rights or with his views." Carter had rejected only two of Cleaver's travel requests, when the Presidential candidate asked permission to attend the Republican and Democratic National Conventions as a reporter for *Ramparts*. "When we heard there were going to be 50,000 National Guardsmen and police there, it seemed too explosive to allow him to go," Carter explained. He was as sanguine about the

Black Panther Party as he was about his model parolee. "I don't look on them as hoodlums," he said. "They're going for social reform. I consider them to be gentlemen among the Oakland black community. They are acquiring respectability in the black community."

Not many Americans aside from the few who actually knew Eldridge and had observed the Panthers would have agreed with Carter, but I did and so did many others who looked upon the growing pressures against the organization and its most notorious spokesmen as a form of persecution, "unbecoming, to say the least, of the law enforcement paraphernalia," in the words of Judge Sherwin. For, while Carter and I mused about the good Eldridge, Governor Reagan, and the state's Board of Regents, which controls the vast California university system, were fuming and creating an international *cause célèbre* over what they conceived to be the bad one.

Cleaver had been invited to deliver ten lectures on racism to a faculty-sponsored, full-credit course called Social Analysis 139X at the Berkeley campus of the University of California. When the projected course was announced, Reagan hit the ceiling. Cleaver, after all, had routinely asked his listeners to "Fuck Ronald Reagan" as often as he had made the same suggestion concerning the more tolerant Stan Carter. At the governor's urging, the Regents voted 10 to 8 to ban Cleaver's proposed lecture series. However, since it probably would have been unconstitutional to specifically deny him, by name, the right to speak, they adopted what they thought to be a clever subterfuge. The Regents passed a new university system rule forbidding guest lecturers from delivering more than a single lecture in any college course if they lacked proper academic credentials (advanced degrees or teacher certificates). Their action was both hasty and ill considered. For one thing, it threw the normally volatile Berkeley campus into a pro-Cleaver uproar because it was perfectly clear that the Regents were acting solely to deny the controversial black man's right to free speech, as well as the university's right to shape its own curriculum. More than 200 students were arrested during demonstrations to protest the action. But the protest was even more far-reaching, because the hasty action affected more than just Cleaver's proposed appearance at Berkeley; it affected the entire university system, and it thereby gained for Eldridge a few improbable allies. A typical one was the School of Business Administration, which complained because some of its most valuable instruction came from self-made businessmen-lecturers who had no academic credits at all and therefore could no longer share their wisdom with the students. But the most anguished protest of all came from Berkeley's famed School of Criminology. Under the new rule, the criminologists lamented, "we will be able to talk at length about crime, but rarely with criminals, about police work, but only briefly with policemen."

Cleaver chose an ironic setting for his response. At the Irvine campus of UC, in conservative Orange County, where he had been invited to appear as a paid ($400) panelist in a discussion of racism, he told the audience:

"The buffoons said I could only deliver one lecture instead of ten. I am going to deliver 20 . . . I'm sorry for the little old ladies with tennis shoes in the audience, but I have only one thing to say to Ronald Reagan: 'Fuck you.'"

Reagan called Cleaver "subversive" and stoutly insisted that "no tiny faction of malcontents are going to be allowed to tear down our institutions of learning."

Cleaver challenged Reagan to a "duel to the death. I could beat him to death with a marshmallow."

To Reagan's discomfort and Cleaver's delight, the duel continued, verbally. The Regents retreated toward compromise when the University proposed that the unwise new rule be rescinded and that 139X be conducted as planned, but as a non-credit, almost unofficial course. And when Cleaver, at last, appeared on the campus to give his first lecture, the publicity inflated confrontation of the puritanical governor and the violently obscene black revolutionary seemed to collapse like an open-necked balloon.

Eldridge delivered a carefully-wrought, scholarly, sober, and utterly anti-climactic academic lecture on the development of color symbolism in Western society, the rise of white as a symbol for purity and black as the mark of fear and evil. To the 300 quiet students who heard him, he offered his own guess concerning the origin of the symbolism; it had its roots, he thought, in primitive man's feelings toward day and night, lightness and darkness. Darkness brought fear of marauders, a threat to survival, while light brought everything good. "I think then man developed a negative feeling about darkness, and that feeling later became intermingled with racism when the slave class was separated from the master class along color lines," Cleaver said. The only possible reason that Cleaver's lectures might hurt Governor Reagan's "institutions of learning" turned out to be the likelihood that the non-credit course would lose its star lecturer before the end of the term, because Eldridge would be back in prison before he could complete the series.

After my pleasant but disappointing meeting with Huey Newton's mother, I had decided to give up my research efforts, and I had called him because I wanted to see him again before leaving town. We met at the headquarters on Shattuck Street.

"Do you have any hope of beating the Adult Authority in court?" I asked him.

"We're appealing to the Supreme Court," he said. "I don't know. I don't think it'll do any good."

"What will you do?" I asked.

"I'll never go back to prison," he said.

"Where will you go?" I asked. "To Cuba? To China?"

"China? I'd like to go there sometime," he reflected. "I'm fascinated by China. But I don't think it would be good for me right now. Maybe Cuba. Maybe Africa. I'm fascinated by Africa, too."

Two weeks later the California Supreme Court affirmed the appeal court's ruling that he would have to return to prison on November 27. Charles Garry urgently asked the first black Supreme Court justice of the United States, Thurgood Marshall, to intercede by staying the order, but Marshall rejected his plea. On November 25, Eldridge dropped out of sight.

# CHAPTER 10

*"I vacillate between saying nothing and saying too little. In between, I say too much."*

While two-month-old Baby Maceo screamed piercingly at his distracted mother from their cluttered cell of a bedroom in the Algiers apartment, Eldridge thrust his finely structured head and broad shoulders forward from the creaking wicker chair in the darkening living room and spoke calmly of shooting his way into the Congress of the United States, removing the head of Senator John McClellan of Arkansas, and shooting his way back out again. His three Black Panther lieutenants-in-exile, all fugitive airplane hijackers standing over me with arms crossed like soldiers at ease on a parade ground, smiled in anticipation. Then in almost the next breath this handsome black paradox of the new American revolution slipped back into the character of the old gentle Eldridge and quietly decried guns and violence. The thing he most detested about his last home in exile, he explained to me, was the ubiquitous pistol strapped on the hip of every petty bureaucrat in Cuba. "Where you have so many guns, you have tyranny," he said. Again the three black American hijackers, whom I had come to know as Muerzi, Rahim, and Akili—new names for new men—nodded and smiled their agreement.

There was no such dichotomy in the personality of Baby

Maceo, whose birth in Algeria on July 28, 1969, Eldridge
hailed as "a new problem for the pigs." He continued his
lusty bellowing for milk, or a fresh diaper, or burping. Kathleen, to whom the child definitely was a new problem, wasn't
sure which. "She didn't find out until last week that you have
to burp a baby after it's fed," Eldridge mused. "Can you
believe that?" Kathleen's mother, a tidy, fashionably coiffed
teacher now separated from her diplomat husband and visiting Algiers to help her recuperating daughter, picked up the
baby and burped him, rocked him gently in her arms, and
tried to ignore the disorder of the sparsely furnished apartment.

This was the last of our Algiers interviews and, after days
of frequently interrupted, chaotic talks, it was coming to a
sticky end. Partly to break the solemn tone of it, and partly
because I had exhausted all questions with which I thought
he was willing to deal, I tried to switch his interest to a distinctly non-revolutionary subject.

"What will be Maceo's full, formal name?" I asked.

"You know," Eldridge said, "when you think about a name
for a child, everybody that I know and relate to, my friends,
they're all seeking to perpetuate revolutionary tradition, so
they want revolutionary heroes to relate to and they want their
children named after revolutionaries. I think one would be
outcast, for example, to name his child Roy Wilkins . . . *Roy
Wilkins Cleaver??* Argh!

"Say, Kathleen," he called to his wife, now fussing with
baby bottles in the adjacent kitchen. "Would you dig Roy
Wilkins Cleaver? Or Thurgood Marshall Cleaver? Or James
Farmer Cleaver?" He laughed at his own irony.

"Not 'til you turn into a Tom like them," she called back.

"Would you dig it then?"

"That's an insult to me," she said.

"But what if I did do that? Would you dig it?"

"No," she laughed. "I'd quit you altogether."

He laughed, and the wicker chair shook as if verging on
collapse. Then he became serious again. I should have learned

by now that it is not possible to divert Cleaver, even incidentally, from thoughts of revolution.

"We have to talk about people who have related to what we relate to," he said. "Then the shining symbols come pretty distinct and clear. There's a kind of rush on heroes these days. There are many Malcolm X's, you know? But I'm very fascinated by Antonio Maceo. He's one of the most important black men in history, you know? I did quite a bit of study on him. He's a man who actually liberated Cuba from Spain. He's the man who carried on the struggle even when others gave it up, when others capitulated. It was Antonio Maceo who, for decades, year after year, continued the struggle and in a very honorable, heroic fashion. I feel that it's an honor to name my son after him. Can't just give a child one name, though. So I would just like to say, Antonio Maceo Dedan Kimathi. Dedan was prime minister of the Mau Mau, you know? Dedan goes very well with Maceo. And then there was the national hero of Algeria who I'm very fascinated by also, Abdel Kadar. But you look at it and you wonder, 'Well, why not Mao, you know? Or why not Stalin? Or why not Kim Il Sung? Why not all of that?' So I don't know at what point we really have to stop being ecumenical about it and decide on one or two, but certainly we know that Maceo will be there, and it seems pretty clear that Dedan will be there.

"But definitely not Eldridge Cleaver, *Junior.* That's presumptuous. This was brought to my attention by a brother from Zimbabwe—the country known by the imperialists as Southern Rhodesia—he was saying that it would be a disservice, potential disservice, to the child to name him after yourself while you're still alive, because you'll maybe sell out later on, you know? You don't know what you're going to do. And its no good to name a child after someone who is still alive, because you don't know how it will come out. That makes a lot of sense to me. I would not think of naming him Eldridge Cleaver, Junior."

*There's a kind of rush on heroes these days . . .*

*Maybe you'll sell out later on, you know?*

After almost a year in exile, a fugitive from the California courts and prison system, wanted by the FBI, missed terribly by the anxiety-ridden Panthers and their radical white allies, was Cleaver beginning to doubt his own heroism, his ability to stay the course? He didn't elaborate, but from my point of view, he had ample grounds to doubt himself, not alone as a result of the alien surroundings or the uncertain motives of the men around him, but from within his own mind, which seemed to me to have fallen off the bridge of reality on which it had tenuously perched in San Francisco and Oakland the year before. Where once there was ordered thinking, an almost ferocious commitment to articulated ideas and a nature that was at once loving and angrily determined to assert itself, there was now chaos, doubt, a mental process that seemed to me to be as disordered as the exile's small, new apartment in Point Piscade, west of Algiers.

I had left Eldridge at Panther headquarters that day in November, 1968, expecting never to see him again, but curiously confident that somehow the man would prevail over the system that was determined to take away his freedom. I was capable of as much romanticism, I discovered, as the most wild-eyed of the Panthers. He had told me and announced publicly that he would never return to prison. But I had thought that he would, and I had accepted as an act of faith that the courts ultimately would recoil at his persecution even as Judge Sherwin had done that previous July. In a year, perhaps less, I thought, Cleaver would emerge from prison with a new appreciation of the American system's innate capacity to right itself. I was not long in being disabused of that sentimentality, but on reflection I think it was justified.

Before he dropped out of sight, disappearing literally inside his own house on Pine Street in San Francisco, an international campaign of petitions and fund raising had been launched with the aim of financing a court fight that would set him free. I joined it. So did large numbers of whites, in-

cluding many of the most prominent names in the American
literary establishment, men and women who had been moved
by the verbal strength and critical power of *Soul on Ice* and
who were convinced, as I still am, that the state wanted to
shut Cleaver up, not because of his alleged crimes, but for
his political radicalism alone. I was convinced that despite the
repressive intransigence of the police, the open hostility of
the FBI, and Governor Reagan's clear antagonism, justice at
the level of the Supreme Court certainly would prevail. His
could have been a landmark case, with profound impact upon
the growing political misuse of police power throughout our
society and particularly against blacks.

At that moment in time, Cleaver obviously stood close to
the edge of total hopelessness, the brink beyond which there
could be no reconciliation, yet he was still able to say with
sincerity, "If I can reserve some room for reconciliation based
on change, there's no reason it can't happen to others, is
there?" The Panthers stood there with him, angered by the
loss of their leader Huey Newton but still willing, I thought,
to interpret their own menacing slogan, "any means necessary" as a guide toward legal solutions to their and society's
problems. I was convinced they were capable then of stepping
back to more realistic ground from which to assist and even
help lead the struggle for institutional reform in America, a
struggle that would demand above all that they define, soon,
which institutions required what reform. I was convinced that
those who took seriously what the Panthers were then saying
—their cries of fascism, imperialism, the power of bullets,
armed revolution, blood in the streets—were overreacting to
the provocative gibberish of immature youths who were still
in the process of growing up to more effective and more peaceable words and actions. The Panthers had not yet evolved
beyond their first awful cries of outrage against the police,
expressed in the morally debilitating tactic of "focusing" on
the institution by dehumanizing its members with the derisive
term, "pigs." Their guns, although utterly repugnant, were

too few in number to be much more than a symbol, the re-
gained phallus of emasculated men, only a little more menacing than and symbolically no different from Lester Maddox's
axe handles. Their economic goals were only dimly understood and vaguely expressed in unspecific condemnations of
"capitalism" and support for public ownership of everything
under Cleaver's glib phrase, "Yankee-Doodle Dandy socialism." Their politics were primitive, and even their most benign
slogan, "Power to the People," was a *non sequitur* in a nation
of universal suffrage where in recent years the power of the
public has been eroded more by its own ignorance and apathy,
black and white, North and South, than by any conspiracy
of an "establishment" ruling class. To me, at least, the Black
Panthers remained at that time what my surge of empathetic
identification that day at DeFremery Park had pictured them
to be: angry young victims of spoken and unspoken American
racism, who were only just beginning to act to break out of
the unearned, unwanted inferiority that society had cruelly
assigned them. I was confident that they would soon work
their way out of organizational and political schizophrenia
and focus effectively on racism itself as the single, most perva-
sive injustice in America that must be expunged. It was this
struggle that motivated them to begin with, and it was to this
struggle alone that I was certain they eventually would shift
all their energy as well as their rhetoric. If, down the line,
they became more sophisticated politically than they had yet
shown themselves to be, and continued to cling to socialist
or Communist ideologies, that was their bag. As far as I was
concerned, they were welcome to stay in it. But I really didn't
see them marching on toward an armed revolution, a new
civil war, because it was perfectly obvious to me, as I thought
it was becoming to them, that such a course meant certain
suicide for them as individuals and for the Black Panther
Party as an organization. They were angry young men, most
of them ill-educated, banding together to express understandable rage over injustice, determined to defend themselves and

in the process to break away from their victimization. I did not see in them the vanguard of an army of blind Samsons, leaning vengefully against the pillars of the entire American edifice.

Then Eldridge leapt from the precipice—he fled rather than stand as he had before for a legal fight that would strip away all doubts about the Oakland shoot-out and reveal to all the magnitude of his persecution. Beginning with the moment on November 25, 1958, when he vanished inside the front door of his house on Pine Street, his total despair became official and irrevocable. Like many other sympathetic white liberals, including the hundreds of demonstrators who gathered outside his house those last few days to show their admiration for him, I told myself, "Well, it was predictable; he said he wouldn't go back to prison. I really don't blame him for running." It occurred to me much later that my reaction was like that of a man who joins an impatient crowd, standing expectantly beneath a potential suicide, crying, "Jump, jump, we'll pay for your funeral."

Not surprisingly, I found it difficult on the basis of my own uncertain experiences in San Francisco and Oakland to come to grips with the Panthers as an organization of people to write about, because, as time amply demonstrated, I had become more confused than enlightened by my researches. I had been rebuffed by the official establishment in Oakland, and I had been accommodated in a good-natured way, but not confided in, by the Panthers. Professionally I had accomplished very little beyond proving to myself the truth of an old saw that only a black reporter can truly relate black experience, if for no other reason than that not many black men will speak candidly to a white interviewer. The Black Panthers had been a mystery to me when I began my almost fruitless research, and they were a paradox to me at the end.

My only gains from the experience were personal, completely internal. I knew that now, for the first time in my life, I had literally felt and understood the disastrous effects of the racism all of us have visited upon the black people of this country, and I could thank Cleaver and the Panthers for that. This understanding had come from direct physical experience with them, however tentative, fearful, naive, and bumbling my efforts may have been. Also, for the first time in a "liberal" life of surface cordiality to black people and remote support for their causes, I had gotten beyond orthodox liberal sympathy, really only a superficial expression of guilt, to a true and deep feeling of friendship for a particular black man who was so much the opposite of me in every way that I couldn't escape the irony of the experience. If, by such modest physical and intellectual effort, I could know, admire, and experience genuine friendship for an ex-rapist, ex-convict, revolutionary fugitive bent on upsetting by any means necessary the life I was living, how much easier would it have been for me, years before, to form stronger friendships with other black people whom I had met cordially but made no effort to know? Knowing Cleaver had led me to recognize the subtle reality of my own racism: the amiable impassivity with which I had reacted to the black people whom I had met in all walks of life during and since my segregated childhood.

So I came away from a professionally unrewarding experience with a better understanding of racism, a better understanding of myself, and a new friendship. I left Oakland and the paradoxical Panthers with at least the beginnings of a better conscience, but, while my interest in them remained strong, I abandoned my writing plans. My own direct experience with them and with Cleaver had come to an end, I thought.

I was puzzled, as were many others, when weeks, then months passed by with no sound from the fugitive Cleaver, who seemed literally to have vanished from the face of the earth. It was unlike him to remain silent—even prison had not silenced him—and rumors rushed like air into the vacuum. He had been kidnapped and killed. He had hijacked an airplane to Cuba. He had been smuggled aboard a ship to North

Korea or Red China. He was living in disguise in San Francisco. I even heard, while completing a long-planned book in Vientiane, Laos, that winter, that he had been seen by a U.S. Government information agency official, walking down a crowded street in Marrakesh disguised as a black Arab. I had no doubt that he was alive, somewhere, probably in Cuba. I imagined him holed up there with a typewriter, free of the chaos that accompanied his brief celebrity, and ready, at last, to assume his natural role: to be what Maxwell Geismar, in his foreword to *Soul on Ice,* called "Simply one of the best cultural critics now writing."

In the spring, a British correspondent named James Pringle discovered him in Havana and reported that Cleaver's silence was the price he had to pay for his exile there, a price demanded by the skittish Cuban government. There was no public reaction either from Cleaver or the Cubans to the reporter's disclosure, but there seemed little doubt that the story was accurate. Then in July, he surfaced, no longer in Cuba but in Algeria, as a guest of that country's young, anti-American revolutionary government. Kathleen, who quietly left the United States in the last month of a pregnancy that had barely begun when Eldridge fled San Francisco, joined him there. Ironically, it had required the same nine months of his first baby's gestation for the formation of a new and quite different Eldridge Cleaver.

Unlike the Cubans, the Algerians did not muzzle their new American guest. On the contrary, they recognized the Black Panthers as a legitimate revolutionary movement and promoted him as one of the featured speakers at the Pan-African Cultural Festival in Algiers in August. The indulgence of his virulently anti-Israeli hosts was quickly explained by Cleaver's first speech and a press conference. He condemned the Jews and endorsed the Arab terrorist organization Al Fatah as a revolutionary guerrilla army the Panthers must emulate. Many Jewish radicals in the United States explained away Cleaver's sudden hostility to Israel as "bread and butter" talk, a pay-off to the Algerians in exchange for his asylum. They dismissed the notion that he might be serious.

A month later, with the support of *The Atlantic Monthly* and *True* magazines, I flew to Algiers. After checking into the opulent Saint George Hotel, a crenellated relic of French colonialism high on a hill overlooking the overcrowded city, I called on Eldridge. He was living then in the Aleti, another former French luxury hotel downtown, near the Mediterranean waterfront. I found him seated at a table with three other young black men, behind a screen of potted plants on the Aleti's streetside terrace. Physically he was the same man I had last seen at the Panthers' headquarters in Berkeley, dressed as always in a pale blue turtleneck shirt and dark trousers, and hiding his confident green eyes behind almost opaque sunglasses.

"Hey, Don, over here." He waved me to the table, removed his glasses, and stood to clasp my right hand. The greeting was warm but not effusive, as if no time or events had passed since our last encounter in Berkeley. His smile said we could pick up where we had left off the year before. He introduced his companions: "This is Rahim, this is Akili, and this is Byron."

Rahim, a short, powerfully built man of about 28, looked at me with undisguised suspicion, tugged nervously at a goatee styled after the whispy beard of Ho Chi Minh and excused himself. Later he told me that his name before Rahim was Clinton Smith and that together with Byron he had broken out of Chino State Prison in California earlier in the year and hijacked an airliner from Los Angeles to Havana. Byron Booth, an inch taller and more heavily muscled than Eldridge, was about 25, boyish looking and handsomely clean-shaven. He said that his African name was "Muerzi," but everyone still called him Byron because it was easier. There was a clean air of surprised innocence ever present in his smooth, light-brown features, and I found it hard to imagine him escaping from prison and threatening the lives of a planeload of innocent people to make an international getaway. The third man, Amiri Akili, never told me what his name had been before he adopted the new one, but acknowledged that in September, 1968, he, too, had emplaned for Havana with his wife, Gwen, in temporary command of an airliner that they boarded in Philadelphia. He was tall, rangy, and his features were as grimly set as if carved on a cocoanut beneath a frizzy, flat-topped haircut. All had come to Algiers from Havana with Eldridge.

I told Eldridge that many people suspected him, too, of hijacking a plane to make good his escape from the United States. "I didn't, but these cats did," he laughed. Then he repeated a caution he had given me on the telephone when I called him from New York before leaving for Algiers.

"I vacillate between saying nothing and saying too little. In between, I say too much. I'll talk to you about anything except how I got out of Babylon and where I went before I came here," he said. "Look man, it isn't important to me, but it is to the people who have helped me. Ask the FBI. I'm sure they know exactly how I got out of the country and everything I've been doing since then, you know? But it just isn't correct for me to say where I've been, what countries I've visited, how I went. If I say anything about that, it'll just make big problems for a lot of other people. I don't want to do that."

While Byron and Akili quietly sipped orangeade, Eldridge and I drank Scotch and chatted idly for a few minutes about small things such as the high cost of the two luxury hotels. "This hotel and the Saint George are used mostly by European and American businessmen and the prices are deliberately set very high by the government," he said. "It's a policy of 'soak the imperialists.' Not a bad idea, you know? But we've got to get out of here and into our apartment. It was hard as hell to find an apartment here. They're scarce, you know? Now we're trying to furnish it. I've got to go out and buy some mattresses today. If I can get Kathleen to finish packing all the stuff in our room we'll check out of here tomorrow. It was all right at first because the government of Algeria paid for our room during the Cultural Festival, you know? But the day the Festival ended we had to start paying for it ourselves. I think I'm going to owe about $1500 by the time we check out."

Much of the expense was reflected in daily trans-Atlantic telephone calls. "I've got to stop doing that, you know? It's just too easy to pick up the telephone and call New York or San Francisco. It only takes a couple of minutes to get a number, then you talk, and before you know it you've spent a hundred dollars."

"Aren't you afraid all of your phone calls are tapped on the American side?" I asked.

"Probably on both sides," he said, "but I don't care. They know I'm here. What do I have to hide? Yesterday I got the overseas operator in New York and before she connected me to the number I was calling, I told her she'd better let J. Edgar know I was calling.

"She said, 'J. Edgar who?'

"I said, 'J. Edgar Hoover, Adolph Hoover, the chief of the Gestapo.'

"She said, 'I never heard of him. Is he a little fat man?'

"I didn't know whether she was putting me on or what, so I said, 'Do you know J. Edgar is probably listening to this call?'

"She laughed and said, 'I don't care, I don't think I'd like him.'

"I said, 'Oooh, you've got guts,' and she laughed again and placed the call."

Most of the calls, he said, were to his lawyers in San Francisco, who were trying to free his frozen assets in the United States, and to David Hilliard, the last of the early Panther leaders who was still free and able to direct the beleaguered organization. His greatest problem and the one that required the most telephone time was getting across his ideas and thoughts on what to do about the plight of Bobby Seale.

Seale was in jail in San Francisco, awaiting extradition both to Chicago for his upcoming conspiracy trial as one of the Chicago 8, and to New Haven, Connecticut, where he faced charges of complicity in the torture-murder of another Panther, a suspected police agent, named Alex Rackley.

"Bobby is in the position now at this moment that Huey Newton was in October, 1967," Eldridge said. "At the time that Huey was first arrested, I was very conscious of the fact that no matter how long it takes, eventually they will put a guy in the gas chamber. I was very conscious of that fact because of the amount of time I spent in San Quentin where they have the gas chamber. At a certain point it becomes too late to do anything about it. You have to really do something about that early, you see? The whole process is inexorable. No one seems to be able to stop it. I remember when we first started mobilizing support for Huey, a lot of people had that attitude. Why worry now? Something can be done later. But something had to be done immediately, see? That's the scene with Bobby right now, because I think it would be very easy for them to railroad Bobby into the electric chair. Murder and kidnapping and conspiracy to commit murder, you know? They have the experience of the Huey Newton trial—and this one is being held in an area where we don't have numbers of supporters or potential supporters. I think they're just sorry that they didn't get Huey to the gas chamber, and they want to make up for it with Bobby."

"But what can you do from here other than pass along your ideas?" I asked.

"I think it's necessary to build up intensive international support," he said, "and I can do that. I think that by starting now the way we have started, that Bobby will become a major cause. By the time it really becomes crucial, we should have some massive support going. I'm going to go to Sweden and maybe to Belgium."

"Won't you have a problem in those two countries, espe-

cially in Belgium? Don't you risk being arrested and sent back
to the United States?"

"I don't know. Belgium's NATO headquarters. It's not at
all certain that I won't have problems in Sweden, too. If the
two governments give me official visas, then they'll have far
more problems than I will. We have, more than anywhere
else in the world, very deep and very broad support in Sweden.
Strange things are happening in Europe today. I've got this
invitation to go throughout the Scandinavian countries. Also
to Belgium and France and England, Oxford, and all that shit.
I'm not about to go, you know? Only the ones that the lawyers
clear."

"Wouldn't you face the same danger in all of those countries? Couldn't they arrest and extradite you?"

"I think they could. The provisions of the extradition
treaties cover it, even in Sweden. People in Sweden sent me
a copy of the extradition treaty between the United States and
Sweden, and it covers everything conceivable. They really
confuse the issue, you see? They can't extradite me just for
parole violation. They did a very tricky thing. It really comes
out early on in the FBI wanted poster on me. They had this
surrender date for me set before my court dates were coming
up, so when I did not show up for the parole violation thing,
about a month later they were able to issue a bench warrant
for me for not showing up at my court appearance (on the
charges stemming from the Oakland shoot-out). So they were
able to issue an FBI warrant for unlawful flight to avoid
prosecution, because they don't have a charge of unlawful
flight to avoid parole violation. They actually twisted the language to fit the particular case. I didn't leave the United States
in order to avoid going to court. But this is the way they're
able to talk about it. I don't care about that any more, either.
I don't think I face any risk from any legal exposure, because
I'm not going to go anyplace where I will risk that. I can go
anywhere. The only question is where I want to go."

We chatted a while longer on the terrace that morning, but

as Eldridge rambled on I was conscious of a mild paranoia, certainly understandable, in most of what he said.

"It seems to me that you're in a position where you really can't trust anyone," I observed.

"That's right, you're right," he said quickly. "You could be an FBI or a CIA agent. These cats think you are," he nodded toward Byron and Akili. "Maybe they're right. But so far as I know, you've never done anything to cross me, so I'll accept you at face value."

"I know you don't want to be specific about where you've spent the last nine months," I said, "but can you tell me something about your last few days in the United States? You vanished so abruptly and completely that some people even thought you had been kidnapped."

"I made very careful plans ahead of time, you know?" he said. "And I was trying to be very, very careful that they didn't get fucked up. They almost did. Three days before I left, I was eating with Bob Scheer at a Chinese restaurant in North Beach (San Francisco). When we came out of the place there was this police car parked down the street with a young cop, a pig, sprawling in the front seat, just sitting there. I didn't know if he was there to watch me or what. When I walked by I looked over at him and said, 'Oink!', then I walked on. He cruised up beside us and said, 'Did you call a police officer?' Then he got out of the car and started talking real close to my face. He was very uptight. I was sure he was going to arrest me, that the pigs were just looking for an excuse to arrest me before the date I was supposed to surrender. Then Scheer identified himself as the editor of *Ramparts* and faced off the cop, asked him if he was trying to arrest me, and on what charge. The cop said, 'No, I thought someone called a police officer,' and got back in his car. That incident shook me, because I had made my plans, and I was afraid of being arrested before it was time to go."

"Do you think the authorities turned their backs deliberately, to avoid the trouble and embarrassment of picking you up and creating another martyr?" I asked.

"I don't know," he shook his head. "I wondered about that. Kathleen said she thought they did. But if they were trying to catch me, I think my cover was good enough to fool them. I'm sure it fooled them."

"What did you do?"

"We scripted and taped a lot of phony telephone conversations, with my voice on tape. After I left, someone who knew what to say would call and carry on his side of the conversation, and my voice would come back, from the tape, so it sounded like a natural conversation, like I was still there. Then there was another cat, a Panther. I don't know whether you saw him around Oakland, but he was about my size and build, and he looked kind of like me. He was inside my house. We fixed him up so that he looked almost exactly like me . . . beard, glasses, my clothes, everything. Kathleen and I drove up to the house. There were a lot of people milling around, demonstrating for me, you know? All of them saw me, and the pigs who were taking pictures from the house across the street saw me. We went up the stairs and in the front door. My double was on the other side. In a little while he and Kathleen went out the door and down the steps, and all the dudes down on the street and the pigs across the street thought it was me, because he looked just like me. They didn't know that at just that exact moment I was down in the basement, cutting through the side, the back, and all around a very devious route. Out! I don't think they know to this day how I got out of that house. When my double went back in with Kathleen, they thought it was me. I'm sure they listened to my voice on the telephone. They never saw me again."

"Can you go on from there and tell me what happened next?"

"No, I was in seven or eight places after that, but I think that's all I'd better say about it."

"I heard one rumor last winter that you were in Marrakesh, posing as an Arab."

"Marrakesh? Where's that? In Morocco? I've been in Morocco. I ran into people everywhere that I've gone that I know. I ran into a newsman who recognized me. He was an American. This was during the time that I was really hiding. He really could have caused a lot of trouble for a lot of people. I really wasn't supposed to be there. I wasn't supposed to be seen there. I thought he was going to blow it but he didn't."

"Why was it so important for you to remain under cover until you surfaced here in Algeria?"

"It wasn't important to me. It was important to other people. I have to say that the Algerians were the only people who were willing to deal with the problem. There were other Arab countries that wouldn't deal with it. All the other countries were afraid."

"Why? Because they had AID agreements with the United States?"

"Some of them who didn't even have any AID agreements just didn't want the problem. You find that it's one thing to have a liberation struggle in Africa or Asia; it's another thing to fool around directly with Sam. They didn't want that. The extent that that's true really came as a surprise to me."

"Were their reasons basically economic ones?"

"Some were not economic. Some were political. Some of the countries don't have more than economic hopes. There's a lot of phony posturing involved in a lot of these so-called diplomatic breaks, you know? You think of mediaries; the United States owns other countries. Like Japan. Japan belongs to the United States. All those Japanese companies belong to the United States. They function in a lot of areas where the United States cannot go directly itself. People want their transistor radios, you know?"

Kathleen walked up to the table just then, her arm linked to that of a slight, dark haired, middle-aged American woman.

Always pale in complexion, Kathleen looked almost jaundiced now. She had not yet fully recovered from the birth of her baby six weeks before. She grinned broadly and exclaimed, "Hey, Schanche, it's good to see you," as if I were an old and dear friend. The greeting surprised me, because she never had shown even the slightest cordiality to me in San Francisco and I had expected her to be just as indifferent to my presence in Algiers. She introduced her companion as Elain Klein, and I stifled an unworthy impulse to ask, "What's a nice girl like you doing in a place like this?" Miss Klein was a Leftist in the late Forties who had moved from New York to Paris during the McCarthy era and become an active supporter of the Algerian revolution. She was now employed as an information ministry official by the government of Algeria. As such she had become unofficial Jewish den mother to the two-dozen or so international revolutionary groups which were formally sanctioned and sheltered in the Arab country. The groups ranged in interest and nationality from moderately left-wing Spaniards to Maoist revolutionaries from Chad and, of course, the Black Panthers of the United States. For a dedicated political activist who had played a dangerous role in a North African revolution, she seemed incongruous not only in her Jewishness, but in her curiously girlish and light-hearted manner. She flirted coquettishly with Eldridge and asked me to call on her at the Information Ministry if I needed help in arranging interviews while I was in Algiers. Then she reminded Eldridge that he had a date that afternoon with the Ambassador of North Korea. She stood close to his shoulder, reminding me of women I had seen touching him in Oakland and San Francisco. While Eldridge scribbled in a notebook and Miss Klein enjoyed her proximity to him, Kathleen touched my shoulder and motioned me away from the table with her. We walked to the other side of the terrace. She turned around so that her body blocked Eldridge's view of what she was about to do.

Wondering what revelation was coming, I watched as she opened a voluminous handbag. She held it toward me.

"Schanche, I don't want El to know this," she whispered, "but I need some bread. Just drop as much as you can in here and swear you'll never tell him." Were the Cleavers broke? Or was Kathleen's impulsive panhandling simply a postpartum aberration? Or was she shaking me down? I dropped $50 in the bag. "Right on," she said.

A few minutes later, without revealing to him what I had done, I asked Eldridge if he had enough money to meet expenses.

"I took quite a bit of expense money with me when I left," he said, "but it's just about run out now. People send me money, little sums here and there. But it's against the law for any American to give me money. *Ramparts* can't pay my salary and my agent can't forward any of my book royalties to me. I think I'm worth about a half a million dollars, you see, but I can't touch it. After the story that I was in Havana, the Treasury Department declared me a 'resident of Cuba,' or a 'citizen of Cuba,' which was ridiculous. They can't just arbitrarily say that a United States citizen is a 'citizen of Cuba.' But they treated my assets like Cuban assets—they froze them. If anyone gives me money, they're guilty of 'trading with the enemy' or something. So you might say it's getting a little bit tight right now."

Kathleen rejoined us and a few minutes later they left with Miss Klein to buy mattresses for the new apartment.

# CHAPTER 11

> *"He's a very uptight cat,
> very paranoid."*

ELDRIDGE asked me to wait for him on the terrace
when I arrived at the Aleti the next day. He came down from
his fifth floor room with Rahim a few minutes later, and as
he hurried across the terrazzo terrace, I could see that he was
highly agitated, clearly furious about something. I wondered
if he had discovered that I had given Kathleen money.

"Don, let me ask you something," he said briskly without
sitting down. I stood uncomfortably, rapidly growing more
afraid of what he was about to say. He was far too angry in
manner and appearance simply to be upset about a $50 gift
to his wife. Wildly, I guessed that Rahim and the others had
convinced Cleaver that I was a police agent of some kind,
come to do him in. It was foolish, but for a moment I became
quite frightened, a good reason, I suppose, why even if I
wanted to I could never carry off the necessary deceptions of
a clandestine agent. Paranoia is not a symptom exclusive to
fugitive exiles. I had more than my share.

"Listen, this is important," he said. "Do you think the FBI
could arrest a dude, smuggle him out of here back to the
United States and hide him away without anybody knowing
about it?"

Rahim nervously stroked his wispy beard and stared steadily
at me. I was wide-eyed, wondering what Cleaver was leading

up to. Could it really be that he thought I was an FBI agent,
come to kidnap him and carry him home in secret?

"I doubt it," I stammered. "If they arrested him, they'd
have to charge him with something in the States to hold him,
wouldn't they? I mean, it would be public record. Somebody
would report it."

"Maybe. Maybe not," he said, cryptically. He sat down
and drummed his fingers nervously on the terrace table.

I might as well get this over with, I thought; it will only
make things worse if I stand here staring at him.

"Why do you ask?" I sighed, sitting down.

He looked at me for a moment as if uncertain whether to
reply, then he said, "There was this dude who was coming
here from Cuba to join us. I knew him there and I knew him
before. I think they've got him. I think he's defected. Or maybe
I should say he's defecated."

"The way you say the words, maybe they mean the same
thing," I joked weakly in my enormous relief to discover that
someone else, not me, was the object of his angry suspicion.

"He is a very uptight cat, very paranoid," said Eldridge.
"He's always been a little crazy, a wanderer, you know? He
wandered around the States and he couldn't stand that. Then
he wandered around South America, and he thought people
were after him all the time; then he came to Cuba. He was
very useful to the Movement there, but I worried about him,
you know? He could be very useful to the Movement here.
On the other hand, he could be very dangerous if he defected.
I think he has. He was due to arrive here on August 26. We
know that he arrived here. He was on the plane when it landed
at the airport. Then he just disappeared. I think he went
straight to the American mission and gave himself up. They've
spirited him out of Algeria some way."

I asked him how the Americans could possibly sneak someone out of Algiers. The tiny American mission—a dozen
nervous diplomats—probably were watched too closely by the
Algerians to engage in clandestine activity. Since Algeria

broke diplomatic relations with the United States during the Arab-Israeli six-day war, the American mission consisted only of this tiny caretaker group that kept the old United States Embassy open under the diplomatic protection of the Embassy of Switzerland.

"They have agents everywhere in the world," said Eldridge. "I'm sure they have them here."

I promised to check with the FBI when I returned to the United States to see if any Black Panther had been returned under arrest from Algeria.

"Here, take this," Eldridge said. He scribbled a few notes on a page of his notebook, tore it out and gave it to me. "This is the cat." The notes read:

"Earl Ferrell—Mosia Kenyatta. Parole Violator, California. Hijacked plane from Mexico, March, 1968. Arrived Algeria, August 26, 1969."

Eldridge asked me to come back that afternoon, excused himself and returned to his room. I caught a cab up the hill to the former American Embassy, now decorated with the official seal of the government of Switzerland, and called on the chief U.S. consular officer, an open-hearted and voluble young American named Conrad Drescher. I asked him if he had heard of Earl Ferrell, or if any black American had come to the mission asking to be sent home. Drescher said no Americans had been shipped out of Algiers since the diplomatic break. He had never heard of Earl Ferrell, but he had met Eldridge and Kathleen, and he seemed genuinely worried about them.

"They're American citizens, you know, and they're entitled to just as much official protection as any other American citizen," he said. "I suppose Cleaver doesn't want to ask us for help, but they really ought to think about the baby. They'll have to bring him in here so he can be registered as an American citizen."

When I rejoined Eldridge at the Aleti that afternoon, I passed along Drescher's concern over the baby's citizenship.

"Yeah, we've been thinking about that," he said. "We need to get Maceo registered, because we're Americans. I have Third-World origins, you know, but I'm of the First World and my life, my goals are in Babylon. Maybe we can do it tomorrow, I don't know. There's so much to do. We've got to check out of this place and move in to the new pad. And I've got to get things together to go to North Korea."

"North Korea?"

"Yeah. Byron and I are going to Pyongyang next week. We're going to a conference of Communist journalists. I really dig those cats. Kim Il Sung. They beat the imperialists. Do you think the clothes we have here will be warm enough there?"

"It'll be a lot colder there than it is here," I said, recalling my own first October in Korea eighteen years before.

"Will my leather jacket be warm enough?"

"Probably not," I said.

"So little Conrad wants to see us up at the Embassy," Eldridge returned to the subject of Maceo's registration. "Maybe we'll just go up there and take that building away in the name of the people," he mused. "It belongs to the people, you know? To us. It doesn't belong to Conrad's little clique up there. Hey, that'll be great! When we all troop in there with Maceo, they'll think we're invading. Won't that get them uptight? You come on with us and take pictures. When we get Maceo registered, I'm going to demand that they give me an American passport, too. I'm an American citizen, and I have a right to a passport. It's a very useful thing, you know? An American passport."

We ordered a drink, and as the waiter hurried to the terrace bar to get it for us, a group of heavyset men in baggy Western suits emerged from the front door of the hotel. From the cut of their clothing, I guessed they were members of the 3,000 to 5,000-man technical and military mission maintained in Algeria by the Soviet Union. Eldridge came to the same conclusion.

"There go the revisionist pigs," he said.

"Are you down on the Soviet Union, too?" I asked him.

"I find it very difficult to relate to them," he said, "although I find it necessary to relate to people who are dependent upon them. There are certain countries of the Third World who are totally dependent upon the Soviet Union. If I would exercise my freedom of speech and talk about that, then I would find myself having problems. I think they're necessary problems for them, they need those problems. I would like to be in a position fully to relate those problems. But there's no point in getting off into a heavy poker game when you can barely meet the table stakes.

"I'd rather stay out until it becomes a practical problem for us. Because I don't think that it's cool to just brush over things and take positions on things in which you're not involved. Do you understand what I mean? We're not that deeply involved in the ideological conflict between Russia and China. Although it's very important, very interesting to us, we have to understand that, and we'll really have to take a position on that. But at this time in our lives, our whole program doesn't depend on that, you know?"

I asked him why, in view of what he had just said, he had found it necessary to take the position he had at the Pan-African Festival concerning Israel, which did not strike me as any more pressing a problem for the Black Panther Party in the United States than the ideological conflict between Russia and China. He started to reply with some heat, but before he uttered a full sentence, Byron strode to the table and interrupted.

"I've got to have some bread, El," he said as he sat down.

"What did you do with the money I gave you this morning?" asked Cleaver sharply.

"Look, man, I had to pay my hotel and buy some lunch and get the stationery and stamps you wanted," Byron replied in a pleading voice, like a child explaining where his allowance has gone.

"Did you write it all down?"

"I forgot," said the chagrined Byron.

"Byron, I know you had an accountancy course in prison. I've told you to write down all expenditures against all the money you get. Debits and credits, you dig? I'm serious. Every dinar you spend has to be accounted for, in writing."

The colloquy continued for a quarter of an hour, during which Rahim and Akili joined us at the table. Each of them, too, needed money and each received a similar lecture from the leader. It was late in the afternoon now, and the same air of agitation that he had displayed when we met in the morning had returned. It was obvious that he didn't want to answer more questions from me just then.

"What's your schedule for tonight and tomorrow?" I asked him.

"What's the schedule in chaos?" he replied. "I can't see you tonight and I'm going to try to get Kathleen to finish packing so we can get out of here tomorrow. Look, meet me here at noon and we'll have lunch. We can talk then."

I stood to go.

"Don't forget to leave some money to pay for the drinks," said Rahim.

# CHAPTER 12

## *"You see very touching extremes of tenderness and cruelty here."*

As we waited for fresh Mediterranean shrimps and wine to be brought to us, Eldridge stared vacantly out of the open, table-side window of the Aleti's third-floor dining room. The busy activity on the street below hardly seemed to penetrate his consciousness. His gaze reflected the loneliness of a stranger in a crowded city.

"Feeling isolated?" I asked him.

He turned away from the window and looked blankly at me for a moment. Then his face became animated as if consciousness had just returned.

"Not really," he said, "just thinking about Babylon. I have a dread of becoming isolated. I can see how it could happen. I would hate to get caught up in a kind of meaningless existence, based on things past, and living off of past laurels, and all that shit. I think it's more functional to concentrate on organizational activities and always relate back specifically to the United States. Everything that we do out here is directed to people there. They're reaching toward us, we reach back, collect this shit up."

"It probably would be pretty easy to assume the role of a local celebrity and get caught up in a ceremonial life, though, wouldn't it?"

"Yeah, it could happen, you know. I see it happening. I see

a lot of people who are caught up in that. They don't seem to know what they're all about. For example, I've encountered in many places many people who for various reasons have had to leave various countries. Some of them have been gone for years. Some of them for short periods of time. I remember one guy—a big fat guy—people telling me that he was once a very gung-ho guerrilla type cat and that he had encountered a lot of problems, personal problems, and also problems with various host governments. It ended up that he got fat and nonfunctional. Those dreams that he had when he left his country are physically impossible now. He never realized it, and he's a very bitter guy. Very twisted in many ways. I don't want to get involved in that. You just have to make the right choices of what you're going to do. The right choices of how you spend your time. Right choices even about what you're going to write. For example, if I started writing fiction, I think I'd drift off into a private thing. It would be very easy to do that. To forget about certain things. But I'm never able to forget that Huey Newton is in prison."

"Are you getting a lot of writing done now?"

"That's the trouble, I'm not. It used to be, every morning I would get up very early and I would write for several hours, then I would go about other things. This was when I was out of prison, before I left. When I was in prison, I would write all day sometimes. But now I have to start planning to write a few days from now and set that day aside. It gets all fucked up. I want to write certain things, because I decided a long time ago that this would be my bag. It used to be a vague ambition, but now it's something that, practically, I can do. But all these things seem to be coming up. I'm not sure whether or not I do things correctly, you know? I make the arrangements that block me from doing it. I make arrangements today that will interfere with my doing things two weeks from now. It causes me a lot of discomfort."

"Is the trip to North Korea a case in point?"

"That's one of the reasons I feel so pressed for time. Every time I think about it, I feel like calling off these trips. But people have a way of arranging things so that it would be a personal insult to the president or someone to call it off. But I can work when I'm traveling if I prepare right. That's the time I'm able to get reading done. When I do go to a strange place I find it so frustrating trying to relate at first that the best thing for me to do is get to work. I have a little suitcase with my pencils and my paper and my books. And I'll be able to read several things. I have a series of things I want to write about. What I have to do is communicate my analysis of what's going on, you know?"

"What kinds of analyses? I read before I came here that you felt the whole theme of starvation and oppression in America was overdone, that compared to the poverty and oppression you have seen in other countries, oppressed Americans were being 'crushed between two pieces of silk.' Does that mean your analysis of what's happening in America has changed?"

"Yeah, I think that a lot of people don't know what they're talking about, you know? I mean, I've always kind of felt that. People are repeating rhetoric, you know? Look, I've never been motivated to revolutionary activity because I was starving. It hasn't been that with me. There've been periods in my life when I've had inadequate foods, when I was younger and when my family was uptight. But starving? That hasn't been my case, you see. That's not the case with a lot of people. They're not starving. They have all the materials there, you know? A lot of it is psychological, spiritual torture that motivates people. Sometimes it's just an intellectual understanding of what it's all about. But yet they still talk as if there was famine in Babylon. And the rhetoric doesn't really fit the situation. That bothers me, to have people functioning off of an analysis that is not accurate. It really controls your activity. That's what distinguished the Black Panther Party from a lot of those other organizations. It was based on certain things, and action was keyed to this analysis. We never would have done certain things unless it was felt that we really understood it this way."

"Such as what?" I asked.

"Like fucking with the cops," he said. "We didn't fuck with the cops just because they were there, you know, just because they were visible. They're visible, but they're very deadly, you know? We always repeat this analysis of the cops as the occupying army. And the key force that has to be dealt with. The key repressive force. I don't care what Nixon and his whole clique want to do, if they didn't have those strong-arm troops to back it up, we could just walk in there and grab him by his little fuckin' neck and break it, you see? But he's got those guards with guns.

"We're having a lot of trouble right now in the United Front Against Facism (an organization of radical groups including the Panthers that had just completed a conference in San Francisco). We're trying to get people across the country, like a lot of white radicals, to relate to this police program of the Panthers. They say, 'Well, let's reform this and that instead, and blah, blah, blah,' you see? It might be all of that, but when they start fuckin' with those cops, they're gonna find out that they're not so soft, you know? If white radicals would start doing that on a national scale, then a lot of things would be liberated. But because they have all this other ideology, all different analyses, they can't see the very practical side of that. They can see the police problem just fine in the black community, you know? They define it as a black problem. To us the police are a class problem. To some of the white radicals the police are a black problem. They say the whites already have control of their police. That's bullshit. They're not controlling the police. So we have to make an analysis to carry that further in order to separate them from the police.

"The lack right now is some very effective theoretical analysis. Everything is hung up on theoretical analysis. There's a real need for clarification of a whole lot of shit. I think you

have to make an analysis that proves to a lot of people that
this is not inconsistent with Marxist ideology, that in fact a
Marxist analysis of the American situation has to deal with
that, you know?"

I asked him if he could accept this new role as a frustrated,
exiled theoretician in place of the more active part he had
played when he was in the United States.

"I would rather be a soldier," he said. "I have a real desire
to pull some triggers. I'm not saying I want to get all fucked
up, you know. I'm saying that out there are a lot of targets
that I actually want to aim at and I want to pull the trigger.
This is something that I want to do. At the same time, I want
to do these other things. That's the way to take a long-range
shot at them. I know that if I can really define this shit, it
will be like shooting a thousand of them. It's not immediate,
though. I need them both."

By then our lunch had been served, and each of us paused
to sip our wine and look out of the window. On the street
below us an altogether too common illustration of uncon-
trollable temper was taking place. A gowned Arab man, perhaps the father of the object of his ire, was furiously kicking
a ragged little boy. After a particularly vicious thrust, he
grabbed the child and hugged him warmly as if to mitigate
the pain. It shocked me, although I had seen the same kind
of scene many times before in the Middle East. Eldridge had
been talking about being "a soldier," and suddenly it seemed
to me that the same kind of hate-love that he had once reflected was being acted out for us on the street.

"You're talking about pulling triggers now, yet you used
to talk often of your hatred for guns and violence," I observed.

He looked at me for a long moment, then glanced out the
window again as the man and the boy hurried away together.

"You see very touching extremes of tenderness and cruelty
here," he said, quietly, and I knew that he was describing
himself.

"Is there any small hope left in your soul that we can solve our problems without violence?" I asked him.

"A lot of things are always accomplished nonviolently, but only because of the presence of violence," he said. "Not the threat of it, the presence of it. The threat of it is a poor substitute for the presence of it. When good men are silent, evil men take over. When evil men are very active, people are actually doing violent things to each other; then people throw up both hands and start dealing with this shit. That's the whole gamble of the vanguard: that by doing these things and throwing this shit out there, other people are forced to acknowledge the reality of this. Before it happens, people are so terrified of reality that they don't want to acknowledge it. When it's there, they find out it's not so terrible . . . well, it is terrible, but what they're called upon to do is not so terrible. It's not suicidal. Just take a position on the issue. That's what Huey forced a lot of people to do. He put his life out there. A lot of people looked at that and they were able to say things that before they were unable to say. They were really only called upon to speak out, that's all. They weren't called upon to involve themselves in gunfights with cops."

"Do you mean the 'vanguard' is gambling on the hope that by its own violence it will provoke middle-class people like me into forcing revolutionary solutions?"

"It seems pretty clear, man," he said. "Pretty fuckin' clear. You must accept us as a liberation movement that is seriously trying to deal with the problems of the people. What can people like you do? You can go wherever the action is. We either have to reaffirm traditional freedoms and liberties of the American people, or we have to redefine them. Because at the present moment, the shit is confused. The present status quo is unacceptable to us. You don't have to be a radical. We're not talking about different species of people. We're talking about people caught up in the same situation and having different reactions to it. But in this situation, either we reaffirm those values or redefine them. If you can't reaffirm it, then the process of redefinition means that it's up for grabs. The process of redefining, in order to have a sort of continuity, calls for another constitutional convention. When we have a revolution in the United States, establish a socialist system, we'll still have to go back to the last constitutional convention to explain what we're doing. You have to deal with all the documents and articles of the government on that level. It would be either a reaffirmation of those rights or a redefinition of them. I personally feel that a redefinition is what's in order, but a redefinition would only be a reaffirmation. The situation has changed so much that the traditional way of saying those things is no longer apt. The meanings have become distorted. The point is that nothing would be lost. The values that were there from the beginning are really precious and eternal values. But because of all the limitations that were placed upon them, they've never been really active. I think that now it's possible to gain more of those liberties, to gain them for everybody."

We left the dining room and Eldridge hurried upstairs to see if Kathleen had finished packing. He said he still hoped they would get out of the hotel that day. A few minutes later I saw them in the lobby with a matronly Negro woman, whose soft, straight hairstyle and neatly tailored suitdress made her look the very image of middle-class American respectability. Outwardly, she was the kind of person I often in the past had heard some of the Panthers scorn as a "black bourgie," "bourgeois bootlicker," or "Uncle Tom." Kathleen introduced the woman as her mother, a language teacher from Washington who had taken her two-week vacation to see her new grandson and help her daughter. The three of them were going shopping for a refrigerator for the new apartment. It was clear that they would not check out of the hotel that day.

Rather than waste the afternoon tagging along or waiting for the shopping trip to end, I walked to the place where Rahim had told me he was staying, a second-rate hotel called

the Cornovailles, about five blocks uphill from the Aleti. I
wanted to reassure him that I was not a dangerous enemy
agent. Also I was interested in learning more about his hijacking experience, if I could get him to talk about it. The Cornovailles was a seedy place with a mixed clientele of European
tourists and Algerian businessmen. The elevator was broken
so I walked up four floors to Rahim's disordered room. It was
two o'clock in the afternoon, but he was not yet dressed.

"I stayed up all night rapping with some really cool Algerian cats," he explained, yawning.

"Do you speak French?" I asked, since few Algerians speak
English.

"No, man, and they didn't speak English, but I can communicate, you know? I related to them, dig? I mean on a
political level we relate even if we don't understand each
other, dig?"

I didn't dig, but it was no particular concern of mine how
Rahim spent his evenings, so I nodded. When he finished
dressing we went down to the hotel's mezzanine lounge. I
asked him if he had learned Spanish during his stay in Cuba.

"Enough to get along, you know?" he said. "We call Cuba
'the rock.' I didn't dig that . . . I mean it was a bad scene for
me. Maybe they had their reasons, being a revolutionary country and all that, you know, but I didn't dig it. Shit, I mean
we're making a revolution, too, ain't we? I mean they put me
on this state farm, you know? Wouldn't let me have my freedom, just put me to work, see? There's as much racism on the
rock as there is in Babylon."

We had sat in the mezzanine lounge for only a few minutes
when a wizened, dissipated little man of about 50 who looked
more French than Algerian joined us. He was a Pepe LeMoco
kind of character named "Eddie" who had attached himself
to the small party of Black Panthers not long after they arrived
in Algiers. Eddie interpreted and ran errands for them in exchange for small tips. He had picked up their jargon.

"You deeg hash?" he asked me. "Anytheeng you deeg—hash, pot, anytheeng—you tell me. Sky's the leemeet."

"Go get me a ham sandwich and a coke, Eddie," said Rahim, explaining that he had to have his meals brought in because the hotel had no dining room.

"Ham ees from the peeg," said Eddie. "I breeng you roast bif."

Akili came in just as Rahim began to bite into the roast beef sandwich. But before he could sit down, an uncomfortable illustration of the international pervasiveness of racism began to unfold.

Akili had barely uttered "hello" when the hotel manager, a dapper Algerian who could have stepped comfortably into a fashionable Paris salon, walked stiffly up to us, fingers playing over the lapels of his tailored continental jacket, and ordered Rahim to take his sandwich out of the hotel. In French he told Eddie to inform Rahim that it was not permitted to eat in the public rooms of the Cornovailles. I knew that wasn't the reason for his imperious behavior, because just a few minutes before I had seen him smiling and chatting indulgently with a white European couple who were finishing a similar snack just a few chairs away from us. Akili didn't require even that much evidence. He turned his slender frame and, from a height of six feet two inches, glared down at the diminutive hotel manager.

"Racist, pig, bourgeois bastard," he said fiercely.

The hotel manager coolly stood his ground and repeated the order to leave.

"He's hassling us because we're the only black people here, not because you're eating in the lobby, Rahim," said Akili. I'm sure that Akili was right, but Eddie nervously implored us to do as the manager said lest Rahim be evicted for good, so we left. Rahim calmly finished his sandwich in a run-down cafe across the street, where the proprietor was only too happy to see a take-in meal provided we bought some beer to go with it. Rahim remained unruffled by the incident, but Akili wouldn't let it go.

"I was staying in that hotel during the Cultural Festival," he said, "and the day the Festival ended, that same dude called me and the only other three black people in the hotel down to the desk and told us we'd have to leave. He said he needed the rooms. Only the black people's rooms? He's a racist, bourgeois pig. There's racism here. Not as bad as the rock, but it's here. I guess it's everywhere, huh?"

"Yeah," said Rahim. "Don't get so uptight about it."

"Shit," said Akili.

I asked Rahim to tell me about the hijacking in which he and Byron had escaped the United States.

"I might do that," he said. "I might talk it all in my tape recorder and give it to you and you can sell it to some magazine, you know? I need some bread, man, gotta get me a job. You think somebody would pay for it? My story, I mean."

I told him that I could think of two or three magazines that might pay for the authentic confession of an airline hijacker if it was interesting.

"Oh, it's interesting all right," he said. "I don't mean just the hijacking. Shit, everybody knows about hijacking. I mean what goes through your head when you do it, you know? You gotta work yourself into a frame of mind where you really mean it, dig? I mean you can't have any question about it. You know that you gonna make it or you gonna die, and that's it. You gotta be ready to die. And to take all those people with you. That's the interesting part."

He said he would think about it for a few days, then perhaps let me help him transcribe his story of the experience on tape.

As Rahim turned over in his mind the possible financial rewards of public confession, Eldridge, I discovered, was turning over in his own mind the whole question of continuing his expository interviews with me. When I met him at the

Aleti the next day he was ready, at last, to check out. Byron and a bellboy were hauling cardboard cartons and luggage from the lobby to a taxicab and Eldridge was just paying his bill which, as he had predicted, totaled slightly more than $1,500. He joined me on the terrace as Byron loaded the taxicab.

"I've got time for a drink with you now," he said, "but I'm not going to have any more time to talk today. I've been wondering whether all this talk is useful, anyway, you know? Don't take this personally, because that's not how I mean it. My experience with you has been that you use material in a responsible and conscientious manner, otherwise I wouldn't want to talk with you. So I've decided that until Byron and I leave for North Korea you can stay and we'll talk when there's time. But I'm not going to get involved with any more interviews after this. I think the type of questions that can be dealt with in an interview have been dealt with. I don't think there's anything more I can say about it, you know? The only things I want to talk about now are policy. All the psycho-social analysis—'Why did that happen?,' 'Why do you feel this way?'—all that is obsolete. It's even insulting, you know?

"This morning Byron and I had a discussion with the Ambassador from North Korea, the Democratic People's Republic of Korea, I mean. The man shows understanding and respect and solidarity for our cause. He knows the history of the Black Panther Party, and he never wasted one minute asking questions on that kind of level. With that kind of thing happening, and it is happening that we're being accepted as a liberation movement that's seriously trying to deal with the problems of the people, I think that puts us in a bag where we don't have to go through a lot of those things that we used to have to go through, you know?"

That afternoon I discarded the list of personal and "psychosocial" questions I had intended to ask Eldridge. The firm and unequivocal tone of his voice and words were clear: He would cut me off without another word if I asked anything that he considered unpolitical or frivolous. Frankly, I was at a loss. Aside from the question of Israel, which I still intended to explore, he would not discuss his own history or that of the Panthers, nor would he deal with the future, nor attempt an orderly critique of any American institution, other than the police, that he felt critical about.

When I saw him the next day I reached back to our luncheon and asked him to clarify the distinctions he had made between the police as a "class" problem and as a "black" problem. His reply was cryptic and unenlightening.

"You have to go back to the concept of America, the melting pot," he said. "The whole thing about America as a melting pot. You deal with two basic things: the class struggle and the ethnic struggle. The fact is that the class struggle in the United States has been hidden or concealed behind the ethnic struggle, which has been made to seem primary. When you go back you end up talking about how the Irish and the Italians became policemen, then you get those dynamics working and it comes pretty clear. It's something that we went into thoroughly at the University of California, in my lectures, you know? I've got all those tapes and one of the things I want to do is collect them, with what would have been the last two lectures. When all that shit comes together, I think it will be very much to the point."

I told him that aside from the first of his Berkeley lectures on the possible origins of color consciousness, I did not know what he had said there. I was still confused. The remarks he had just made were like the opening dialogue of the third scene of a play for which I had arrived late. I simply didn't understand what he was talking about.

"I'm kind of down on Irish, Italians, Anglo Saxons and Jews," he said, as if sweeping my bewilderment aside. "I think it's very functional to be that way. I think there's been a lot of abdication of responsibility by the ethnic groups in those

countries. I think ethnic groups have to talk to each other.
The way that they're . . . what they did, they took all those
ethnic groups . . . uh . . . when you take them from the United
States and put them back in Europe, they're part of nations,
and they have very strong hostilities toward one another. Then
when they go to the United States, they redefine themselves as
ethnic groups and then, in order to get rid of those traditional
hostilities and rivalries, they put them all in the melting pot
and redefine them all as White Man. That's why I don't like
to talk about white men. I'd rather talk about the Irish, *vis
à vis* the Anglo Saxons, and the Italians, and the Jews.

"Are you saying that you are personally hostile to these
ethnic groups?"

"No, no, no, no," he said. "I think that black people have
an interest in exacerbating the antagonisms between these
ethnic groups. I'd like to see them at each other's throats.
That's why I dig what is happening in Ireland (Protestant-
Catholic rioting in Ulster). In San Francisco, the mayor
(Mayor Alioto) is Italian. Chief Cahill (since involuntarily
retired by Alioto) is Irish. Alioto was actually plotting to get
rid of Cahill to put in this Italian chief of police. When we
started talking about that in public, it created problems for
both of them. I want to create more problems like that. Blew
his game! He really got enraged when we talked about that.
We really fucked it up for him."

I shook my head over what he had said, because most of
it made little sense to me. The only sentences he had spoken
that linked rationally together were the ones describing the
tactic of exacerbating tensions between ethnic groups, which
were a far cry from Huey Newton's idealistic dream of multi-
leveled cultural maturity in a "nation of nations."

I tried to describe to him Newton's prison remarks to
Ed Keating, recalling that Huey had foreseen the peaceful
flowering of many ethnic cultures, side by side, without antagonism. It didn't seem to square with what Eldridge had just
said.

"When did Huey say that?" Eldridge asked.

"Last year," I said, "when he was at Vacaville, not long after the trial. He appeared to have been deeply impressed by B. F. Skinner's *Walden Two*. Do you know the book?"

"Yeah, I know *Walden Two*. I wouldn't know how Huey reacted to it."

Abruptly he gazed off with unfocused eyes, just as he had stared out the window of the Aleti during our lunch, and his big hands fidgeted nervously with a ballpoint pen, stroking it softly, then tightening over it and jabbing the automatic point out and in, out and in.

I responded by fussing with my portable tape recorder, as if something had gone wrong with it, but I was only covering my own uncertainty about continuing. He was nervous and I was bewildered. I wondered if perhaps he was speaking a kind of verbal shorthand, an extension of things he had said or written that he assumed I was familiar with. Perhaps he was. I'm still not sure whether I briefly glimpsed Cleaver's mind in a state of agitated disorder or whether he was simply telegraphing verbal signals without amplification and my receptors were too weak to receive them. I gathered only that he believed in the tactical wisdom of a multiplicity of ethnic wars to hasten some kind of apocalypse. We parted a few minutes later.

The next day he seemed as completely in control of himself as he ever had in California. Although Eldridge had only a few minutes to spare, he was relaxed, and we sat comfortably together on the terrace of the Aleti while he waited for Kathleen and her mother to conclude another shopping trip. They were to pick him up shortly to return to their new apartment which was about a half an hour by cab from the center of Algiers. It seemed a good time to return to the question that Byron had interrupted with his financial problems as we sat on the same terrace a few days before. I asked him to explain the strident public position he had taken on Israel at the Pan-

African Festival. "Were you knocking Zionism as a movement,
or were you knocking Jews as a race?" I asked.

"I'm talking about Zionism, but I think that all Jews, particularly in the United States, have a responsibility to understand what Zionism is, what's actually happening in their
name," he replied. "They must understand how they have
been victimized by a lot of manipulation by Jewish capitalists,
strong supporters of Zionism like United Jewish Appeal. I
used to work for a place in Los Angeles called the Jewish
Community Center. I always considered the Jews to be a good
model to study, because there are a lot of historical similarities
in their situation and the situation of black people. It caused
me to make a study of Theodore Herzl and all those people
who founded Zionism. I know that people who call themselves
Zionists today have nothing in common with Herzl or what he
was really about, what he was trying to do with the people.
Moshe Dayan has nothing in common with that cat except
that historically they grew out of each other. There were certain crucial periods when that whole direction was decided,
and it has everything to do with British colonial policy. The
whole situation has gotten out of hand, and it is turning people
who should be allies into enemies. This is why I think it's
necessary to make that kind of distinction between Zionists
and Jews—the same distinction between slumlords and Jews,
Jewish capitalists and Jews, you know? Jerry Rubin is a Jew.
Mark Rudd is a Jew. Many important people in the Movement in the United States are Jews. People active and functional in the Movement are Jews. But when it comes to this
whole question of Israel, they're all paralyzed. These cats
don't want to face that. It creates a lot of problems for them."

I observed that many people who were morally upset by
the manner in which Palestinian refugees had been pushed
aside had decided that it was unrealistic to keep bemoaning
the fact, and that it was more realistic now to seek an end
to hostilities and solutions in the Middle East based on the

fact that Israel exists as a viable state. It is, after all, twenty years old and it is thriving. Eldridge responded angrily.

"That's the Zionist position," he said, glaring at me. "That's like saying you come home one night and there's a burglar hiding under the bed in your house. He's making use of your belongings. He's doing this, so you've got to relate to that and accept him as a boarder in your pad. Does it matter if he's been there twenty years? I don't think there's any statute of limitations on crimes of that caliber. Statutes of limitations are granted according to the caliber of crimes. For a misdemeanor it is very short. For murder there is none. For genocide, invading people's land, there's no statute of limitations. It takes people sometimes hundreds of years before they can reclaim what has been taken from them. To negate the right of the Palestinian people on the basis of time would be, by inference, to negate our own claims for justice. I don't think time has any importance."

I wanted to ask him why he felt it was so important for the Black Panthers, fighting for racial justice in the United States, to turn their attention to conflict in the Middle East, but my question was cut short by Kathleen, her mother, and Elain Klein.

"C'mon, El," Kathleen cried across the terrace. "Elain's going to drive us home in her car. Schanche can talk to you later."

Cleaver stood to go. "Byron and I are going to Pyongyang the day after tomorrow," he said. "Come on out to the pad tomorrow night. You can finish this shit off then."

# CHAPTER 13

### *"The people's war should be escalated . . ."*

THE Cleavers' apartment above a malodorous auto repair shop on the main thoroughfare of Point Piscade, west of Algiers, seemed to have been calculatedly constructed to make an ex-convict feel at home. It was a five-room walk-up suite cast entirely of reinforced concrete on cold floors of polished stone. Three small, windowless bedrooms, lined up along the street side of the apartment, were as jail-like as solitary prison cells. Bare mattresses lay on each of the bedroom floors: one for Eldridge, Kathleen, and Maceo; one for Mrs. Neal; and one for Gwen and Amiri Akili and their year-old child. Heaps of clothing, cardboard cartons, and books were scattered around the unmade Cleaver and Akili mattresses. Mrs. Neal's room was uncluttered and the mattress was neatly covered with sheets and a blanket. The sleeping rooms were connected by a shoulder-wide corridor whose other wall separated them from an irregular living-dining area that was illuminated by a large casement window with metal frames resembling prison bars. A small kitchen abutted the larger room. At the end of the corridor, where narrow stairs descended to the street, was the doorway to a bathroom that was only slightly larger than a telephone booth. The toilet was typically North African, a tiled hole in the floor connected directly to a four-inch drain. Its flush tank was broken. The Cleavers and their houseguests used a slop bucket for sanitation. It was hard to determine whether the odors that permeated the apartment emanated primarily from the diapers of the two babies, the bathroom, the auto repair shop or the wretched Arab neighborhood that spilled down the hillside behind the building. The only furnishings in the living-dining area were four flimsy wicker chairs, a radio-record player, a dozen cardboard boxes, a black and white cowhide throw rug, a poster of Huey Newton holding gun and spear, and a footlocker that served as a coffee table. Neatly stacked on the footlocker were *Baby and Child Care* by Dr. Benjamin Spock, *It's All in Our Stars,* by Zolar, The World's Most Popular Astrologer, *A Dictionary of Philosophy,* published by the Ministry of Foreign Affairs of the U.S.S.R., and two long-playing records, *Dr. Martin Luther King, Jr., In the Struggle for Freedom and Human Dignity,* and Aretha Franklin's *Lady Soul.* The apartment's only other esthetic salvation was its lovely view of the Mediterranean shore a few hundred yards beyond the window.

With unusual formality, Eldridge placed two wicker chairs near the window and asked me to sit in the one that faced the sea vista. He sat with his back to the window so that as my eyes searched his dark face, they were partially blinded by the sharply contrasting light of the evening sky, brightened by the fading sunlight that reflected from choppy Mediterranean waves. Byron and Rahim took positions on each side of my chair and Akili moved directly behind it. They stood motionless, arms folded across their chests. This was not to become an evening's discussion with a white acquaintance from Babylon, or even an informal, give-and-take interview; it was a formal audience, granted by the Minister of Information of the Black Panther Party, bodyguards and all. If the purpose was to intimidate me, it succeeded. I had never in the past made a point of pressing what he might consider "unfriendly" questions on Cleaver, because I didn't want to anger him to the point of silence, but I had the feeling now that if I attempted to ask even a mildly critical question, I would find myself at the foot of the narrow stairway with three stern black soldiers at my back.

Without preliminaries, Cleaver began in a sonorous tone, like a head of state beginning a press conference with a prepared statement.

"You were asking about our position on Palestine. We're primarily concerned with the struggle in the United States, and so we take a position on the struggle in Palestine, and we do that not just because there's an issue available and it's possible to take a position on it. We know that there's a very real connection between policies that the U.S. Government pushes outside and policies that they push in New York or in Oakland, California. The same people, the same ruling class or power structure has pushed all these policies. We're interested in stopping the repression and eliminating the ability of these people to do these kinds of things to our people. So we have to take a close look at what's going on in Palestine: to interpret it from the point of view of trying to solve intricate problems that are intricately connected. When we take a position on these things, in effect we're just taking or extending a position that we've already taken. It's not only a question of showing international solidarity, it's just a question of having a consistent position in opposition to an enemy who is consistent in his oppression everywhere.

"We were talking earlier about the fact—you stated that a lot of people feel that no matter what the rights or wrongs of the situation, Israel exists as a state and that we have to be realists about that and try to solve the problem within the context of that reality. I feel that's very erroneous because once you concede that, then it's kind of inevitable that there aren't too many alternatives left in terms of what conclusions you come to. So we go back beyond that and recognize the atrocities committed against the Jewish people, the fact that there's a great outpouring of sympathy for the Jewish people because of the persecution. We cannot endorse what the Nazis did to the Jews. We cannot endorse that. But at the same time, we take a dim view of Zionists taking this humane response that people have and harnessing it through propaganda as part of their campaign to justify the aggression that they've committed against a people. We say that the problems of the Jews cannot be solved by giving problems to the Arabs. The Arab people who lived there, the Palestinian people who were there and who constituted a majority, they're calling to us through their organization, Al Fatah.

"The voice that makes the most sense to us is the voice of Al Fatah, you know? There's a very clear difference between what they say and a lot of other voices over there, you know? I've never been able to relate to any call for genocide, and people who say, 'Well, we will just run people into the sea, we'll just crush people.' That doesn't seem to be a viable solution. But when they start speaking of a democratic republic in which every man would have his political rights and there will not be distinctions between people on the basis of their religion or their ethnic group, then it begins to sound like a classic solution to that problem. I don't see why people should be timid about that.

"Another reason I am very concerned about this is that in the United States, the Left, the Movement, has quite a few cadre militants who are Jews, very active people who play very significant roles in the Movement, very positive roles. When it comes to confronting the issue of Palestine, I've noticed— and this has been a stumbling block to a lot of our activity in the Movement—that they want to avoid confronting that issue. They want to look elsewhere or confuse the issue by advancing these positions that say, 'Well, the Arab governments are corrupt; you've got monarchies backing the regimes,' you know? 'What we need over there is a total socialist revolution.' They start going off into that bag because they don't want to face the basic problem presented by Zionism and policies that they've followed, that they've instituted over there. So I've found that the entire Movement becomes stultified, and I think that this whole stultification reaches all kinds of other problems, too. There's a kind of spirit that comes out of it, because when you see someone who's being equivocal on a very important issue, and then you have to deal with him on other issues, you tend to not really have faith in him and you tend to suspect him and you're angry at him. This has been a big problem.

"So we feel that it is necessary to confront that issue and to inject it into the Movement, so that people will be forced to define their position on it, whatever it might be. If all of the Jewish radicals in the United States feel that they must support the policies of Zionism, then we need a clear line of demarcation, because they become part of the problem then. As it is, by not advancing clear solutions or taking a position, they're still part of the problem. You have to define it because the Palestinian people are fighting for their rights. They've launched an armed struggle, and it's becoming more and more intense, and the United States Government is supporting the Zionist regime. They just recently sent over, very provocatively, fifty jets. This incenses the Palestinian people and it has a direct bearing on attitudes toward the American people as a whole. So we certainly have an interest in making our position clear on that. We oppose those policies and we oppose people who support those policies."

He had spoken clearly and without pause, as if reciting from memory, as perhaps he was. He stopped abruptly with the final word and waited in formal silence for me to take the cue. I guessed that he wanted to talk about white radicals in the Movement since they obviously were the intended target of the first monologue.

"Does this mean you are changing your views concerning alliances with white radical groups?" I asked dutifully.

"No," he began another monologue. "I think they've matured and developed. When you go back to the first attempt that we made at the founding convention of the Peace and Freedom Party, March 15, 1968, we advanced our position on coalition. At that time people were not relating to each other. Black radicals, white radicals, militants, progressives, whatever you want to call them, were all going their various ways. We always regarded that as being self-defeating, and we took our position in the face of a lot of opposition. But since that time, I think that our position has been vindicated. A lot of the opposition has either withered away or been revealed as absurd. So I think that it was a very positive contribution that we made. At the time that we first started, the leadership of the Black Panther Party had a better understanding of that than did many of the members of the Party, so we had to wage a very intensive educational campaign within the Party to get people to understand that and to accept it, and there were some very tight occasions relating to that. But now people are very strongly supportive of that position. They recognize the value of it and the justice of it. And one other thing that was very important. When the delegation from the Party came over here to the Pan-African Cultural Festival, we were in the position of not really having had contact with the outside world. We didn't have very detailed and sophisticated knowledge and understanding of some of the subtleties of problems and positions that people were taking around the world, particularly in Africa. So that when we got over here, people were asking us for our positions on these various questions, and we really didn't know where other people were at. We had a kind of hard-nosed attitude that we'd have to defend our position here and fight for it and all of that. But we found out that people, through their struggles here, had also arrived at the same conclusion.

"Historically, there has been a trend that is very similar, the same with different terminology. What we call cultural nationalism, they defined in Africa as Negritude. So there were several years of the prevalence of Negritude as a kind of philosophy and this created a lot of antagonisms between the people above the Sahara—it's obvious that the people north of the Sahara are white or Semitic people—and although they could be very revolutionary, when people confronted

them with the category of Negritude, they found it difficult
to relate, see? It created a lot of problems. It was a divisive
thing that was used by the common enemy. It was very destructive. So they found that they needed a unity that was
based on revolutionary principles. When we got here and
articulated our position on the very same points, we found
that we had a lot of support. A lot of people felt the very
same way. That was very helpful to us, the fact that we had,
without any prior consultation with anyone, worked out
through the necessities of our struggle these same points that
other people had reached in the same manner. This was a
very clear case study for them. It went a long way for us over
here. It strengthened—that's the point I want to make—it
strengthened the people who came over here in the delegation. There were about eight people who came over here from
the Party. These people, some of them I have seen change
from a position where they opposed coalition, to one of support, to one of enthusiastic support. They came over here and
it was very important to see how those positions that we had
taken were in the international scene, so they went back with
more dedication to the Party and the way that the Party made
that particular analysis."

Again he stopped abruptly and waited for me to continue
or conclude this one-man press conference. "When you speak
of cultural nationalism and Negritude, I guess you are talking
about the futility of black exclusivity, black nationalism," I
observed. I was trying to find an inoffensive way to question
the apparent schizophrenia of the all-black Panthers on the
subject. "Not long ago you wrote a very critical piece about
Stokely Carmichael . . ."

"You'd need Frantz Fanon to analyze Stokely," he cut me
off, "or somebody with his ability for psychological analysis.
I cannot say why the man doesn't see this. I cannot say that
he doesn't see it. I can only say that he doesn't act as if he
sees it. And he says that he disagrees with it. He's not the
only one who can't see it. Elijah Muhammad can't see it. Papa

Doc Duvalier can't see it. There are a lot of people who can't see it. That means that there's a lot of other things that they can't see, because behind all those points there are considerations of what the human race is all about, where history is moving, what kind of world we're going to have. If they can't see some of these other things, that makes them a very destructive element as far as I'm concerned."

I decided not to press on with my own theory about the poorly buried streak of black nationalism in the Panther Party. "A year ago when I asked you where the human race was heading and what kind of a world you wanted to have, you said you didn't want to talk about such things because they fell in the realm of fantasy," I said. "You called it 'counter-revolutionary' to project that kind of thinking into the future."

"My response is just the same, simply because we take the position that history is moving toward socialism and we feel that socialism is superior to capitalism, so we want a socialist society. Now there's a process of achieving that society. We're more concerned about the process. We're conscious of the fact that we are part of the process of revolution. What we are doing is part of the process. What we want to know is how to do that more effectively, how more effectively to make the revolution. It really gets to be academic, precisely what are to be the contours of the new society. We can save that for others whose duty that would be."

"Huey described his ideas about an ideal future when Ed Keating interviewed him for me at Vacaville. Won't you do the same?"

"No, because I don't think it's useful or helpful. There are moments when you can do that, there are even moments when I have done that. I'm not saying that theoretical analysis is not relevant. I'm not saying that. It's just that, it's already been done. Karl Marx did it. Mao Tse-tung has extended it. Until some of that is implemented, I don't see any great need for further elaborations on it. I don't think our struggle is suffering for lack of that type of analysis. I think the great need is relating these classical analyses to our practical situation. That's where we need to be."

"I described you as a kind of Utopian Socialist a year ago because I thought you had not been specific enough about your political ideals to fit any other category. Would you describe yourself now as a Maoist?" I asked him.

"Don't categorize me," he said. "You can't categorize me because I'm not any of those things. I think we are developing now, in the United States, a new and uniquely American Marxism, an indigenous Marxism. It's not Chinese Marxism or Russian Marxism. It's American Marxism. Yankee Doodle Dandy Socialism."

"If you won't speculate about the actual form of that kind of socialism, then what needs to be done, in your view, to achieve it?" I asked.

"I think that the people's war should be escalated in terms of revolutionary violence against the system, specifically designed to destroy the system. By all means that are consistent with the goals, by all sectors of the society. The great sabotage to the revolution that is taking place is the great foot-dragging that is going on in the white community by people who claim to be concerned about humanity, by people who must understand and realize that there is no sanctuary for anyone on the face of the planet earth. These problems have to be solved, and the solution to doing that is by smashing and disrupting the machinery of the oppressors. I don't feel that there's any other way of doing that. I really feel that's the way it has to be done. So I want to see people doing that."

"Can't people do that peacefully, by voting?"

"I don't think you can do it that way. They'll vote one set of pigs in for another, that's all. I think it is a very vicious attack upon the American people, upon humanity, when you question whether or not they can make a revolution. I don't think that's the question at all. I don't think there's any doubt at all that the American people are capable of making a revolution and of coping. You see, people get uptight and bugged by the vast technological development of the United States, by all the machines. So they say, 'Gee, it's just impossible to make a revolution here,' you know? I think that's very myopic and even absurd, because why should we say that history has ended with Babylon? People managed to make a revolution inside the Roman Empire, the British Empire, the French Empire. So why can't they do it inside of Babylon? I think it's really part of the propaganda of the system to debilitate the revolutionary potential of the people by making it seem impossible.

"Even repression or resort to these openly fascistic tactics is what we call trying to sell a ticket to the people, trying to bluff the people, trying to frighten the people, and to overpower and overawe their ability to strike! This is something that you learn in prison. You'll see thousands of convicts in the yard. And you'll see a handful of cops controlling all those dudes. If some trouble breaks out at one end of the yard, what happens is that a signal is given and all those cops will rush to concentrate on that point, so that the two people involved in the fight will be surrounded by ten cops. They're outnumbered and overpowered and there's nothing they can do. But this is really a form of guerrilla tactics that the cops are using, and they use the same tactic outside, because there are more people than there are pigs. If people understand that, they can deal with it. I think that in the United States, people will be able to make a revolution just as they are able to do in other places."

"You mention foot-dragging in the white community. I presume you're talking about people like me. What do you have to say to us?"

"I'm through. I've said everything I can say about that. I cursed them out and everything else trying to express that. I think the only real and effective way of doing that is through action, by moving and creating a situation where they have to do something, have to move, where they can no longer sit back and fat mouth about it because the country will be on fire. There will be gestapo raids at night, and there will be dead pigs in the street, and the pigs will be killing people. People will then want to know what the country is about. They will then be forced to take actions to see to it that their liberties are safeguarded, you see? Because if the Black Panther Party's offices are raided and shot up, it's just like another episode on the T.V. or the news—they watch the news to get their goodies; they run the action in Vietnam, then local news, state news, national news and everybody gets to see a good cowboy shoot 'em up, or a modern analogy of that. But if they look at the T.V. and they see themselves being shot by pigs or someone that they relate to being shot, or their own house or the house next door burns down, then they'll come away from the T.V. set with a different attitude. The Chicago convention of the Democrats was something like that. In Berkeley, too, with the people's park incident, where the cops used strictly military tactics against them, where they threw over a proud campus of the University of California, indiscriminately tear-gassed students and not only students, but the surrounding community, where they went out in the streets and actually murdered a man. So people can't live in that kind of situation. They have to stop that. They have to ask themselves, 'Who are these people running amok in our streets? Is that what it means to be a guardian of the law? What is the nature of law that it's being enforced in this manner? This is not what I want.' They have to either very stupidly accept that, or they have to see to it that the guardians of the law actually guard the law."

"If people are moving toward that state of awareness of the misuse of police power, don't you think they're capable of correcting it by nonviolent political means?" I asked.

"If you do research, you see that there have been some brilliant advances for humanity that have been made in the legislative process," he said, "but I don't think there's ever been anything done outside an atmosphere of controversy and conflict. So, under certain conditions, it's absurd, it's even counterrevolutionary to be talking about a nonviolent alternative to defending people when the people are being viciously attacked with guns and all kinds of military equipment by pigs. I think if the pigs became nonviolent—if they would put down their guns—then we could start talking about some peaceful transitions.

"If they didn't have armed guards around Congress, it would be possible for us to go in there and get Senator McClellan and kick his ass and just kick him out in the streets without killing him, you see? But the way it is now, when we make up our minds to go into that Congress, we have to make military calculations, because there are armed guards there. We have to talk about shooting our way in, and shooting out way out, so we wouldn't be in a frame of mind to shoot our way in, kick Senator McClellan in his ass and leave him there and walk out. We'd go in there and take his head, then try and get out. So it's a question of the tactics and the policies with the power structure. McClellan is from my home state, from Arkansas. He's a man who's persecuting black people from his seat in the Senate, and he has that seat because black people and poor white people, too, in the state of Arkansas are caught up in a critical situation that really hasn't allowed them to express their will. The man is illegally holding the seat, and then he's persecuting people with his investigations."

"You speak of doing all of these things, making a revolution in America. How can you accomplish that from this apartment in Algiers?"

"I'll go back to Babylon at a time and in a way of my own choosing," he said. "If they let me come back openly, I'll come back openly. If they won't, I'll return the same way I left. The FBI won't find me. One of the tactics we are going to pursue, and it will be a very effective tactic, is make underground sanctuaries all over the United States where people can flee. When anyone faces trial, he will resist trial. When anyone faces arrest he will resist arrest. He will go to a sanctuary.

Prisoners who escape from the jails in Babylon will have these sanctuaries to go to. I will be in one of those sanctuaries. I will go to all of them. People who escape from the pigs will know that I'm there. It will give them a sense of security, because I'm there."

It was becoming quite dark in the apartment now and the only light was a low wattage bulb in the kitchen which cast a yellow corridor into the living area. Byron stood in the center of it. Neither he nor Rahim nor Akili had moved since I took my seat other than occasionally to nod eager assent to what Eldridge was saying or to shift his weight. Suddenly Eldridge stood up and is if by signal all three relaxed and moved away from me.

"Time for some supper," he said, peering into the small kitchen. "Kathleen, let's get some supper," he called to the bedroom, where Maceo was crying. Then he walked to the narrow corridor and entered the bedroom.

"Don, there's something I've got to have from you," said Byron after Eldridge left the room. "I mean, we're here making a revolution and all that, and it looks like you ain't doin' shit."

Under certain circumstances, I am quite easily intimidated, and at this moment after a distinctly uneasy audience with Eldridge, I felt that any prudent man would feel the same. Byron's remark scared hell out of me.

"Uh, what's that?" I said as he strode to my chair and looked down at me.

"The Minister of Information of the Black Panther Party and I are leaving for North Korea tomorrow," he said, "and you've got something that we need. The Movement needs it."

"I have something you need?"

"Yes. I need a camera so I can document our trip. The pictures will be very valuable to the movement. I see you carrying two Nikons and a case full of lenses."

"But that's professional equipment," I said. "I need it. I can't give it away."

"I tell you what. With us making a revolution and all, you got to make a positive contribution too, right? I mean if you ain't prepared to make a positive contribution, how come the Minister has been wasting all this time talking to you?"

"Look, Byron, I'm a reporter, that's all. I'm not a revolutionary. I don't agree with you guys at all. I don't believe in violence or . . ."

"Tell you what," he interrupted. "It'll make you feel better, I'll just 'borrow' one of those cameras. How's that? I'll even send you some pictures of Eldridge in Pyongyang and Hanoi, and you can put them in some magazine. That'll be a fair capitalist trade, right?"

Eldridge poked his head in the door of the living room and rebuked Byron. "You're not going to send any pictures to him or to any magazine, Byron. You will send your pictures to *The Black Panther*. The Party will determine whether our pictures will be sold to the imperialist press." He retreated to the bedroom.

I attached a 58 millimeter lens to the older of my two Nikons and handed it to Byron. He was squinting through the viewfinder when Eldridge returned to the room. "You gave Byron a camera? Good. Thanks," he said. "We need it for our trip."

"Eldridge," I said, smarting from the polite shakedown, "aren't revolutions often followed by tyrannies that are as bad or worse than the ones they were fought to replace?"

"They might seem that way. I've seen countries where that appears to be true. But a lot of the things we consider to be tyrannies to a lot of the people involved are actually progressive steps. Consolidation of the revolution, you know?"

"What countries, for example?" I asked him.

"I don't think it's nice to give examples. There are some examples I'm very anxious to give, but it's a question of when you do that, you know? Now is not a good time to give examples."

"Cuba?"

"Maybe Cuba is an example. I'll tell you one thing about Cuba, the thing that bothered me most about Cuba. They are going to very unnecessary lengths to threaten the people with arms in Cuba, and I don't think you need to do that after the revolution is won. Every civil servant in Cuba wears a gun strapped to his hip, no matter what he does; if he's got a government job, he's got a gun. Most of them were not even true revolutionaries when Fidel fought. Wherever you have so many guns you have tyranny." He paused, sitting down again in the wicker chair. I thought he was prepared to continue talking, but he stretched and said, "I'm through talking. I don't want to talk any more."

That's when I asked the question about Maceo's full, formal name, hoping it might lead him to relax and continue. But except for the ironic raillery with Kathleen over names like Roy Wilkins and James Farmer, he gave the question the same sonorous weight as he would give to his analysis of police power. His humanity returned, briefly, when he expressed slight doubt about himself. But after that remark he politely excused himself, and I left. Byron went downstairs with me, holding his newly liberated Nikon, and generously helped me find a taxicab.

The next afternoon I went to Dar El Beida airport outside of Algiers and watched Eldridge and Byron, assisted by the press attaché of the North Korean Embassy, board a Czech airliner for Prague, where they were to connect with a flight for Pyongyang. I never saw either of them again, although I did see Byron's picture in a recent edition of *The Black Panther*. I was somehow not surprised to read the legend under the head shot which showed Byron's boyish face sprouting a mustache of almost handlebar proportions.

## BYRON BOOTH:

## WANTED

Next to his picture was the smiling image of an attractive black girl named Louise Soloman Wibecan, also "Wanted." A headline above the two pictures said, "Repudiating Lies of Renegade Bandits Byron Booth and Louise Wibecan," and there was a brief proclamation about them below, signed by David Hilliard. It accused the two "renegade bandits" of stealing $20,000 from the Party, and "desperately spreading factionalizing progaganda against an indefatigable fighter and patriot, our Minister of Information, Eldridge Cleaver, with the ultimate plot of being to set him up for a reactionary coup instrumented by the C.I.A." The paranoia in Algiers, I thought, is flowering. So, apparently, were Byron's larcenous instincts.

I hung around Algiers for a few days after Eldridge and Byron left, waiting for Rahim to decide whether he wanted to bare his psychological soul concerning the airplane hijacking, but in the end he told me the experience was too shattering to be recounted in my presence. He didn't think it should be interrupted with questions. I left him two blank cassettes of recording tape in case he should be moved to speak his confession in private. He promised to send me the tapes if he got around to confessing after I left. I never heard from him.

The day before my own departure, I went with Kathleen on one of her shopping expeditions, to the open-air flea market at El Harash, east of Algiers. She bought two bulky armoires, an old garden picnic table and four benches. I helped her move them into the disordered apartment, shot a few pictures of her and Maceo, and left.

After passing through immigration and police procedures at the airport, I wandered around the almost barren departure lounge as I waited for my flight. The departure lounge, as in all international airports, was an official "no man's land" where passengers waited before formally "entering" the country and after formally "leaving" it. I was relieved to be out of the city, away from its Black Panthers and en route to a Pantherless Paris. But I wasn't away from them yet. I took a seat.

Sitting beside me on a hard wooden bench was a thin, bearded young American black man who looked both exhausted and utterly frustrated. I said hello to him and asked him if he, too, was waiting to leave Algiers. He shook his head and told me his story.

"I got here on August 26," he said, "and there was something wrong with my visa. The Algerians wouldn't let me in. They kept me here in the departure lounge for a couple of days, wouldn't even let me make a phone call. Then they put me on a plane to Morocco. They wouldn't let me in there, either. The Moroccans put me on a plane to Sierra Leone, and they sent me back to Morocco, which sent me to Liberia, which sent me back to Sierra Leone. In the last few weeks I've been to eight different countries, some of them three times. None of them would let me through customs and immigration. I've been sleeping in departure lounges and eating whatever I can get. I've been here three days this time. They still won't let me make a phone call. I've got friends here. I think, finally, they're going to let me in."

I told him I had been in Algiers interviewing Eldridge Cleaver.

"That's who I'm supposed to be with," he said. "How is he?"

"He's in North Korea."

"Oh," he grunted.

"What's your name?" I asked him.

"They call me Kenyatta," he said. He wouldn't elaborate. I guessed the young man was Earl Ferrell. He had not defected, as Eldridge had feared. He had simply been caught up in the bureaucracy of international immigration procedures. A man without a country, bouncing from airport to airport. I don't know whether Eldridge greeted him warmly or not when he and his soon-to-become renegade companion, Byron, returned from Communist Asia, but I do know that the relationship was short-lived. About three months after I saw him in the airport departure lounge, Earl Ferrell called a press conference in Paris to announce that he had left the Black Panther Party and wanted the American Embassy to send him home.

About two months after I left Algiers, *True* magazine published the story I wrote about Eldridge there. Near the end of the piece, after recounting his remarks about pulling triggers and writing, I had observed:

While he has not yet pulled a trigger, he has written, but the quality of his writing has suffered terribly both from the chaotic life conditions of exile and from his own deliberate decision to disdain art for politics. *Ramparts* recently published two of his pieces, one of them a commentary on his exile and the other an open letter to Stokely Carmichael whose violent anti-white feelings are anathema to Cleaver. In style and content, neither was much more than a hurried political tract. The slick, radical magazine followed in the next issue with the beginning of a partially completed autobiographical novella which Cleaver wrote while he was still in prison in 1966. The rhythm of the prose was commanding, the style simple and bursting with power. To one whose admiration of Cleaver came through the strength and eloquence of *Soul on Ice,* also written in prison, the contrast was symptomatic of Cleaver's condition. He has lost power, both literary power and real power, as a result of his exile and his almost exclusive preoccupation with Marxism. If he remains in exile, a prospect which horrifies him, he will almost certainly fade away as a leader of the radical New Left.

My last conversation with Eldridge was on the telephone and it was extremely brief. He had asked someone in Paris to send me a cable urging me to call him, which struck me as a curious way to get in touch. Perhaps they wouldn't let him place a collect call from Algiers, and he took this roundabout means of reaching me in order to save paying for the call himself. All he said when I reached him in Algiers was this:

"What are you trying to do, man? You got the whole world uptight."

"Why?" I asked.

"Because of what you wrote."

"Have you read it?"

"No, man," he replied, "we don't get any magazines here. My lawyers told me about it on the telephone. What are you trying to do?"

"To show some critical objectivity," I said.

I sent him a copy of the article, but he never acknowledged it.

# Afterword

O N September 24, 1969, a few days after I left Algiers, the ordeal of Bobby Seale, seven white radicals, and the American judicial system began in the Federal courtroom of Judge Julius Hoffman in Chicago. Seale immediately became the focal point of the Chicago 8 trial; not because of the role he allegedly played in the Government's weak depiction of a "conspiracy" to incite violence during the 1968 Democratic Convention (Seale was in Chicago less than 48 hours at that time, made only one speech, and never even met some of his alleged co-conspirators), but because he translated what previously had been only wild Panther rhetoric into courtroom action.

("When anyone faces trial, he will resist trial," Eldridge said. "When anyone faces arrest, he will resist arrest.")

Seale quite reasonably asked for permission to act as his own defense attorney in the absence of Charles Garry, who was under gall bladder surgery. When his request was denied, he adopted tactics of obstreperousness and insult to disrupt the procedures of a court that he complained was denying him his constitutional rights. In the context of traditional courtroom decorum, the veneer of polite procedure that is essential to objectivity and justice under any rule of law, his tactics were utterly self-defeating, including calling the judge, among other things, a "racist," a "liar," a "fascist dog," and a "son of a bitch."

Unhappily, Judge Hoffman reacted with almost equal anger, hostility, and judicial indecorousness, arguing with Seale, peremptorily dismissing all his remarks, ordering him physically restrained by chain and gag, and finally severing his case from that of the others and sentencing him, without benefit of jury, to four years imprisonment for contempt of court. Hoffman deserved an award from the Black Panthers for so perfectly illustrating Cleaver's falsely oversimplified challenge, "if you're not part of the solution, you're part of the problem." By his failure to act with dignity and justice in a nasty courtroom situation created by a defendant who was determined to destroy his own rights in the name of pleading them, Judge Hoffman epitomized the ethnic and social polarization Eldridge Cleaver and the Black Panther Party are seeking.

Lawyers who have studied the transcript of the Chicago conspiracy trial have expressed confidence that Seale's contempt sentence will be reduced or reversed on appeal, and that higher courts probably will find that Hoffman was in error in refusing to permit Seale to defend himself. The American judicial system, whatever its human and procedural flaws, is specifically designed to correct such errors. A year earlier, Seale probably would have followed the example of Huey Newton and let the appeals process serve as the means of gaining justice "by any means necessary." But in Chicago, I think it is clear that his purpose was not to seek justice from the system. That would have meant making a record of his reasonable plea to defend himself, then sitting decorously through the trial, even enduring a flawed conviction, while awaiting the appeals process to consider and affirm his rights. Instead, I think, his purpose was simply what it appeared to be: to perform a "revolutionary act" by attacking the judicial system frontally.

("I think that the people's war should be escalated in terms of revolutionary violence against the system, specifically designed to destroy the system. By all means that are consistent with the goals, by all sectors of the society," Eldridge said.)

In the name of his civil rights, Seale demanded that he be destroyed, hoping like Samson to bring the system down by his own judicial suicide. To thus attempt to politicize a courtroom *is* judicial suicide. To react as Judge Hoffman and the prosecuting attorneys did, by their own failures of dignity, would be judicial suicide, too, if theirs was a court of last resort. Fortunately, the system is such that their failure to comprehend that they were being used as political foils of the Black Panther Party and its radical allies can be corrected. So can the original act of courtroom politicization, the so-called "Rap Brown Law," that so loosely defines the kind of conspiracy under which the Chicago 8 were tried. Few lawyers doubt that it is unconstitutional.

Judge Hoffman was not alone in illustrating acts of "oppression" against the Black Panthers in Chicago.

At 4:45 A.M. on December 4, 1969, fourteen Chicago policemen, acting on a tip from the Federal Bureau of Investigation, burst into a Black Panther apartment with a legal warrant to search it for weapons. They claimed that they were subjected to "a deadly assault by firearms" from within the apartment and they opened fire on its nine occupants. Twelve minutes and many rounds of police gunfire later, two Black Panthers, Fred Hampton and Mark Clark, were dead, and four others suffered multiple gunshot wounds. In reporting the incident officially and to the press, the police said the Panthers were the aggressors and that the incident was a "shoot-out" with heavy fire from both sides. A Federal Grand Jury in May confirmed what many already suspected, that the entire raid was a police "shoot-in," not a shoot-out. During all of the furious gunplay, the Grand Jury found that only one shot could have come from a Panther weapon. The police had misrepresented the truth of the incident. Their guilt was shared by a coroner's court that absolved them and by an unknown number of Chicago police and political officials who condoned their brutality. Even the Grand Jury shared it to a degree. After finding the police version of the incident untrue, the jury failed to return a single indictment of any of the policemen involved. The jury's reason was that none of the aggrieved victims had come forward to testify.

The surviving Panthers refused to testify before the Grand Jury that found them blameless, on grounds that the jury was not made up of their peers.

A similar police raid against a Panther headquarters in Los Angeles occurred four days later. Again, the police characterized the incident as a Panther shoot-out. While there seemed to be more truth in the official story of the Los Angeles police than there was in Chicago (the Los Angeles Party headquarters was heavily fortified with sandbags and the Panthers had a machinegun inside), the credibility of the police raiders was weakened by the blatant lying of the police in Chicago.

Moreover, the timing of the two raids raised questions of a nationwide police conspiracy against the Panthers, sanctioned by the Federal Bureau of Investigation. FBI Director J. Edgar Hoover did his own credibility no good when he testified in his annual appearance before the House Subcommittee on Appropriations on March 5, 1970. Two months after the Chicago Grand Jury, with FBI assistance, began unearthing the truth of the riotous police violence in Chicago, Hoover told Congress:

"In keeping with its intense hatred of and vindictive hysteria against local police, two BPP chapters *engaged in shoot-outs* [italics mine] with local police during December, 1969. On both occasions the police were attempting to execute duly authorized search and/or arrest warrants. In Chicago, Illinois, on December 4, 1969, seven heavily armed Panthers were arrested and two were killed. One police officer was wounded by gunfire and one injured by flying glass . . ."

Hoover made no attempt to acknowledge the guilt of the police and still characterized the Chicago incident as a "shoot-out," although his own men, working with the Chicago Grand Jury, presumably knew better. Whether his testimony reflected sloppy staff work or deliberate imprecision, only Hoover knows; however, he showed the same disregard for accuracy the year before when the FBI Annual Report stated that "Huey P. Newton was stopped for a traffic violation, and he shot and killed an Oakland police officer and wounded another." Granted, Newton was convicted of killing Officer Frey (since reversed), but he was found *not guilty* of wounding the other officer, Herbert Heanes.

In the most stirring section of his 1970 testimony, Hoover said that "a free society is in trouble when blatant propaganda so overshadows truth that the rule of law is jeopardized. Currently, law enforcement agencies throughout the country are wrongly accused of harassment by many well-intentioned but uninformed voices echoing outright lies generated by the lawless BPP."

One wonders whose "blatant propaganda" to believe. There is no doubt that members of the Black Panther Party have performed many lawless acts, not the least of which was the possession of weapons in both the Chicago and Los Angeles incidents. In every case that they are caught performing a lawless act, they should be arrested and tried under due process which guarantees their rights. It is even perfectly understandable, in fact essential, that as a result of their avowed revolutionary aims and madly intemperate statements (such as David Hilliard's alleged threat against the life of the President in a speech in November, 1969), the Black Panthers warrant special surveillance by the police wherever they operate. But they do not warrant *illegal* repression by the police.

Just as there is no doubt that many Panthers have behaved lawlessly, as Hoover charged, there is no doubt that the police have, too. Since their beginnings in Oakland in October, 1966, there has been a great deal of police harassment of the Panthers. Much of it has been provoked or invited by the Panthers. Newton's original brandishing of loaded weapons, for instance, certainly was not designed to calm police fears of possible Panther violence. Nevertheless it was legal. The police raid on Cleaver's first apartment in San Francisco, the forcible entry of Seale's apartment, the attempt by armed policemen to enter Father Neil's church, the first Oakland police attack against Panther headquarters, and the murderous Chicago police raid on the Panther apartment were not. To recount them is not to become one of Mr. Hoover's "well-intentioned but uninformed voices echoing outright lies generated by the lawless BPP." Rational men may differ in accepting the police or the Panthers' versions of other incidents, such as the Oakland shoot-out and the killing of Bobby Hutton; but my own examination of the house that was destroyed by police gunfire left me with the distinct feeling that Cleaver, not the police, had truth on his side.

The problem is not so much the "intense hatred . . . and vindictive hysteria" of the Panthers, which is demonstrable, but the degree to which the same emotions have influenced the police throughout the United States. In the process of reacting against the threatening and dehumanizing cries of the Panthers, the police establishment in America appears to be acting in concert, outside the law, to get them "by any means necessary." More and more the police reflect a self-concept dangerously like that described for me by Lieutenant McKee in Oakland: they see themselves as an autonomous power group in conflict with other power groups. Hoover's downright scary characterization of the Black Panther Party (rather than of the sources of black rage) as one of the greatest threats to internal security is, in effect, a sanction from America's chief policeman of almost any repressive act against the Panthers that frightened cops on the street want to perform. In that sense, there seems little doubt to me that there is an unuttered police conspiracy acting against the Black Panther Party. It doesn't take much imagination to see that kind of lawless police hostility expanding to include the repression of other "power groups" in our society, such as their own civilian political leadership, the press, disagreeable political parties and any other group that threatens police freedom of action. Such a prospect is far more terrifying than the cries of enraged black children to "off the pigs."

On the other side, the Panthers have demonstrated by their words and actions that they are not the "gentlemen of the ghetto" that parole officer Stan Carter, I, and many others thought they were becoming two years ago. I was woefully slow in seeing the stupidity of that, as this volume demonstrates. In brief, I thought of the Panthers then as simply a tough-talking NAACP and of their chief spokesman, Eldridge Cleaver, as a street-raised, prison-educated Martin Luther King.

I dismissed their revolutionary sloganeering as an immature cry for attention. I thought of them as angry young boys and girls, not as black Samsons. I was slow to see Cleaver's flight to avoid facing peaceful judicial procedures as the Panthers' watershed. After his official pronouncement that all hope was lost and that the only chance of salvation lay in Bakunin's "root and branch" destruction of the entire American society, all the Panthers, like all Bakunin's revolutionaries, were doomed. They rushed thereafter toward personal and organizational suicide. Their rhetoric became terrifyingly heated: "We will kill Richard Nixon," said David Hilliard in a San Francisco speech, according to Hoover's 1970 Congressional testimony. Seale wildly attacked the system frontally in Judge Hoffman's court. His tactics were emulated in New York during pre-trial hearings of thirteen of the "Panther 21," indicted for conspiracy to bomb public buildings. As I write this there are indications that the Panthers will spring more of their tactical surprises—revolutionary acts against the system—in New Haven, Conn., where eight of them, including Bobby Seale, are under indictment for the torture-murder of another Black Panther named Alex Rackley. (The murder was committed, according to the Panthers, by police provocateurs.) The tactics are what they seem to be: suicidal acts of doomed revolutionaries. If the will to suicide is insane, then the Black Panther Party is insane without doubt.

One can detect enough vengefulness in this insanity to characterize it as Samsonism. Cleaver's remarks in Algiers made it clear to me, at least, that the so-called "vanguard party" has only the will to destroy, not to build and certainly not to reform. That kind of destructiveness ("smashing and disrupting the machinery of the oppressors,") can only be described as an act of revenge, not of revolution. I use the term "insane" in a figurative sense, but it doesn't matter whether the insanity of the Panthers is figurative or literal, it is demonstrable.

This fact, which most liberals, like me, have been slow to realize, is the source of our dilemma, for the Panthers confront us with utterly unacceptable alternatives: if we support the Black Panther Party in any way, we encourage what psychiatrists Grier and Cobbs called "black rage, apocalyptic and final"; if we condone the unuttered, unwritten national police conspiracy to deprive the Panthers of their constitutional rights, we take the first awful step toward the loss of all liberties for minorities and majority alike. Normally, this kind of dilemma is easily resolved under the broad principle attributed to Voltaire: "I disapprove of what you say, but I will defend to the death your right to say it." Easy enough, then, to support bail and legal defense fund campaigns as many liberals, including me, have done for the Panthers, and to dismiss the madness of their rhetoric as inherently self-defeating. But the Panthers, by extending their rhetoric to "revolutionary actions" with the aim of destroying civil liberties not only for themselves but for all of us, have become the leading anti-civil libertarians of our time. Their cause, clearly stated and now clearly being acted out, is the "root and branch" destruction of the entire American "system," which, whatever its improvable faults, remains for most of us the best and most responsive form of government man has yet devised. Every dime contributed to their various legal funds simply strengthens that destructive cause, because this "civil liberties" money only frees their own considerable resources for the purchase of more guns, and for more of their tragically suicidal indoctrination of aggrieved little children.

Although the Panthers refused to make any accounting of their financial resources to me, I believe they have access to considerable sums of money. One source, for example, is *The Black Panther*. David Hilliard claims, and the FBI confirms, that the party sells roughly 100,000 copies of the paper, at 25 cents a copy, each week. People familiar with newspaper production costs place the per copy cost of the skimpy tabloid at from 10 to 18 cents, depending upon the number of pages in a given issue. The weekly net profit from circulation, therefore, is between $7,000 and $15,000 which, incidentally, makes it one of the world's few successful newspapers that does not rely on advertising revenue. Hilliard also claims that the Panther breakfast program currently includes about 50,000 ghetto children. Some of the costs of the free hot breakfasts are met by donations from ghetto merchants, some of whom reportedly have complained of being shaken down. Black Panther speakers have earned a good deal of money on college campuses, where they are in demand, and all of that goes into the party treasury, too. In addition, there have been substantial sums of money raised in the various Free Huey, Free Eldridge, Free Bobby, and Free the Panther 21 legal defense campaigns. Those of us who contributed to these causes were never reassured that our money was being spent for the purpose for which it was raised. To me this lack of candor raised questions of whether these funds were being diverted in the name of "civil liberties" to other Panther activities including arms purchases, international travel expenses, and assistance to fugitives from the law. Those questions have never been answered to my satisfaction.

Recently, the Black Panthers have shifted the emphasis of their public fund-raising attempts from simple legal defense to raising bail-bond money for jailed members awaiting trial.

The most notable case is that of the Panther 21 in New York, where most of the defendants have been held in lieu of bail as high as $100,000 apiece. The prohibitive bail figures were first assessed by Judge John Murtagh in whose courtroom preliminary trial hearings were rudely disrupted by the Panther defendants and sympathetic spectators. Months later, similarly high bails were set for a group of young blacks arrested during police raids against Panther offices in Philadelphia. These high bail figures aroused the ire of many liberals because the sums asked seemed by their excessiveness to be a form of official repression. The defendants were being unfairly imprisoned in advance of their trials, as Judge Sherwin found Eldridge Cleaver to have been unfairly imprisoned after the Oakland shoot-out in 1968. But was it that simple? The purpose of bail is to assure the court that the defendant will remain within legal jurisdiction between indictment and trial. What other assurance, beyond very high bail limits, did the court have that the Panther defendants would not flee the country, particularly if the cost of doing so was nominal? Their ideological leader and chief spokesman jumped high bail himself; moreover he has since publicly counseled them to resist trial and to resist arrest. I think judges can be forgiven if they allow reasonable suspicions of possible flight to influence them in establishing bail limits for the Panthers.

If financial support of the *legal rights* of the Black Panther Party is, in effect, a contribution to the destruction of the legal system, then what can be done in the name of civil liberties, because however insane the organization may be, the question of its *legal rights* is fundamental to the legal rights of all of us? It remains the absolutely basic cause Voltaire counseled. Whether the victims of illegal police repression happen to be Black Panthers or White Minutemen or Democrats or Republicans makes no difference, because we know that we cannot condone the limitation of any individual's legal rights without imperiling the liberties of all.

The Panthers are a paradox, a seeming absurdity, a self-contradictory thing that, as a paradox must, illustrates a truth. The Panther paradox, in fact, could be the most useful illustration ever to face our society despite the fact that I think there is nothing we can do for or about the members of the Black Panther Party other than lament the fact that they have gone over the brink of sanity. For what really matters is not so much the madness and suicidal rage of the poorly educated, well-indoctrinated kids of the party, but the conditions that made them such ripe subjects for their indoctrination in total despair. The most dangerous of these wretched conditions, as the very origin of the party *against* the Oakland police demonstrates, is police misbehavior on a massive, national scale.

Such real Panther repression as we have seen so far has stemmed almost entirely from the attempts of frightened policemen, with the sanction of the FBI, to stamp out, often by devious and illegal means, an organization whose words and goals are repugnant. Police fears are understandable. As Oakland's Chief Gain noted, the Panthers *are* a vigilante group. They have, by dehumanizing their opponents with the derisive term, "pigs," made the next mad step, assassination, imaginable. They have made an almost religious symbol out of one of civilization's most awful tools, the gun. And they have, without any doubt, often acted lawlessly. The police, not the Panthers, have had truth on their side in many Panther arrests.

But as we all saw in Chicago and as I believe I saw in Oakland, the police have been devious, deceitful, and downright untruthful as well. They also have been unforgivably brutal: the ruthless beating, for example, of six Black Panthers and their supporters by a crowd of off-duty policemen in a Brooklyn courthouse two years ago; the killing of unarmed Bobby Hutton; the violent, fatal raid on the Chicago apartment; the jailing, without medical attention, of a chronically ill defendant among the Panther 21 in New York.

Although I am sure that peaceful reform was not Eldridge Cleaver's intention when he spoke of the urgent need to focus attention on the national police problem, that is what the Panthers may accomplish, and that is the truth of the Panther paradox. Police power, applied outside the law, as it obviously has been in a number of the police-Panther conflicts, is far more corrosive to the cause of civil liberties than the revolutionary insanity of the Black Panther Party. Unlike the madness of the Panthers, who I think are both politically and socially unsalvageable, police behavior is subject to citizen control. Here lies the solution to the dilemma raised by the plight of the Panthers, and it does not depend upon the question of whether they are madly provoking their own persecution, or whether they are innocently suffering it as many still want to believe.

The solution lies not in polite *legal defense* of Black Panthers up against the law, but in *legal offense* by private citizens and concerned politicians against police misbehavior. Unlike the madness of the Panthers, the "intense hatred ... and vindictive hysteria" of the police can and must be peacefully corrected. A good place to begin, I think, would be with an unequivocal campaign for the resignation of the author of those phrases, J. Edgar Hoover.

The cause of police reform, of course, touches only one of the worst of the conditions that created the rage and frustration which the Black Panthers exemplify. The "iron ring of frustration" which Thomas Merton found surrounding the American black ghetto has more rigid links to it than police brutality and the official lawlessness of some other elements of the judicial system. *"White institutions created it, white institutions maintain it, and white society condones it,"* said the Kerner Commission. There is no further need to analyze or to intellectualize about American racism. It has been done. Each of us who is white knows that the germs of the disease of racism grow within us. Its cure is nothing more complicated than genuine commitment to equal justice and equal opportunity for all.

If it is not cured soon, the military tradition of the Black Panthers, whom we ourselves have driven to their madness, will spread, and not just the revolutionaries, but all of us, will be doomed.